Unless Recalled Earlier

PLANE TRIGONOMETRY

WITH PRACTICAL APPLICATIONS

OTHER BOOKS BY
PROF. LEONARD E. DICKSON

COLLECTED PAPERS, 4 vols., in prep.
ALGEBRAS AND THEIR ARITHMETICS
ALGEBREN UND IHRE ZAHLENTHEORIE
ALGEBRAIC INVARIANTS
COLLEGE ALGEBRA
ELEMENTARY THEORY OF EQUATIONS
FIRST COURSE IN THE THEORY OF EQUATIONS
HISTORY OF THE THEORY OF NUMBERS, 3 vols.
INTRODUCTION TO THE THEORY OF ALGEBRAIC EQUATIONS
INTRODUCTION TO THE THEORY OF NUMBERS
LINEAR ALGEBRAS
LINEAR GROUPS, WITH AN EXPOSITION OF THE GALOIS FIELD THEORY
MINIMUM DECOMPOSITION INTO FIFTH POWERS
MODERN ALGEBRAIC THEORIES
MODERN ELEMENTARY THEORY OF NUMBERS
NEW FIRST COURSE IN THE THEORY OF EQUATIONS
ON INVARIANTS AND THE THEORY OF NUMBERS
STUDIES IN THE THEORY OF NUMBERS

PLANE TRIGONOMETRY

WITH PRACTICAL APPLICATIONS

BY

LEONARD E. DICKSON, P$_H$.D.

CORRESPONDANT DE L'INSTITUT DE FRANCE
PROFESSOR OF MATHEMATICS IN THE UNIVERSITY OF CHICAGO

CHELSEA PUBLISHING COMPANY
BRONX, NEW YORK

THE PRESENT WORK IS A REPRINT, WITH MINOR TEXTUAL CHANGES, OF A WORK FIRST PUBLISHED AT CHICAGO, ILLINOIS IN 1922. PRINTED ON ACID-FREE PAPER. NEW YORK, N.Y., 1970

©, 1970, BY CHELSEA PUBLISHING COMPANY

INTERNATIONAL STANDARD BOOK NUMBER 0-8284-0230-2

LIBRARY OF CONGRESS CATALOG CARD NUMBER 70-114597

PRINTED IN THE UNITED STATES OF AMERICA

PREFACE

Distinctive features of this book are its immediate justification of the study of trigonometry, its emphasis on the practical applications, its sensible problems, its model solutions of sample problems, its concreteness, simplicity, and clearness, and its use of a traverse table in addition to the usual tables.

Trigonometry here justifies itself The great majority of students of trigonometry, whether in the high school or the college, take it as their final course in mathematics. Hence the course should justify itself at the time, and not be merely a stepping stone to further mathematical subjects. Without overlooking the needs of the few who will go further in mathematics, we may justify trigonometry to the others by demonstrating its great utility by means of simple applications to various subjects which are vital in the practical world today.

Practical applications This book introduces at an early stage concrete applications of trigonometry to the elementary parts of navigation and surveying, which are the two simplest exact sciences, as well as to the two elementary topics of physics which are known as composition of forces and refraction of light. There is, too, a full explanation of the theory and construction of a Mercator map, a subject of great importance also in geography. Three separate chapters are devoted to these subjects. The necessary terms and ideas are explained at length and illustrated concretely. We thereby obtain an abundance of simple problems whose importance is so convincing that they cannot fail to arouse real interest. Actual experience with classes has firmly convinced the author that these practical applications offer the best means to drive home the principles of trigonometry and to make the subject truly vital.

Sensible problems The problems are simple and sensible. Puzzle problems have been discarded, as well as those serving no purpose beyond the scourge of endless computation. Instead of the usual dull problems calling for the solution of a triangle in which certain sides and angles are given, the problems here proposed are real and reflect some activity of actual life.

Sample problems solved   The problems which present continuity of thought are collected into a set of exercises and given an appropriate descriptive heading. This plan will greatly aid the instructor in his selection of problems for assignment. Before each such collection of problems are inserted examples worked out in detail which together illustrate all of the different types of problems occurring in that collection. This feature will commend itself to both student and teacher. The harder problems (marked *) may be proposed for extra credit.

Concreteness   Several informal illustrations of the tangent and sine are given prior to the formal definitions. The concrete information about angles of any size and their measurement, which is acquired in the chapters on navigation and surveying, furnishes a desirable background for the introduction of general angles. And the same is true as to familiarity with latitude and longitude before coördinates are introduced for the sake of defining the trigonometric functions of a general angle. But above all, the book is concrete on account of the practical applications included and the practical nature of the problems.

Simplicity Clearness   The development of the subject is leisurely and the student is given ample time in which to digest each idea. There are given full and lucid explanations of all new terms and ideas. Lack of the precise knowledge of the mathematical meaning of terms is one of the chief sources of difficulty in the study of mathematics. Various terms which should already be familiar to students are re-defined. On the basis of careful readings both of the manuscript and proof sheets by various experienced teachers in high schools and colleges, it is believed that the presentation is throughout both simple and clear.

Tables   The tables are as simple as possible, and accurate for computation to four significant figures, which are ample for all ordinary practical purposes. It is true that some delicate astronomical measurements justify computations with 5, 6, or 7 place tables; but no new theory is involved. The traverse table, which is necessary for navigation and surveying, is really a systematic list of the sides and angles of all right triangles of moderate size. Its additional headings aid in making the present exposition of navigation much simpler than was possible heretofore. The traverse table is extremely useful in all parts of trigonometry and its applications, partly by relieving the monotony of logarithmic computation, but chiefly for the instantaneous checking of computations.

PREFACE

A suggestion to teachers The chapters on navigation and surveying are each divided into two parts, this making possible either a brief, wholly untechnical, introduction to those applications, or a fuller treatment. When these chapters are reached, it is suggested that henceforth two hours a week be devoted to these applications and the remaining class periods to general trigonometry, which begins with page 103. Under this plan the student will be applying the theory of the right triangle, which he has already learned, while he is acquiring the theory of the oblique triangle, and will complete the former applications just when he is ready for the applications of the latter theory. Under such a program the student will understand at all times why he is doing what he is doing, will have real respect for the subject, and will take a genuine interest in it.

Acknowledgments Valuable suggestions were made, after reading the entire manuscript, by Dr. J. M. Kinney and Professor O. M. Miller, both of the Hyde Park High School, Chicago, by the author's colleague, Dr. Mayme I. Logsdon, and by Dr. E. J. Moulton of Northwestern University, while the latter read also the proof sheets critically. An earlier form of the chapter on navigation was read by Professors Moulton, R. G. D. Richardson of Brown University, and the author's colleague, J. W. A. Young. The chapter on surveying was read by the author's colleagues, Professors K. Laves and G. W. Myers, and by G. D. Tompkins of the Bureau of Maps and Plats of the City of Chicago; while the proof sheets were carefully read by Professor B. F. Yanney of the College of Wooster, Ohio. The author is greatly indebted to these experienced teachers, and especially to Professor Moulton for his generous help at all three stages of the book. Plates for the cuts of the surveyor's compass and transit were kindly loaned by the instrument makers, W. and L. E. Gurley, of Troy, New York.

L. E. DICKSON

UNIVERSITY OF CHICAGO
DECEMBER 3, 1921

CONTENTS

CHAPTER I
Trigonometric Functions of Acute Angles

ARTICLE | PAGE
1. Nature of Trigonometry 1
2. Drawings to scale 1
3. Absolute and relative errors 3
4. Horizontal and vertical lines, planes, angles 4
5. Angles of elevation and depression 5
6. Illustrations of the tangent of an acute angle 5
7. Definitions of the trigonometric functions of an acute angle . 6
8. Problems on heights and distances 9
9. Given one trigonometric function, to find the others . . . 11
10. Relations between the six trigonometric functions of an acute angle 12
11. Further formulas true for every acute angle 14
12. Relations between the functions of complementary angles . 16

CHAPTER II
Solution of Right Triangles by Means of Tables of the Natural Functions

13. How to use tables of natural functions 19
14. Solution of right triangles by means of tables of natural functions 21
15. Cases when an angle cannot be accurately found by Table II 23

CHAPTER III
Traverse Table; Solution of Right Triangles by Inspection; Problems on Forces and Refraction of Light

16. Description of Traverse Table VI 26
17. When and how to use Traverse Table VI 26
    Exercises on heights and distances 28

CONTENTS

ARTICLE		PAGE
18.	Force	29
19.	Resultant of two forces	29
20.	Parallelogram of forces	29
21.	Component of a force	30
22.	Refraction of light	31

CHAPTER IV

Logarithms, Slide Rule

23.	Powers of 10, index laws	34
24.	Logarithms	36
25.	Significant digits	38
26.	Mantissa and characteristic of a logarithm	39
27.	To find the logarithm of a number by Table VII	40
28.	To find the number with a given logarithm by Table VII	41
29.	Extraction of roots by logarithms	41
30.	Logarithmic scale	43
31.	Slide rules	44
32.	Logarithms of trigonometric functions	46

CHAPTER V

Solution of Right Triangles by Logarithms

33.	Results in Chapter II recalled	48
34.	Solution by logarithms	48
35.	Given the hypotenuse and a leg	49
36.	Errors of computation	51
37.	Area of a right triangle	53
38.	Isosceles triangles and regular polygons	53
39.	Problems on heights and distances	55

CHAPTER VI

Navigation: Dead Reckoning

40.	Navigation and its subdivisions	59
41.	Geographical terms	59
42.	Nautical mile	60

CONTENTS

ARTICLE	PAGE
43. How distance is measured	60
44. Ship's course, compass card	61

Part I. The Sailings (True Course Assumed)

45. Plane Sailing	62
46. Unfavorable case in the use of a traverse table	63
47. Traverse Sailing	64
48. Parallel Sailing	66
49. Middle Latitude Sailing	68
50. The Mercator chart, meridional parts	71
51. Angle and distance on a Mercator chart	73
52. Mercator's Sailing	73

Part II. Finding the True Course; Compass Corrections

53. The mariner's compass	76
54. Variation and deviation of the compass	76
55. Leeway	76
56. Courses, compass course, true course, corrections	77
57. Dead reckoning	79

CHAPTER VII

Land Surveying

58. Branch of surveying treated	82
59. Chains, tapes, area	82
60. Course	83
61. True bearing	83

Part I. Balancing a Survey, Area (True Bearings Assumed)

62. Latitude and departure	84
63. Balancing a survey, error of closure	84
64. Double meridian distances	86
65. Area of a field	86
66. Plotting	88

Part II. Surveying Instruments; Finding True Bearings

67. Verniers	89
68. Surveyor's compass	91

CONTENTS

ARTICLE		PAGE
69.	Bearing with respect to any course	93
70.	Magnetic bearing	94
71.	Magnetic declination, variation charts	94
72.	Surveyor's transit	96
73.	Measuring angles with a transit	99
74.	Traverse	99
75.	Direct angle	100
76.	Deflection angle	100
77.	Azimuth	100
78.	Balancing a transit survey	101

CHAPTER VIII

Trigonometric Functions of Any Angle

79.	Rectangular coördinates, plotting	103
80.	Radius vector	104
81.	Generalized notion of angle	105
82.	Trigonometric position of an angle; the four quadrants	106
83.	Trigonometric functions of any angle	107
84.	Trigonometric identities	110
85.	Reduction of the trigonometric functions of any angle to functions of an acute angle	111

CHAPTER IX

Solution of Oblique Triangles

86.	Altitude and area of any triangle.	115
87.	Law of sines	115
88.	Law of tangents, Mollweide's equations; solution of a triangle, given two angles and a side or two sides and the included angle	116
89.	Solution of a triangle, given two sides and the angle opposite to one of them	121
90.	Law of cosines	126
91.	Area of a triangle in terms of its sides	128
92.	Radius of the inscribed circle	129
93.	To compute the angles of a triangle, given the sides	129
	Exercises on resultants and components of forces	131

CONTENTS

CHAPTER X

Relations Between Functions of Several Angles

ARTICLE		PAGE
94.	The addition theorem for sine	133
95.	Functions of $A + 90°$	135
96.	The addition theorem for cosine	136
97.	The subtraction theorems for sine and cosine	136
98.	Heights and distances	137
99.	The addition and subtraction theorems for tangent and cotangent	138
100.	Functions of double angles	140
101.	Functions of multiple angles	141
102.	Trajectories	142
103.	Functions of half angles	144
104.	Sum or difference of two sines or two cosines expressed as a product	145
105.	Trigonometric equations	147

CHAPTER XI

Graphs of the Trigonometric Functions and Their Inverses, Radians

106.	Line representations of the trigonometric functions	150
107.	The sine and cosine curves	152
108.	The tangent curve	153
109.	Graphical solution of trigonometric equations; harmonic curves	156
110.	The radian unit of angle	157
	Reduction of degrees, minutes, and seconds to radians	159
111.	Approximate values of sines and tangents of small angles	161
112.	Equations involving both an angle and its trigonometric functions	162
113.	The inverse trigonometric functions	164

LIST AND INDEX OF FORMULAS 169
INDEX, INCLUDING INDEX TO DEFINITIONS 171
ANSWERS TO CERTAIN OF THE FIRST FIVE EXERCISES OF EACH SET 173

TABLES, SEPARATELY PAGED

PLANE TRIGONOMETRY WITH PRACTICAL APPLICATIONS

CHAPTER I

TRIGONOMETRIC FUNCTIONS OF ACUTE ANGLES

1. Nature of trigonometry. The word *trigonometry* means literally the measurement of triangles. For example, if we are given the lengths of two sides of a triangle and the size of their included angle, we can, as we shall learn, compute the size of each remaining angle, the length of the third side, and the area of the triangle. Computations are made by means of tables and checked against gross errors either by a drawing made to scale or more quickly by a traverse table (see Table VI).

Trigonometry is a prerequisite to engineering, physics, astronomy, and other exact sciences. Applications to navigation, surveying, and a few simple topics of physics, are introduced early in this text, with a full explanation of the terms involved.

2. Drawings to scale. Angles of a drawing are measured by means of a *protractor*, which in its simplest form (Fig. 1) consists of a semicircle graduated to degrees. It is recalled that a right angle is divided into 90 degrees (90°), each degree into 60 minutes (60′), and each minute into 60 seconds (60″). Thus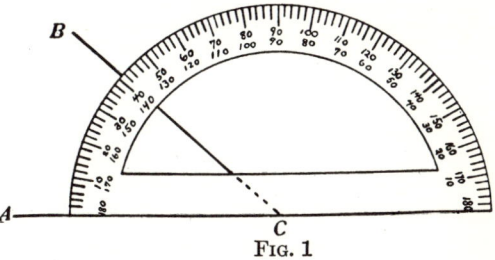

FIG. 1

one-sixteenth of a right angle equals 5°37′30″. To measure ∠ACB, in Fig. 1, place the protractor with its center at C and with its diameter along one arm CA of the angle, and note the reading (about 41°) at the intersection of the other arm CB of the angle with the semicircle.

There will be given in Chapter VII (on Surveying) a description of instruments used to measure angles between lines, and lengths of lines, on the earth's surface. Angles may be measured with a transit correctly to minutes or even to within 20 seconds.

The length of a straight line of a drawing can be estimated by means of a graduated ruler, or by counting divisions in case the drawing has been made on square-ruled plotting paper (Fig. 2).

EXAMPLE 1. Draw to scale a right triangle whose legs are 15.4 ft. and 12.7 ft., and measure its acute angles and hypotenuse.

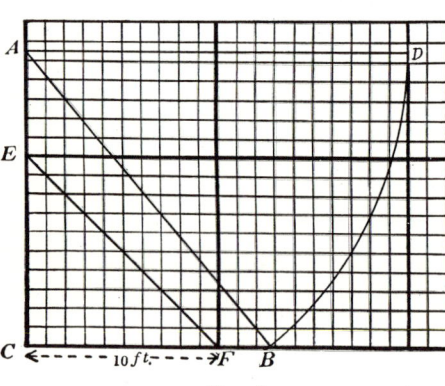

Fig. 2

Solution. Select a point C of intersection of two heavy lines of the square-ruled paper to represent the vertex of the right angle of our triangle ABC (Fig. 2). Let a small division represent 1 foot. Locate the point A by counting off $15\frac{1}{2}$ small divisions from C on one arm of the right angle. Locate B on the other arm of the right angle. To measure AB, transfer it to a position AD parallel to a ruling line by means of a pair of compasses (or by placing a strip of paper along the line AB and marking the points opposite to A and B, and then moving the strip of paper into the desired position AD). Or we may measure AB by means of a strip of the square-ruled paper cut as a permanent ruler. The approximate results are

$$AB = AD = 20 \text{ ft.}, \quad \angle A = 39\frac{1}{2}°, \quad \angle B = 50\frac{1}{2}°.$$

In any triangle ABC, the side BC opposite to angle A is denoted by a, the side opposite to B by b, and the side opposite to C by c.

EXAMPLE 2. Construct a triangle in which $a = 12$, $b = 9$, $B = 25°$, and measure side c and angles A and C.

Solution. Construct $\angle ABC = 25°$ and lay off $BC = a = 12$. With C as a center and 9 as a radius, draw an arc of a circle cutting BA at A and cutting BA produced at A' (Fig. 3). Thus both of the triangles BAC and $BA'C$ satisfy the requirements. By measurement, the first triangle has the required parts

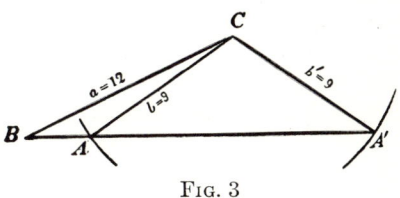

Fig. 3

$BA = c = 3.5$, $\angle BAC = A = 148°$, $\angle BCA = C = 8°$,

approximately, and the second triangle $BA'C$ has the required parts

$BA' = c' = 18.2$, $\angle BA'C = A' = 35°$, $\angle BCA' = C' = 119\frac{1}{2}°$.

3. Absolute and relative errors. The scales used in making measurements are not perfect and the reading of them involves an estimate by the eye. Hence all measurements involve errors. If, in Fig. 2, we measure the diagonal EF of one of the larger squares, whose side represents 10 ft., we obtain a number representing 14.1 ft., approximately. The length of the hypotenuse EF of the right triangle CEF can be found exactly by applying the theorem of Pythagoras that the square of the length of the hypotenuse is equal to the sum of the squares of the lengths of the two legs of the right triangle. Thus

$$\overline{EF}^2 = 10^2 + 10^2, \quad EF = 10\sqrt{2}.$$

The true length of the diagonal is therefore $10\sqrt{2} = 14.14\ldots$ ft. Its length by measurement was 14.1 ft., so that the (absolute) error just exceeds 0.04 ft. The ratio of the absolute error to the true value is called the *relative error*, and in this instance is 4/1414, approximately; or, if we prefer, 0.28 per cent.

EXERCISES ON DRAWINGS TO SCALE

1. Draw a triangle at random, measure its angles and find their sum. What is the error? What is the relative error?

2. Draw a quadrilateral at random, measure its angles and find their sum. What is the error? What is the percentage of error?

3. What is the simplest way to draw, on square-ruled paper, a right triangle whose acute angles are each 45°? Draw such a triangle having a leg equal to 10 small divisions, measure the hypotenuse and compute the error.

4. On square-ruled paper select a line AB along a ruling and containing 10 small divisions. What is the simplest way to locate the vertex C of an equilateral triangle having AB as its base? Measure the altitude from C and compute the error.

5. At the points A and B in Ex. 4, construct angles each of 60° by use of a protractor and hence find C. What is the present error in the altitude?

If in a triangle ABC the side opposite angle A is called a, etc., construct the triangles in which the following parts are given and measure the parts not given:

6. $a = 7.4, b = 9.8, c = 5.1$.   7. $a = 11.3, b = 13.4, C = 24°$.
8. $a = 8.5, B = 36°, C = 68°$.   9. $a = 8.5, b = 10.5, A = 54°$.

4. Horizontal and vertical lines, planes, angles. The *vertical line* through a point P is the straight line determined by a *plumb line* or cord one of whose ends is at P, while the other end is attached to a suspended weight. Any plane which contains a vertical line is called a *vertical plane*.

A *horizontal line* or *plane* is one which is perpendicular to a vertical line. A more convenient test for horizontal position is furnished by a *spirit level*, which is composed of a tube filled so nearly full of alcohol that a single air bubble is left. A line is horizontal if, when the level is placed along the line, the bubble is at the middle of the tube. To test whether a plane is horizontal or not, place the spirit level along it in two different directions in turn.

A *horizontal angle* is one whose arms are in a horizontal plane; a *vertical angle*[1] is one whose arms are in a vertical plane.

[1] This term is not to be confused with the usage in elementary geometry, where two opposite angles formed by two intersecting lines are called vertical angles.

5. Angles of elevation and depression. The angle which the line (of sight) from an observer's eye to an object makes with a horizontal line in the same vertical plane is called the *angle of elevation* or *angle of depression* of the object, according as the object is above or below the horizontal plane of the observer.

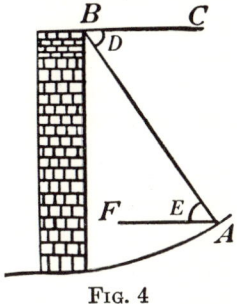

Fig. 4

Thus, in Fig. 4, if the observer is at A and the object is at B, the angle of elevation is the angle E which AB makes with the horizontal line AF in the same vertical plane with AB. But if the observer is at B and the object is at A, the angle of depression is the angle D which BA makes with the horizontal line BC in the same vertical plane with BA.

6. Illustrations of the tangent of an acute angle. A sufficiently short portion of a railroad track may be regarded as having a constant grade or *slope*, as 3/100 if it rises 3 feet for each 100 feet in a horizontal direction. A wagon road or the roof of a house may have a greater slope, as 2/5. In trigonometry, we speak of the slope of the road or of the roof as the *tangent* of its angle A of inclination with the horizontal plane, and write it "tan A." Thus, for the roof, tan $A = 2/5$; while, for the railroad, tan $A = 0.03$.

Now a roof which rises 2 feet per 5 feet horizontal will rise 4 feet per 10 feet horizontal. Whether in Fig. 5 we use the right triangle with the legs 2 and 5, or the larger right triangle with the legs 4 and 10, each triangle having A as an acute angle, we obtain the same value for tan A, viz., the ratio of the opposite side to the adjacent side. It is clear that if we use a right triangle with the legs $2n$ and $5n$, we again have tan $A = 2/5$.

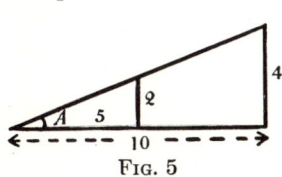

Fig. 5

In mathematics, when the value of one quantity is determined by the value of another, the first quantity is said to be a *function* of the second. For example, the area of a circle is a function of the radius. Again, cost is a function of the quantity bought. It is seen that tan A is determined by the size of the angle A, and hence tan A is a function of A.

The same ideas are involved in the ancient method of finding the height h of a tower by measuring the lengths of its shadow

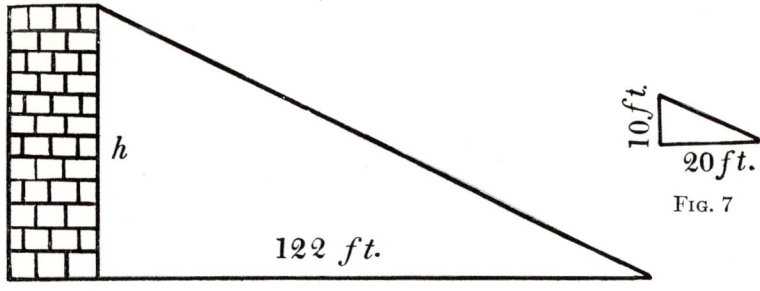

Fig. 6

Fig. 7

and of the shadow of a vertical pole at the same instant. Suppose that the shadows are of lengths 122 and 20 feet, while the pole is 10 feet high. Since the sun's rays are parallel, we have two similar right triangles (Figs. 6, 7), so that $h : 122 = 10 : 20$, whence $h = 61$ feet. The tangent of the angle of elevation of the sun at the moment is $10/20 = 61/122$.

7. Definitions of the trigonometric functions of an acute angle. In the first illustration in Art. 6 of the tangent of an angle, we made use of the horizontal distance beneath a railroad track. But that distance is not so easily or accurately measured as a distance along the track. If we find that the track rises 2 feet for every 100 feet along the track, we speak of $2/100$ as the *sine* of the angle which the track makes with the horizontal plane.

In a right triangle there are, in addition to the two ratios of sides which have been called tangent and sine, four more ratios of sides. The six ratios occur in pairs, and the ratio b/a is called the *reciprocal* of a/b. The six ratios are given names as follows:

The *sine* is the ratio of the opposite side to the hypotenuse. The *cosecant* is the reciprocal of the sine.

The *cosine* is the ratio of the adjacent side to the hypotenuse. The *secant* is the reciprocal of the cosine.

The *tangent* is the ratio of the opposite side to the adjacent. The *cotangent* is the reciprocal of the tangent.

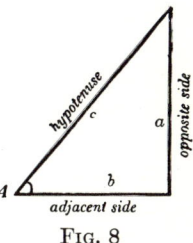

Fig. 8

These definitions should be memorized in these words. The student should repeat the definitions until he also "knows them backwards" and hence can answer the following questions and the two analogous questions of each type:

Which function is the ratio of the adjacent side to the hypotenuse?
Which function is the reciprocal of the tangent?

In symbols we may express these definitions as follows (Fig. 8):

$$\sin A = \frac{a}{c}, \qquad \cos A = \frac{b}{c}, \qquad \tan A = \frac{a}{b},$$

$$\csc A = \frac{1}{\sin A} = \frac{c}{a}, \quad \sec A = \frac{1}{\cos A} = \frac{c}{b}, \quad \cot A = \frac{1}{\tan A} = \frac{b}{a}.$$

Hence the cosecant is the ratio of the hypotenuse to the opposite side, the secant is the ratio of the hypotenuse to the adjacent side, and the cotangent is the ratio of the adjacent side to the opposite side.

As in Art. 6, each of these six trigonometric functions of an acute angle A is a definite number, completely determined by angle A, and that number does not depend on the size of the right triangle, containing angle A, which we may select in defining the function. While the numbers which express the lengths of the sides of such a triangle depend upon the unit of length used, their ratios (i.e., the trigonometric functions of A) are wholly independent of the choice of the unit of length, but depend solely upon the size of A.

By the theorem of Pythagoras, proved in plane geometry,

(1) $$a^2 + b^2 = c^2.$$

EXAMPLE. Find the six functions of the least angle L in the right triangle having the hypotenuse 17 and a leg 8.

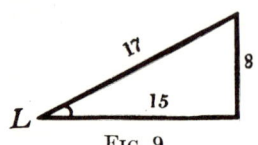

FIG. 9

Solution. By (1), the other leg is 15. Hence, by Fig. 9,

$$\sin L = \frac{8}{17}, \quad \cos L = \frac{15}{17}, \quad \tan L = \frac{8}{15},$$

$$\csc L = \frac{17}{8}, \quad \sec L = \frac{17}{15}, \quad \cot L = \frac{15}{8}.$$

EXERCISES ON THE DEFINITIONS OF THE TRIGONOMETRIC FUNCTIONS[1]

1. Find the six functions of 45°.

Take the adjacent side to be of unit length (Fig. 10). Since the remaining acute angle is 45° (why?), the opposite side is 1 (why?), and the hypotenuse is $\sqrt{2}$ (why?).

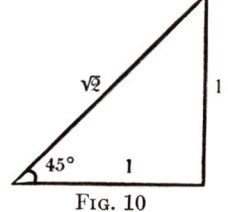

FIG. 10

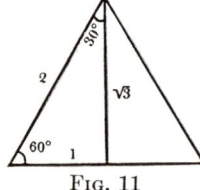

FIG. 11

2. Find the six functions of 60°.

In an equilateral triangle each of whose sides is of length 2, drop a perpendicular from the vertex (Fig. 11). Then each segment of the base is of length 1 (why?) and the perpendicular is of length $\sqrt{3}$ (why?).

3. From Fig. 11 read off the six functions of 30°.

4. Draw a right triangle with an angle of 15° and hypotenuse 10. After measurement of the legs, calculate sin 15° and cos 15°. By drawing more triangles, calculate from measurements the values required to fill out the accompanying table.

A	Sin A	Cos A
15°	0.26	0.97
30°	0.50	0 87
45°	0.71	0.71
60°	0.87	0.50
75°	0.97	0.26

5. Find the six functions of the least angle in the right triangle having the legs 3 and 4.

[1] The first three exercises are needed for many later exercises; the figures should be kept in mind.

6. Find the six functions of the larger acute angle in the right triangle having the hypotenuse 13 and a leg 5.

7. Find the six functions of the least angle in the right triangle having the hypotenuse 41 and a leg 40.

8. Show that neither the sine nor the cosine of an acute angle is greater than unity, while neither the secant nor the cosecant is less than unity.

9. By means of right triangles whose bases have the length unity, construct angles A, B, C for which $\tan A = 0.3$, $\tan B = 3$, $\tan C = p$, where p is any positive number.

Hence show that the tangent of an acute angle may have any positive value whatever. Why is this true also of the cotangent?

8. Problems on heights and distances. For the following problems involving only the angles 30°, 45°, and 60°, exact answers in terms of square roots may be found. Similar problems involving other angles will be assigned later to be solved by use of the traverse table or logarithms.

EXAMPLE 1. When the angle of elevation of the sun is 60°, a vertical pole casts a shadow 50 feet long. What is the height h of the pole?

Solution. We have

$$\tan 60° = \frac{h}{50}; \quad h = 50 \tan 60° = 50\sqrt{3}.$$

EXAMPLE 2. With an instrument I held 6 feet above the level of a pond, a man observes that the angle of elevation of a tree at the edge of the pond is 45° and that the angle of depression of its reflection is 60°. Find the height h of the tree.

Solution. The reflection BR of the tree BT is also of length h (Fig. 12). Since $AB = 6$, we have $AT = h - 6$, $AR = h + 6$. Since $\angle ITA = 45°$, $IA = AT = h - 6$. Thus in triangle IRA,

$$\sqrt{3} = \tan 60° = \frac{AR}{IA} = \frac{h+6}{h-6}.$$

Solving for h, we get

$$h = \frac{6(\sqrt{3}+1)}{\sqrt{3}-1} = \frac{6(\sqrt{3}+1)^2}{(\sqrt{3}-1)(\sqrt{3}+1)},$$

$$h = 6(2+\sqrt{3}).$$

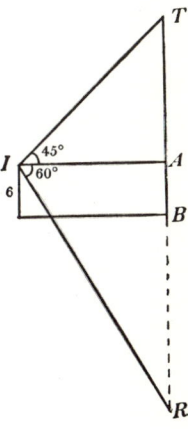

Fig. 12

EXAMPLE 3. The angle of elevation of a balloon B from a station P due south of it is 60°, and from another station Q due west from P and 2 miles from it the angle of elevation is 45°. Find the height h of the balloon.

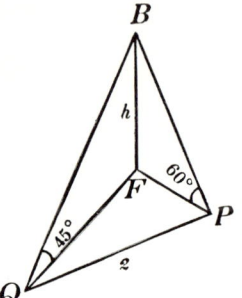

Fig. 13

Solution. Let F be the foot of the perpendicular from B to the ground (Fig. 13). In triangle BFP, $\angle F$ is a right angle and

$$\sqrt{3} = \tan 60° = \frac{h}{FP},$$

whence $FP = h/\sqrt{3}$. In triangle BFQ, $\angle F$ is a right angle, and hence $\angle B = 45°$, so that $QF = h$. Finally, in triangle FPQ, $\angle P$ is a right angle, so that

$$\overline{QF}^2 = \overline{FP}^2 + 4, \quad h^2 = \frac{h^2}{3} + 4, \quad h^2 = 6, \quad h = \sqrt{6}.$$

EXERCISES ON HEIGHTS AND DISTANCES

(Give exact answers, not computing square roots.)

1. At the top of a house 80 feet high, the angle of elevation of the top of a tower is 45°; on the ground floor it is 60°. Find the height of the tower.

2. A man 6 feet tall observes that the angle of elevation of the top of a tree is 45°, while that of the point where the branches begin is 30°. The latter point is 17 feet above the ground. How high is the tree?

3. The angle of ascent of a road is 30°. If a man travels 500 feet up the road, how many feet has he risen?

4. The shadow of a flagpole standing on level ground is 50 feet longer when the angle of elevation of the sun is 30° than when it is 45°. Find the height of the pole.

5. The upper part of a tree broken over by the wind makes an angle of 30° with the ground and its top rests on the ground at a point 75 feet from the root. What was the height of the tree?

6. From a boat at sea the angles of elevation of the top and base of a tree 100 feet high on the top of a bluff are found to be 60° and 45° respectively. Find the height of the bluff.

7. At a point half way between two buildings the angles of elevation of their tops are 30° and 60°. Prove that one building is three times as high as the other.

8. A ladder 24 feet long leans against a house on one side of a street, making an angle of 30° with the street. After the ladder is turned about its foot until the top touches the house on the opposite side of the street, the angle is 60°. Find the width of the street.

9. From the top of a lighthouse of height 120 feet, the angle of depression of an object at sea is 60°, and from the base 30°. How high is the base above the sea?

10. Two persons stand at opposite sides of a pond in positions such that the eyes of one are 6 feet above the pond and those of the other 7 feet. When each person looks toward the pond in a direction making an angle of 60° with the vertical, the reflection of an eye of either is visible to the other person. How wide is the pond?

11. From two points 400 feet apart in a horizontal straight line with the foot of a tower which lies between the points, the angles of elevation of its top are 30° and 60°. How high is the tower?

12. From the top of a tower of height 93 feet, the angles of depression of the top and base of a tree standing on a level with the base of the tower are observed to be 30° and 60°. Find the height of the tree.

13.* A square tower stands upon a horizontal plane. From a point in this plane from which three of its upper corners are visible, their angles of elevation are 45°, 60°, and 45° respectively. What is the ratio of the height of the tower to the breadth of one of its sides?

14.* The angle of elevation of a balloon B from a station P due south of it is α, and from another station Q due west from P and l miles from it the angle of elevation is β. If its height is h, prove that

$$h^2 (\cot^2 \beta - \cot^2 \alpha) = l^2.$$

9. Given one trigonometric function, to find the others. If the value of one of the six functions of an acute angle A is known, we can find the values of the remaining five functions of A either graphically as in the following example or algebraically by means of the formulas in Art. 10. While the latter method has the advantage that we can always compute the required functions to as many decimal places as desired, the graphical method is less liable to gross errors especially when applied later on to angles which are not acute.

EXAMPLE. Construct and measure an acute angle whose cosecant is equal to 9/8. Complete a right triangle and read off the values of the remaining functions.

Solution. Given that csc $A = 9/8$, we have sin $A = 8/9$. Hence in a right triangle one of whose angles is A, the ratio of the opposite side to the hypotenuse is 8/9. To avoid fractions, we therefore take the hypotenuse equal to 9. Then the opposite side is 8. On square-ruled paper, take a vertical ruling line BC containing 8 divisions, and BD containing 9 divisions (Fig. 14). Let the circle with B as center and BD as radius cut the horizontal ruling line through C at the point A. Then ABC is the desired triangle. Since the number of divisions in AC is 4 (more nearly 4.1), we have

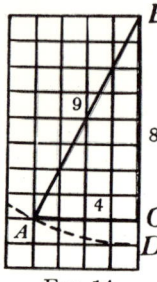

Fig. 14

$$\cos A = \frac{4}{9}, \quad \sec A = \frac{9}{4}, \quad \tan A = \frac{8}{4}, \quad \cot A = \frac{4}{8},$$

approximately, while $A = 63°$, nearly.

Exercises on Drawings to Scale

1. Construct and measure an acute angle whose tangent is equal to 4/3. Complete a right triangle and read off the remaining functions.

2. Construct and measure an acute angle whose cosine is 8/17. Complete a triangle and read off the remaining functions.

3. Construct and measure an acute angle whose secant is 13/5, and find its cotangent and cosecant.

4. Construct and measure an acute angle whose sine is 2/3, and find its cosine and tangent.

5. What is the angle of elevation of the sun when a yardstick casts a shadow of length 27 inches? How high is a flagpole whose shadow is then of length 15 feet?

10. Relations between the six trigonometric functions of an acute angle. For any acute angle A, we shall prove that

(1) $$\sin^2 A + \cos^2 A = 1,$$

where $\sin^2 A$ denotes the square of sin A. By geometry, we have

$$a^2 + b^2 = c^2$$

in the right triangle of Fig. 15. Dividing each member by c^2, we get

$$\left(\frac{a}{c}\right)^2 + \left(\frac{b}{c}\right)^2 = 1.$$

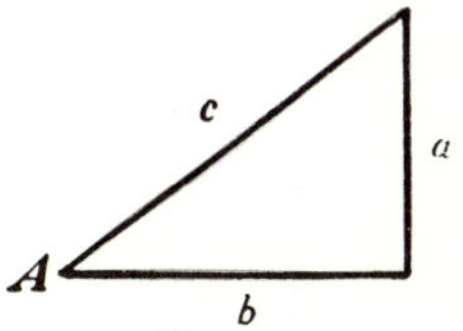

Since $a/c = \sin A$, $b/c = \cos A$, this proves formula (1).

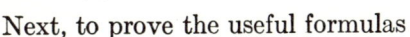

Fig. 15

Next, to prove the useful formulas

(2) $\qquad \tan A = \dfrac{\sin A}{\cos A}, \quad \cot A = \dfrac{\cos A}{\sin A},$

note that

$$\frac{\sin A}{\cos A} = \frac{\frac{a}{c}}{\frac{b}{c}} = \frac{a}{c} \times \frac{c}{b} = \frac{a}{b} = \tan A, \quad \cot A = \frac{1}{\tan A}.$$

Finally, we shall need also the formulas

(3) $\qquad \sec^2 A = 1 + \tan^2 A, \; \csc^2 A = 1 + \cot^2 A,$

which are proved as follows:

$$1 + \tan^2 A = 1 + \frac{\sin^2 A}{\cos^2 A} = \frac{\cos^2 A + \sin^2 A}{\cos^2 A} = \frac{1}{\cos^2 A} = \sec^2 A,$$

$$1 + \cot^2 A = 1 + \frac{\cos^2 A}{\sin^2 A} = \frac{\sin^2 A + \cos^2 A}{\sin^2 A} = \frac{1}{\sin^2 A} = \csc^2 A.$$

Formulas (1)–(3) should be memorized. They enable us to find algebraically all the trigonometric functions of angle A when the value of one function of A is known — a problem treated graphically in Art. 9.

EXAMPLE 1. If A is an acute angle whose cosine is 8/17, find by formulas (1)–(3) the five remaining functions of A.

Solution. By (1),

$$\sin^2 A = 1 - \cos^2 A = 1 - \left(\frac{8}{17}\right)^2 = \left(\frac{15}{17}\right)^2.$$

Since sin A is positive, we take the positive square root and get sin $A = 15/17$. Then, by (2),
$$\tan A = \frac{15}{17} \div \frac{8}{17} = \frac{15}{8}.$$
By definition, cot $A = 8/15$, csc $A = 17/15$, sec $A = 17/8$.

EXAMPLE 2. Given the value v of cot A, find sin A and cos A.

Solution. By the second formula of (3),
$$\csc A = +\sqrt{1+v^2}, \quad \sin A = \frac{1}{\csc A} = \frac{1}{\sqrt{1+v^2}}.$$
While cos A could be found from (1), it is simpler to use the second formula of (2), which gives
$$\cos A = \cot A \sin A = \frac{v}{\sqrt{1+v^2}}.$$

EXERCISES ON THE RELATIONS BETWEEN THE FUNCTIONS OF AN ANGLE

In each of the following 18 exercises, the value of one function of an acute angle A is given. Find by formulas (1)–(3) the values of the remaining functions of A.

1. $\sin A = \frac{4}{5}$.
2. $\cos A = \frac{12}{13}$.
3. $\tan A = \frac{8}{15}$.
4. $\sin A = \frac{3}{5}$.
5. $\cos A = \frac{5}{13}$.
6. $\tan A = \frac{4}{3}$.
7. $\cot A = 1$.
8. $\cot A = \frac{15}{8}$.
9. $\sec A = \frac{17}{15}$.
10. $\sec A = \frac{13}{12}$.
11. $\csc A = \frac{5}{4}$.
12. $\csc A = \frac{5}{3}$.
13. $\tan A = 1$.
14. $\sin A = s$.
15. $\cos A = c$.
16. $\tan A = t$.
17. $\sec A = m$.
18. $\csc A = n$.

19. Prove formulas (3) directly from Fig. 15.

11. Further formulas true for every acute angle. An excellent way to learn formulas (1)–(3) thoroughly is to use them in proving various new formulas.

Ch. I] FUNCTIONS OF ACUTE ANGLES 15

EXAMPLE 1. Prove that, for every acute angle A,
$$(\tan A + \sec A)^2 = \frac{1 + \sin A}{1 - \sin A}.$$

Solution. Replace $\tan A$ by its value $\sin A/\cos A$ from (2), and replace $\sec A$ by $1/\cos A$ (definition). Then the left member of the proposed equation becomes
$$\left(\frac{\sin A}{\cos A} + \frac{1}{\cos A}\right)^2 = \frac{(\sin A + 1)^2}{\cos^2 A} = \frac{(1 + \sin A)^2}{(1 + \sin A)(1 - \sin A)},$$
since $\cos^2 A = 1 - \sin^2 A$ by (1). Finally, we cancel $1 + \sin A$.

EXAMPLE 2. Prove that, for every acute angle $x > 0$,
$$\frac{\sin x}{1 - \cos x} = \frac{1 + \cos x}{\sin x}.$$

Solution. Express each fraction as a new fraction having the common denominator $(1 - \cos x) \sin x$. The new fractions will be equal if their numerators are equal, i.e., if $\sin^2 x = 1 - \cos^2 x$, which is true by (1).

Note that this proof might easily be twisted into the illogical one of manipulating the proposed equation (treated as if known to be a true equation) into the equation $\sin^2 x = 1 - \cos^2 x$ by multiplying both members of the former by $(1 - \cos x) \sin x$. By such a false kind of argument we could "prove" that $4 = 2$ by subtracting 3 from each member to obtain $1 = -1$ and then squaring to obtain the correct equation $1 = 1$.

It is safer for the student to draw a vertical line separating the two members of the proposed equation and manipulate each member *separately* by use of formulas (1)–(3) until he obtains two expressions which are identical.

EXAMPLE 3. Prove that, for every acute angle B,
$$\frac{\sin B}{1 + \cos B} + \frac{1 + \cos B}{\sin B} \;\bigg|\; = 2 \csc B$$

Solution.
$$= \frac{\sin^2 B + (1 + \cos B)^2}{(1 + \cos B) \sin B} \;\bigg|\; = \frac{2}{\sin B}$$
$$= \frac{\sin^2 B + \cos^2 B + 1 + 2 \cos B}{(1 + \cos B) \sin B}$$
$$= \frac{2 + 2 \cos B}{(1 + \cos B) \sin B} = \frac{2}{\sin B}$$

Exercises on Identities

Prove that the following equations are true for every acute angle:

1. $(\tan A + \cot A) \sin A \cos A = 1.$
2. $\cos^2 A (1 + \tan^2 A) = 1.$
3. $\tan^2 x \cos^2 x + \cot^2 x \sin^2 x = 1.$
4. $\cos x + \tan x \sin x = \sec x.$
5. $\sin y \sec y \cot y = \cos y \csc y \tan y.$
6. $\csc^2 y \tan^2 y - 1 = \tan^2 y.$
7. $\tan^4 B + \sec^4 B = 2 \sec^2 B \tan^2 B + 1.$
8. $\cot^2 B - \cos^2 B = \cot^2 B \cos^2 B.$
9. $\sin x \cos x (\sec x + \csc x) = \sin x + \cos x.$
10. $\sec^2 x + \csc^2 x = \sec^2 x \csc^2 x.$
11. $(1 + \tan \beta)^2 + (1 + \cot \beta)^2 = (\sec \beta + \csc \beta)^2.$
12. $\sec^2 \beta \csc^2 \beta = \tan^2 \beta + \cot^2 \beta + 2.$
13. $\dfrac{\tan A + \tan B}{\cot A + \cot B} = \tan A \tan B.$
14. $\dfrac{1 - \tan^2 A}{1 + \tan^2 A} = \cos^2 A - \sin^2 A.$
15. $\dfrac{\sec z - \csc z}{\sec z + \csc z} = \dfrac{\tan z - 1}{\tan z + 1}.$
16. $\dfrac{\tan x - \cot x}{\tan x + \cot x} = 2 \sin^2 x - 1.$

12. Relations between the functions of complementary angles. Two angles are called complementary if their sum is a right angle or 90°. Hence the two acute angles A and B (Fig. 16) of any right triangle are complementary.

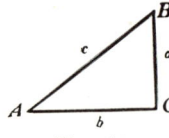

Fig. 16

We have

$$\sin A = \frac{a}{c} = \cos B, \quad \cos A = \frac{b}{c} = \sin B,$$

$$\tan A = \frac{a}{b} = \cot B.$$

Passing to reciprocals, we get

$$\csc A = \sec B, \quad \sec A = \csc B, \quad \cot A = \tan B.$$

Since $B = 90° - A$, these formulas may be rearranged and written in the form

$$\sin(90° - A) = \cos A, \quad \csc(90° - A) = \sec A,$$
$$\cos(90° - A) = \sin A, \quad \sec(90° - A) = \csc A,$$
$$\tan(90° - A) = \cot A, \quad \cot(90° - A) = \tan A.$$

These six useful formulas, which are true for every acute angle A, may be combined into a single formula which is more easily remembered than the six. To this end, let us designate the cosine as the co-function of the sine, the cotangent as the co-function of the tangent, the cosecant as the co-function of the secant, and, vice versa, the sine as the co-function of the cosine, etc. Thus always the co-function is obtained by annexing or deleting the prefix "co" before the function, according as the name of the function does not already start or starts with "co." Hence *any trigonometric function of the complement of an acute angle A is equal to the co-function of A.*

The values of the trigonometric functions of the acute angles greater than 45° can therefore be expressed in terms of functions of angles less than or equal to 45°. For example, $\cos 70° = \sin 20°$, $\cot 65° = \tan 25°$. Hence tables of the trigonometric functions need extend only as far as 45°. Moreover, we can now understand the origin of the names cosine, cotangent, and cosecant. In Latin, the cosine was initially *complementi sinus*, i.e., the sine of the complement, and this term was later abbreviated to *cosinus*.

EXAMPLE. Find an acute angle x for which $\tan 2x = \cot(45° + x)$.

Solution. Substitute for $\tan 2x$ the equal value $\cot(90° - 2x)$. Since two acute angles with the same cotangent are equal, we have

$$90° - 2x = 45° + x, \quad 45° = 3x, \quad x = 15°.$$

Exercises on Functions of Complementary Angles

1. Express as functions of their complementary angles $\sin 65°$, $\cos 20°$, $\tan 55° \, 20'$, $\cot 82° \, 12'$, $\sec 67°$, $\csc 67°$.
2. Express as functions of angles less than 45° all the functions of 70°.
3. Show that $\sin(45° + x) = \cos(45° - x)$,
$\tan(60° + x) = \cot(30° - x)$.

Find the acute angles x for which

4. $\cot x = \tan (45° + x)$.
5. $\cos 2x = \sin (45° - x)$.
6. $\tan 3x = \cot 2x$.
7. $\sin 2x = \cos 4x$.
8. $\cos x = \cos (90° - x)$.
9. $\sin (2x - 30°) = \cos (30° + x)$.
10. Prove that $\tan (90° - A) + \cot (90° - A) = \csc A \csc (90° - A)$.

CHAPTER II

SOLUTION OF RIGHT TRIANGLES BY MEANS OF TABLES OF THE
NATURAL FUNCTIONS

13. How to use tables of natural functions. Tables I–V give the values of the trigonometric functions of every acute angle expressed in degrees and sixths of a degree (10', 20', 30', etc.). In the headings of these tables, the word *natural* is inserted to distinguish them from the tables of the logarithms of the trigonometric functions, which will be explained in Chapter IV.

Tables I and II together give the values of the (natural) sine and cosine to four decimal places of the angles from 0° to 90° at intervals of 10 minutes. When the number of minutes in an angle is not a multiple of 10, we resort to interpolation, as explained in Examples 4–6.

EXAMPLE 1. Find sin 25°20'.

Since we desire the sine of an angle *less than* 45°, we use Table I, marked natural sines at the *top* of its page, and look in the *left-hand* column for 25° and then along its horizontal row until we reach the entry 4279 which occurs in the column marked 20' at its *top*. Supplying the decimal point (as indicated at various places in the second column), we have sin 25°20' = 0.4279.

(The words in italics have the opposite sense to the corresponding words in Ex. 2; for example, *less than* and *greater than*, or *top* and *bottom*.)

EXAMPLE 2. Find cos 64°40'.

Since we desire the cosine of an angle *greater than* 45°, we use Table I, marked natural cosines at the *bottom* of its page, and look in the *right-hand* column for 64° and then along its horizontal row until we reach the entry 4279 which occurs in the column marked 40' at its *bottom*. Thus cos 64°40' = 0.4279.

This result agrees with that in Ex. 1 since the sine of an acute angle equals the cosine of its complement (Art. 12). We now see why a table of sines serves also as a table of cosines when properly labeled.

EXAMPLE 3. Find cos 25°20' and sin 64°40'.

Using Table II and following the instructions given in Ex. 1 in the case of 25°20′, and those in Ex. 2 for 64°40′, we get 0.9038 in either case.

EXAMPLE 4. Find sin 25°23′.

By Table I, sin 25°20′ = 0.4279, sin 25°30′ = 0.4305. Our angle lies between these two angles and is three-tenths of the way from the smaller angle toward the larger. It is assumed that its sine will lie three-tenths of the way from 0.4279 toward 0.4305. The difference of the latter numbers is 0.0026, three-tenths of which is 0.0008 to four decimal places. Hence

$$\sin 25°23′ = 0.4279 + 0.0008 = 0.4287.$$

This work is abbreviated by making use of the tablettes, headed P. P. (proportional parts), given at the right of our table. Opposite to the marginal number 3 (for 3 tenths), we find in the tablette headed 26 the desired correction 8 (to the fourth decimal place).

EXAMPLE 5. Find cos 64°58′.

In Table I, using the labels at the bottom of the page and the angles in the right-hand column, we see that the entry 4253 for cos 64°50′ *exceeds* the entry 4226 for cos 64°60′ by 27. The P. P. of 27 for 8 (tenths) is 22. This correction is to be *subtracted* from 4253 to obtain cos 64°58′ = 0.4231, since we noticed that the cosine decreases when the angle increases.

The use of Tables III–V of natural tangents and cotangents is entirely similar to that of the tables just explained (see Ex. 6). The converse problem of finding an acute angle when one of its functions is given will be explained by the following example.

EXAMPLE 6. Find the acute angle x whose cotangent is 2.

Since Table V does not contain an entry exactly equal to 2, we employ the adjacent numbers between which 2 lies:

$$\left.\begin{array}{l}\cot 26°30′ = 2\,006 \\ \cot \ x \ \ \ \ = 2\,000 \\ \cot 26°40′ = 1.991\end{array}\right\}\begin{array}{c}6\end{array}\right\}\ 15$$

Hence x is six-fifteenths of the way from 26°30′ toward 26°40′. But

$$\frac{6}{15} \times 10′ = \frac{2}{5} \times 10′ = 4′.$$

Hence $x = 26°34′$. Or we may use the P. P. tablette headed 15, look for 6 underneath 15, and at the left of 6 read off the marginal number 4 of minutes in the correction.

Ch. II] TABLES OF NATURAL FUNCTIONS 21

EXERCISES ON THE USE OF TABLES OF NATURAL FUNCTIONS

1. Find the sines, cosines, tangents, and cotangents of
   (a) 18°24'. (b) 36°45'. (c) 71°36'.
2. Find $\tan A + \cot A$ when $A = 55°25'$.
3. Find $\cos B + \cos \tfrac{1}{2}B + \cos \tfrac{1}{3}B$ when $B = 73°6'$.
4. Find the acute angles for which

   $\sin x = 0.4567,$ $\cos y = 0.7654,$
   $\tan z = 2.123,$ $\cot w = 0.1234.$

5. Given $\cos 2C = 0.3456$, find $\tan C$.
6. A ladder 20 feet long leans against the side of a house, its foot being 8 feet from the house. What angle does the ladder make with the ground?
7. What is the angle of elevation of the sun when a vertical pole of height 12 feet casts a shadow 25 feet long?
8. Find the grade (Art. 6) of a railroad track which rises 4 feet per 100 feet along the track.
9. The Grand Canyon of the Colorado River has in places a depth of 1 mile and a width of 8 miles from rim to rim. Assuming that the walls or banks are planes intersecting at the bottom of the canyon, find the angles of inclination of the walls with the horizontal plane.

14. Solution of right triangles by means of tables of natural functions. Not counting the right angle, there are five *parts* in a right triangle, viz., its three sides and two acute angles. If only the angles are given, the shape, but not the size, of the triangle is determined. But if we are given any two parts at least one of which is a side, we proceed to show how we can solve the triangle, i.e., find the remaining three parts.

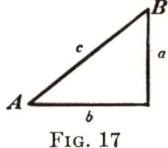

FIG. 17

First, let the two given parts be sides. Then (Fig. 17) in one of the three relations

(1) $\qquad \sin A = \dfrac{a}{c}, \quad \cos A = \dfrac{b}{c}, \quad \tan A = \dfrac{a}{b},$

angle A is the only unknown, so that we can find A by looking in the tables. There remain two relations (1), of which one determines the third side and the other serves as a check. Finally, $B = 90° - A$.

Second, let the two given parts be an angle and a side. Since $A + B = 90°$, we have both angles. Then two of the relations (1) determine the two unknown sides and the third relation serves as a check.

Besides the check mentioned, a further check against gross errors may be secured by inspecting Traverse Table VI, to be explained in Chapter III, or by making a drawing to scale.

EXAMPLE 1. Given $\angle A = 43°15'$ and the hypotenuse $c = 13.20$, find the remaining parts of the right triangle.

Solution. $B = 90° - A = 46°45'$.

$$\sin A = \frac{a}{c}, \quad a = c \sin A \qquad \cos A = \frac{b}{c}, \quad b = c \cos A$$

$\sin A =$	0.6852	$\cos A =$	0.7284
$c =$	13.2	$c =$	13.2
	13704		14568
	20556		21852
	6852		7284
$a =$	9.0446	$b =$	9.6149

Since only four decimal places of $\sin A$ and $\cos A$ were given by our tables, we have suppressed the fifth decimal places in the products. Check: $\tan A = 0.9408 = a/b$.

EXAMPLE 2. Given the hypotenuse $c = 63.12$ and a leg $a = 47.04$, find the remaining parts of the right triangle.

Solution. First find $\angle A$ from $\sin A = a/c$:

$$\sin A = \frac{47.04}{63.12} = 0.7452, \quad A = 48°10\tfrac{1}{2}'.$$

Next find b from $\cos A = b/c$:

$$b = c \cos A = 63.12 \times 0.6669 = 42.09.$$

As a check, compute b directly from the given parts, using

(2) $\qquad b^2 = (c + a)(c - a),$

which is a way of writing $a^2 + b^2 = c^2$.

EXAMPLE 3. Given $a = 27$, $b = 40$, find the remaining parts.

Solution. $\tan A = 27/40 = 0.6750$, $A = 34°1'$, $B = 55°59'$

$$c^2 = a^2 + b^2 = 729 + 1600 = 2329, \quad c = 48.260.$$

Check: $\cos A = 0.8288 = b/c$.

The method of Ex. 3 is not recommended when either leg is expressed by a number containing more than two digits.

15. Cases when an angle cannot be accurately found by Table II. If $\cos A = 0.9994$, we cannot tell by Table II which of the angles between $1°50'$ and $2°10'$ is to be taken as A. Given the cosine of an angle greater than $9°$, we can find the angle correctly[1] to within $1'$, but not if the angle is less than $9°$. Similarly, we may make an error of $2'$ or more if we determine by Table II an angle greater than $81°$ whose sine is given.

Such an error can arise in only two cases of the solution of right triangles and may be avoided as follows. Given leg b and hypotenuse c, with b nearly equal to c, so that angle A is small, do not attempt to find A from $\cos A = b/c$, but first compute a by means of
$$a^2 = (c+b)(c-b),$$
and then determine A by means of its tangent or sine. Similarly, given a and c, with a nearly equal to c, so that angle A is nearly $90°$, do not attempt to find A from $\sin A = a/c$, but first compute b by means of formula (2) and then determine A by means of its tangent or cosine.

In brief, *when the hypotenuse and one leg are given, first find the other leg and then find an angle from its tangent.* The computation is best made by logarithms (Art. 35).

For example, let $c = 4.345$, $b = 4.331$. Then
$$c + b = 8.676, \ c - b = 0.014, \ a^2 = 0.121464, \ a = 0.3485,$$
$$\tan A = \frac{a}{b} = 0.0805, \ A = 4°36'.$$

However, in the practice of trigonometry we are concerned with the results of measurements. Let us therefore assume that c and b are correct only to the third decimal place, so that each may be in error by ± 0.0005. The correct value of $c - b$ is between 0.013 and 0.015, and its product a^2 by[2] $c + b$ is between 0.1127 and 0.130. Thus a is between $.335$ and $.361$. Then $\tan A$ is between $.077$ and $.0834$, whence A is between $4°24'$ and $4°46'$.

If we attempt to find A from $\cos A = b/c$, allowing an error of $\pm .0005$ in both b and c, we find that b/c lies between $.9965$ and $.9970$, whence A lies between $4°47'$ and $4°25'$.

---

[1] As is shown by a five-place table of natural sines.

[2] In practice, we retain only the same number of significant figures in each factor. The product of 8.7 by .014 is .12 to two places, which alone are reliable.

Either of our two methods of finding angle A leads to a conclusion which involves the same doubt. This doubt is not due to imperfections in our tables, but is due to the impossibility of finding angle A accurately from our badly chosen measurements. In fact, our first solution (which is theoretically the best one) shows clearly that a small absolute error in b and c may cause double that absolute error in the very small difference $c-b$ and hence a large relative error in $c-b$, and consequently a large error in A.

The same doubt occurs in the geometrical determination of angle B in Fig. 14, given nearly equal values of BC and AB. A small error in either evidently causes a large error in finding the intersection A of line AC with the arc AD of the circle, since the arc runs practically parallel to AC when AB and BC are nearly equal.

The long multiplications, divisions, and extractions of square roots, involved in the solution and checking by tables of natural functions, are avoided in the solution by logarithms (Chapter IV) or by a traverse table (Chapter III). Hence only relatively few problems are proposed here for solution by tables of natural functions.

EXERCISES ON SOLVING RIGHT TRIANGLES BY NATURAL FUNCTIONS

Solve the right triangles having the following given parts:

1. $c = 300, B = 20°$. 2. $A = 15°, b = 40$. 3. $A = 25°, a = 15$.
4. $a = 115, c = 176$. 5. $b = 17, c = 18$. 6. $a = 3, b = 4$.

7. From one milestone a house is seen in a direction making 60°4′ with a straight road, and at the next milestone the angle is 30°2′, the road between the milestones being an arm of each angle. How far is the house from the road?

8. Two forts are 4 miles apart and one is due west of the other. From one a ship is observed due north and from the other it is 15° west of north (i.e., the line to the ship is to the west of the line to north and the angle between is 15°). How far is the ship from the nearest fort?

9. A tunnel slopes downward at an angle of 10° with the horizontal. How far below the level ground is a point which is 220 feet down the tunnel?

10. A vertical pole 45 feet high casts a horizontal shadow 75 feet long. What will be the length of the shadow when the sun is 10° higher?

11. From a point P in the fifth floor of a building the distances between whose successive stories are all equal, the angle of depression of a point in the street is 48°. What is the angle of depression from a point, directly below P, in the third floor?

Hint: Assume a convenient value, as 100, for the height of the fifth floor.

12.* From a point 5 feet above a lake, the angle of elevation of the top of a tree standing at the edge of the water is 50°, while the angle of depression of the lowest point of its reflection in the water is 55°. How high is the tree?

13.* From a pier 8 feet above the water, the angle of elevation of the top of the mast of a boat is 48° and the angle of depression of the lowest point of its reflection in the water is 56°. What is the height of the top?

CHAPTER III

TRAVERSE TABLE; SOLUTION OF RIGHT TRIANGLES BY INSPECTION; PROBLEMS ON FORCES AND REFRACTION OF LIGHT

16. Description of Traverse Table VI. Table VI gives at sight the values to two decimal places of the legs of each right triangle in which an angle is 1°, 2°,..., or 89° and the hypotenuse is 1, 2,.., 100, 200,.., or 900.

For example, if the angle is 30° and the hypotenuse is 20, we see by the table that the opposite leg is 10.00 (it is exactly half of the hypotenuse), and the adjacent leg is 17.32 (which is the value of $10\sqrt{3}$ to two decimal places).

In this chapter we ignore the further headings[1] in Table VI, dis., lat., dep, D, $D \cos$, $D \sin$, which will be needed in the chapters on navigation and surveying.

17. When and how to use Traverse Table VI. In navigation, farm surveying, and in most practical problems, results correct to only three or four figures are desired, and then the traverse table may be used with a decided saving of time. When greater accuracy is necessary, the computation should be made by logarithms and checked against gross errors by the traverse table, which furnishes a more accurate and more rapid check than a drawing made to scale. When checking by the traverse table, we may omit all interpolation or interpolate roughly by inspection.

There is one case in the solution of right triangles in which the use of the traverse table is inconvenient (though possible, Art. 46), viz., when we are given the two legs and seek the hypotenuse and the angles. None of the exercises in this chapter falls under this case.

---

[1]Only one set of headings has hitherto been printed in traverse tables. Bowditch's *American Practical Navigator* (U. S. Hydrographic Office) gives, in 90 pages, the values to one decimal place of latitude and departure for 1°,.., 89° and distance 1, 2,..., 600. There exist other traverse tables of the same length which read to quarters of a degree and distances up to 100. Much more bulky is Boileau's *Traverse Table, Computed for Every Minute of Arc and for Distances 1 to 10*, published by Van Nostrand & Co.

The method of using the traverse table is similar to that for tables of natural functions (Chapter II) and will be explained by examples.

EXAMPLE 1. Given the angle 44° and the hypotenuse 385, find the adjacent leg.

Solution. Divide the hypotenuse by 5 to obtain the hypotenuse 77 of a similar triangle which is directly within the limits of Table VI and has the adjacent leg 55.39 by the table. Its product by 5 gives the adjacent leg 276.95 of the original triangle. This result may be in error 0.02, or 5 times the possible error, which is at most 0.005, in the reading from the table. To avoid such a material increase in the error, we express 385 as the sum of 300 and 85. For hypotenuse 300, the adjacent leg is 215.80. For hypotenuse 85, the adjacent leg is 61.14. The sum of these legs gives the adjacent leg 276.94 of the original triangle (Fig. 18).

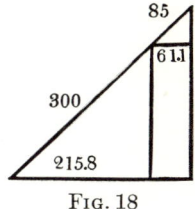

FIG. 18

EXAMPLE 2. Find the legs of a triangle whose hypotenuse is 385 and one angle is 44°20′.

Solution. As in Ex. 1, we read from Table VI the numbers in the first and third lines of the following tablette:

hyp.	angle	adj. leg	opp. leg
385	44°	276.94	267.45
385	44° 20′	*275.37*	*269.04*
385	45°	272.23	272.23
		3|4.71	3|4.78
		−1.57	+1.59

We use $\frac{20}{60}$ or ⅓ of the differences to interpolate the values in the second line.

EXAMPLE 3. Given the angle 77° and the opposite leg 55.80, find the hypotenuse and the adjacent leg.

Solution. Table VI gives the first and third lines below:

opp. leg	hyp.	adj. leg
.97 { .26 { 55.54	57	12.82
55.80	57.27	12.88 } .23
56.51	58	13.05

$$\frac{26}{97} \times 1 = .27, \quad \frac{26}{97} \times .23 = .06$$

Exercises on Heights and Distances

Solve the following problems by means of Traverse Table VI.

1. When the angle of elevation of the sun is 55°, how high is a flagpole which casts a horizontal shadow 42 feet long?

2. How high is a kite if held by a string 1100 feet long making 35° with a vertical line?

3. From the top of a cliff 320 feet above water, the angle of depression of a boat is 15°. How far is the boat from the foot of the cliff?

4. Find the height of a kite whose angle of elevation is 40° if held by a string 500 yards long.

5. From the top of a hill 1240 feet above a level plane, the angles of depression of two houses in the plane, both due south of the observer, were found to be 25° and 35°. Find the distance between the houses.

6. The centers of two circles, whose radii are 16 and 24 inches, are 6 feet apart. Find the length of an exterior common tangent and its angle of inclination with the line of centers.

7. Two stations on a level plane are 6 miles apart. The angle of depression of one from a balloon directly above the other is 8°. How high is the balloon?

8. A man sees a fort 26° north of east, and after walking 500 yards in the direction 40° south of east he sees it due north. How far is the fort from his new position?

9. A spherical balloon 15 yards in diameter subtends an angle of 2° from a point P at which the angle of elevation of the point of contact of the lower tangent from P is 50°. How high is the center of the balloon?

10. The angle of elevation at a point A of the center of a spherical balloon 40 feet in diameter was found to be 65°. At the same instant the angle subtended at A by the balloon was 2°. Find the height of the center of the balloon above the horizontal plane through A.

11. The angle of elevation of the top T of an inaccessible fort observed from a point P in the level plane is 12°. At a point Q, in the plane, 440 feet from P and on a line PQ perpendicular to PT, the angle PQT is 62°. Find the height of the fort.

12. From the ground floor of a building, the angle of elevation of the top of a hotel is 24°, while from a floor 30 feet higher up the angle of depression of the floor of the hotel is 28°. How high is the hotel?

Ch. III] TRAVERSE TABLE 29

13.* There are two routes ABC and ADC from A to a place C on the opposite shore of a lake and 44 miles from A, each route being along portions of two intersecting roads. Given the angles $CAB = 65°$, $BCA = 25°$, $ACD = 61°$, $CAD = 29°$, find the length of the shorter of the two routes.

Resultants and Components of Forces

18. Force. Examples of forces are the exertions of a man in lifting, pulling, or pushing an object; gravity, which causes an unsupported object to fall to the ground; and a stroke which drives a base ball. In general, force is that which tends to change the state of rest or uniform motion of a body.

We speak not only of the magnitude of a force (telling how large or small it is), but also of its direction. Hailstones descending vertically cause little damage in a city, but when descending obliquely often break window panes. Since a force is completely defined when its magnitude, its direction, and the point at which it is applied, are all given, a force is appropriately represented by a directed (arrowed) segment of a straight line (as OB in Fig. 19)

19. Resultant of two forces. Under the force of gravity alone, hailstones descend vertically. But when acted upon also by the force of a north wind, hailstones descend obliquely in a southerly direction, just as if acted upon by a single force in that oblique line. So always, if two forces are acting simultaneously upon a body, there is a single force, called the *resultant* of the two forces, which will produce the same effect upon the body as is produced by the joint action of the two forces.

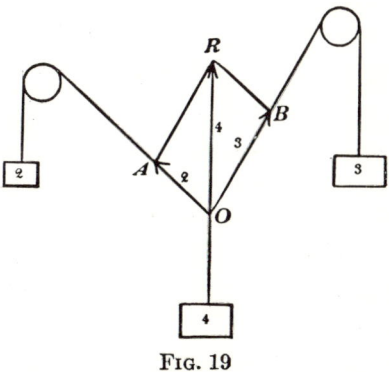

Fig. 19

20. Parallelogram of forces. If two given forces are represented in magnitude and direction by the lines OA and OB, their resultant will be represented in magnitude and direction by the diagonal OR of the parallelogram of which OA and OB are sides (Fig. 19).

This law has been justified by many experiments such as the following. Choose any two numbers, as 2 and 3, and select any third number, as 4, which is less than their sum, but exceeds their difference (whence a triangle OBR can be drawn having 2, 3, 4 as sides). At one end of a cord passing over two pulleys attach a weight of 2 lbs. and at the other end a weight of 3 lbs. At a point O of the cord between the pulleys attach a weight of 4 lbs. After some motion, the system of weights will come to rest. Then, if OA represents 2 units of length, OB 3 units, and OR 4 units, the quadrilateral $AOBR$ will be found to be a parallelogram.

The same principle applies to velocities as well as to forces.

21. Component of a force. When a boat is towed by a horse walking along a bank of a canal, only a part of the force OR exerted by the horse is effective in pulling the boat in the direction OA of the canal (Fig. 20). This part OA, where angle OAR is a right angle, is called the *component* of OR in the direction OA.

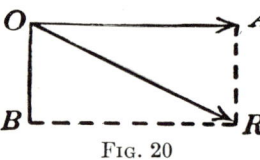

Fig. 20

The component OB, in a direction perpendicular to OA and such that OBR is a right angle, tends to pull the boat toward the bank and is balanced by the resistance of the water on the rudder.

EXAMPLE. A ball weighing 80 pounds rests on a smooth plane inclined at the angle of 20° to the horizontal plane. What force acting parallel to the inclined plane is necessary to keep the ball from rolling down the plane?

Solution. We desire the component c, along a line making 70° with a vertical line, of a force of 80 pounds acting vertically downwards. Hence c is the side adjacent to angle 70° in a right triangle whose hypotenuse is 80. By Table VI, $c = 27.36$ pounds.

Ch. III] TRAVERSE TABLE 31

Exercises on Resultants and Components of Forces

1. Two forces of 5 and 12 pounds act at right angles to each other. Find the resultant force (without using tables) and the angle which it makes with the second force.

2. A sled is pulled along a level road by a force of 65 pounds, the direction of the pull making 50° with the horizontal. Find the forward pull on the sled.

3. Two men lift a weight by means of ropes in the same vertical plane. One man pulls 42 pounds in a direction making 22° with the vertical and the other 63 pounds in a direction making 43° with the vertical. How heavy is the weight?

4. A ship, always headed due east, steams at a speed which would carry it 12 miles per hour in still water. But, on account of a current running due south, its actual speed is 13.5 miles per hour and its track in the water makes an angle of 27° with an easterly direction. Find the velocity of the current.

5.* Each half of a bridge is inclined 8° to the horizontal. Find the vertical pressure and the horizontal thrust (i.e., pressure) upon the two supporting piers at the ends when the bridge bears 40 tons at its middle.

6. A horse pulls with a force of 400 pounds along a towline making 7° with the direction of a canal. Find the effective force on the boat.

7. Find without tables the magnitude of the resultant of a force of 30 pounds acting southwest with a force of 40 pounds acting southeast.

8.* Resolve a force of 100 pounds into two equal components whose directions make an angle of 70° with each other.

22. Refraction of light. When a ray of light AB passes from the air into water, it does not continue in its former direction ABE, but is said to be *refracted* into a new direction BC (Fig. 21). The angle i which the incident ray AB makes with the perpendicular PB to the surface of the water is called the *angle of incidence*. The angle r which

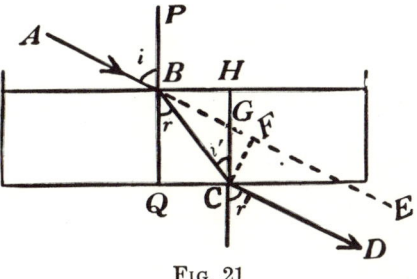

Fig. 21

the refracted ray BC makes with this perpendicular QBP is the *angle of refraction*. Experiments show that the quotient

$$\frac{\sin i}{\sin r} = \text{index of refraction}$$

has the same value, approximately 4/3, whatever be the angle of incidence i. Hence, if $i = 30°$,

$$\sin r = \frac{3}{4} \sin 30° = \frac{3}{8}, \quad r = 22°.$$

The index of refraction from air to crown glass is about 3/2.

To find the index of refraction from water to air, let the bottom of the tank (Fig. 21) containing the water be horizontal and transparent. For the same ray of light passing through the bottom into the air, let i' be the angle of incidence and r' the angle of refraction. Then i' and r are equal, being alternate angles, while, as shown by experiments, $r' = i$, so that the ray CD after passing through the water, with its upper and lower surfaces parallel, is exactly parallel to the ray AB before entering the water. Thus the index of refraction from water to air is

$$\frac{\sin i'}{\sin r'} = \frac{\sin r}{\sin i} = \frac{3}{4},$$

and is the reciprocal of the index of refraction from air to water.

EXAMPLE. A pebble lies at the bottom of a pool of water 4 feet deep. How far below the surface will the pebble appear to be to a man above if his line of vision makes an angle of 5° with the perpendicular to the water?

Solution. The ray of light CBA (Fig. 21) proceeds from the pebble C to the eye at A, the angle of incidence being r and the angle of refraction $i = 5°$. Thus

$$\frac{\sin r}{\sin 5°} = \frac{3}{4}, \quad \sin 5° = 0.0872, \quad \sin r = 0.0654, \quad r = 3°45'.$$

In triangle QBC, adj. side BQ is 4 ft., or 40 tenths of a foot. Table VI shows that when adj. side is 40 and the angle is 3° or 4°, the opp. side is 2.09 or 2.80 respectively, and by interpolation is 2.62 for 3°45′. Thus $QC = BH = 2.62$. Since $\angle GBH = 90° - i = 85°$, the opp. side HG is 30 (tenths) by Table VI. Hence the answer is 3 ft.

Exercises on Refraction of Light

1. A pebble lies at the bottom of a pool of water 6 feet deep. How far below the surface will the pebble appear to a man above if his line of sight makes 8° with the perpendicular to the water?

2. Find the displacement CF (Fig. 21) of a ray of light passing through a crown glass plate 0.258 in. thick at the angle $ABP = 55°50'$ with the perpendicular to the plate.

3. A man whose eye is at a point A, 10 feet above the level of the water BH (Fig. 21), sees at B the image of the foot C of a pile HC driven in the water. His horizontal distance from B is 24 feet, and from the pile 78 feet. Find the length HC of the pile below water.

4. If a ray of light passes through water and makes angle i with the perpendicular to the surface of the water, the largest value of i for which the ray will emerge into the air is C, where $\sin C = 3/4$; while, for $i > C$, the ray is wholly reflected by the surface back into the water. Find this *critical angle* C. Will a ray having $i = 50°$ be refracted or all reflected?

5. If the critical angle (Ex. 4) for crown glass is 42.5°, what is the index of refraction from crown glass to air? A crown glass prism, whose cross section is an isosceles right triangle, acts as a total reflector for rays entering at right angles to either perpendicular face.

CHAPTER IV

Logarithms, Slide Rule

23. Powers of 10. The symbol 10^2 denotes the square of 10 and equals $10 \times 10 = 100$. Again, 10^3 denotes the cube of 10 and equals $10 \times 10 \times 10 = 1000$. The product $10^2 \times 10^3$, being the product of two factors 10 by three factors 10, equals 10^5, which is the product of five factors 10. It follows that the quotient of 10^5 by 10^2 equals 10^3. These facts are expressed by the following equations:
$$10^2 \times 10^3 = 10^5, \quad 10^5 \div 10^2 = 10^3.$$
Similarly, if m and n are any two positive whole numbers,

(1) $\qquad 10^m \times 10^n = 10^{m+n},$
(2) $\qquad 10^m \div 10^n = 10^{m-n} \quad$ (if $m > n$).

Just as $(10^3)^2 = 10^3 \times 10^3 = 10^6$, so always

(3) $\qquad\qquad\qquad (10^m)^n = 10^{mn}.$

Formulas (1), (2), (3) are known as the *first*, *second*, and *third index laws*, respectively.

We next inquire what meaning must be given to symbols like $10^{\frac{1}{2}}$, $10^{\frac{1}{3}}$, 10^{-2} if also these symbols shall obey the index laws. Using the third law (3), we have
$$(10^{\frac{1}{2}})^2 = 10^1 = 10, \quad (10^{\frac{1}{3}})^3 = 10, \quad (10^{\frac{n}{d}})^d = 10^n,$$
so that $10^{\frac{1}{2}}$ is the (positive) square root of 10, $10^{\frac{1}{3}}$ is the cube root of 10, and, in general, $10^{n/d}$ is the dth root of 10^n:

(4) $\qquad 10^{\frac{1}{2}} = \sqrt{10}, \quad 10^{\frac{1}{3}} = \sqrt[3]{10}, \quad 10^{\frac{n}{d}} = \sqrt[d]{10^n}.$

We agree to employ the second law (2) also in the new case $m = n = 2$, whence
$$10^2 \div 10^2 = 10^0.$$

But when 10^2 is divided by 10^2, the quotient is 1. Hence we make the definition that

(5) $$10^0 = 1.$$

Finally, we employ (2) when $m = 0$ and obtain
$$10^0 \div 10^n = 10^{-n}.$$

By our preceding result, $10^0 = 1$. Hence we have

(6) $$10^{-n} = \frac{1}{10^n}.$$

To illustrate these new definitions, let us take the number 10^3 and divide it by 10, then divide the quotient 10^2 by 10, etc. We obtain the powers of 10 written in the upper of the following two rows:

10^3	10^2	10^1	10^0	10^{-1}	10^{-2}	10^{-3}
1000	100	10	1	0.1	0.01	0.001.

Similarly, starting with 1000, we obtain the numbers in the lower row by successive divisions by 10. This process makes clear that each power of 10 in the upper row should have the value written beneath it, and hence that our definitions (5) and (6) are justified.

We have now attached a definite meaning to 10^e when the exponent e is any whole number or fraction, whether positive, negative, or zero, i.e., when e is *rational*.

We may also find a suitable meaning for 10^e when e is any real number, like $\sqrt{2}$, which is not rational. In fact, if we employ the successively closer approximations

$$1.4, \quad 1.41, \quad 1.414, \quad 1.4142, \ldots$$

to $\sqrt{2}$, the corresponding numbers

$$10^{1.4} = \sqrt[10]{10^{14}}, \quad 10^{1.41} = \sqrt[100]{10^{141}}, \quad 10^{1.414}, \quad 10^{1.4142}, \ldots$$

are successively closer approximations to a definite number[1] which is designated by $10^{\sqrt{2}}$.

Conversely, any given positive number can be expressed in the form 10^e by choice of a suitable exponent e.

---

[1] Its value to two decimal places is 25.95, since this is the number whose logarithm is 1.4142, as the reader will soon be able to see by the table of logarithms.

24. Logarithms. If $10^e = N$, we call e the (common) logarithm of N and write it "log N." Hence, by definition,

(7) $$N = 10^{\log N}.$$

Thus the exponent of the power of 10 which gives rise to a positive number N is called the logarithm of N. Expressed otherwise, the logarithm of a positive number N is the number which indicates the power to which 10 must be raised to yield N. Negative numbers do not have logarithms.

From the following results in Art. 23:

$$10^2 = 100, \quad 10^3 = 1000, \quad 10^{\frac{1}{2}} = \sqrt{10}, \quad 10^{\frac{1}{3}} = \sqrt[3]{10}, \quad 10^0 = 1, \quad 10^{-2} = \frac{1}{10^2},$$

we therefore have

$\log 100 = 2,$ $\log 1000 = 3,$ $\log \sqrt{10} = \frac{1}{2},$
$\log \sqrt[3]{10} = \frac{1}{3},$ $\log 1 = 0,$ $\log 0.01 = -2.$

Since logarithms were defined as exponents (of powers of 10), the three index laws in Art. 23 lead at once to corresponding theorems on logarithms, which we proceed to state, prove, and illustrate.

THEOREM 1. *The logarithm of a product equals the sum of the logarithms of its factors.*

Let the factors be M and N. By definition (7),

(8) $$M = 10^{\log M}, \quad N = 10^{\log N}.$$

Hence, by the first index law (1),

$$MN = 10^{\log M + \log N}.$$

Thus, by the definition (7) of logarithms,

(9) $$\log MN = \log M + \log N.$$

For example, let $M = 1000, N = 0.01$. By the above values, we get
$\log MN = \log 10 = 1, \log M + \log N = 3 + (-2) = 1.$

THEOREM 2. *The logarithm of a quotient equals the logarithm of the dividend minus the logarithm of the divisor.*

Expressed otherwise, *the logarithm of a fraction equals the logarithm of the numerator minus the logarithm of the denominator.*

By (8) and the second index law (2), we have
$$\frac{M}{N} = 10^{\log M - \log N}.$$
Hence, by the definition of logarithms,

(10) $$\log \frac{M}{N} = \log M - \log N.$$

For example, let $M = 100$, $N = 10000$. Then
$$\log \frac{M}{N} = \log 0.01 = -2, \quad \log M - \log N = 2 - 4 = -2.$$

THEOREM 3. *The logarithm of the pth power of a number equals p times the logarithm of the number.*

Raising the two members of the second equation (8) to the power p and applying the third index law (3), we get
$$N^p = (10^{\log N})^p = 10^{p \log N}.$$
Hence, by the definition of logarithms,

(11) $$\log N^p = p \log N.$$

For example, let $N = 100$ and $p = 2$. Then
$$\log N^p = \log 10000 = 4, \quad p \log N = 2 \times 2 = 4.$$

If in Theorem 3 we take p equal to $1/n$, we obtain the

COROLLARY. *The logarithm of the nth root of a number is obtained by dividing the logarithm of the number by* n.

For example, let the number be 10000 and let $n = 2$. Then
$$\log \sqrt{10000} = \log 100 = 2, \quad \frac{\log 10000}{2} = \frac{4}{2} = 2.$$

EXERCISES ON THE PROPERTIES OF LOGARITHMS

1. Find the logarithms of 100000, 0.1, 0.001, $\sqrt[3]{100}$.
2. Find $\log \sqrt{10} \times \sqrt{1000}$.
3. Given $\log 2 = 0.30103$, $\log 3 = 0.47712$, find

(a) $\log 8$.   (b) $\log 24$.   (c) $\log \frac{9}{4}$.

(d) $\log \sqrt{3}$.   (e) $\log \sqrt{6}$.   (f) $\log \frac{3}{\sqrt{2}}$.

(g) $\log 5$.   (h) $\log 60$.   (i) $\log 45$.

4. Express in terms of log N and log M the following:

log $N^3 M^2$, log N^3/M^2, log $\sqrt[3]{N^{-3}/M^{-4}}$.

5.* The logarithms of numbers a, ar, ar^2, ar^3, ... in geometrical progression are in arithmetical progression, i.e., have a common difference.

25. Significant digits. The distance from the earth to the sun is not the same at different times of the year, but is said to be 93 millions of miles in round numbers. Since we do not mean to imply that the digits (or figures) which follow 3 are here actually all zeros, it is preferable to write the number in the form 93×10^6 or 9.3×10^7, rather than as 93,000,000. Again, the first measurement of a star's diameter was made by Michelson in 1920, who found that the giant star Betelgeuze has a diameter of about 3×10^8 miles. Since the sun's diameter is less than 10^6 miles, that star is 27×10^6 times as large as the sun.

Similarly, many very small numbers are employed in modern physics, and it is customary to employ the notation 9.3×10^{-6}, rather than 0.0000093. This number and 0.93 and 93 are all said to have the same two *significant* digits, 9 being the first significant digit and 3 the second. In both 93 and 3.7 the digit 3 is said to be in *units' place*. The results

$93{,}000{,}000 = 9.3 \times 10^7$ and $0.0000093 = 9.3 \times 10^{-6}$

furnish two illustrations of the following

PRINCIPLE. *If the first significant digit of a positive number lies p places to the left of units' place, the number can be expressed in the form $N \times 10^p$, where N lies between 1 and 10. But if the first significant digit lies p places to the right of units' place, the number can be expressed in the form $N \times 10^{-p}$, where again N lies between 1 and 10.*

As further examples of this evident principle, consider the numbers 0.93 and 930 in each of which the digit in units' place is 0. In 930, the first significant digit 9 lies two places to the left of units' place, and $930 = N \times 10^2$, where $N = 9.3$. But in 0.93, the first significant digit 9 lies one place to the right of units' place, and $0.93 = N \times 10^{-1}$, where again $N = 9.3$.

26. Mantissa and characteristic of a logarithm.

We have just seen that any given positive number can be written in the form $N \times 10^c$, where $c = \pm p$ is a whole number which may be positive, negative, or zero, while N lies between 1 and 10. Hence the logarithm of the number equals the sum of $\log N$ and $\log 10^c = c$. Further, $\log N$ lies between $\log 1 = 0$ and $\log 10 = 1$ and hence is a positive decimal. This positive decimal is called the *mantissa* and c the *characteristic* of the logarithm of the given number. Thus the positive decimal part of a logarithm is called its mantissa, while the integral part is called its characteristic, which may be positive, negative, or zero.

For example, the two numbers
$$10^{\frac{1}{2}} = \sqrt{10} = 3.162\ldots, \quad 10^{\frac{3}{2}} = 10\sqrt{10} = 31.62\ldots$$
have the logarithms $\frac{1}{2} = 0.5$ and $\frac{3}{2} = 1.5$, whose mantissas are each .5, and whose characteristics are 0 and 1 respectively.

By the principle stated in Art. 25, we have the following

THEOREM. *The characteristic of the logarithm of a (positive) number is $+p$ if the first significant digit of the number lies p places to the left of units' place, but is $-p$ if it lies p places to the right of units' place. If two numbers have the same significant digits, so that they differ only in the position of the decimal point, their logarithms have the same mantissa and differ only as to their characteristics.*

For example, the logarithm of 31.62 has the characteristic 1 since the first significant digit 3 lies one place to the left of units' place. This agrees with the result $\log 31.62 = 1.5$ given just above. Next, we have
$$\log 0.03162 = \log \frac{31.62}{1000} = \log 31.62 - \log 1000 = 1.5 - 3.$$
We do not express this difference in the form -1.5, which is the sum of -1 and the negative decimal $-.5$, since the latter is not a mantissa, mantissas being positive by definition. On the contrary, we write the above difference $1.5 - 3$ in the form $\bar{2}.5$, which means $-2 + 0.5$, and does not mean -2.5. Hence we have
$$\log 0.03162 = \bar{2}.5,$$
whose mantissa is the positive decimal .5 and characteristic is -2. This is an illustration of our theorem, since the first significant digit 3 lies two

places to the right of units' place. Some computers prefer to add and subtract 10 in such cases and write

$$\log 0.03162 = 8.5 - 10.$$

In view of the last part of the above theorem, we may ignore the decimal point in a number when seeking, in a table of logarithms, the mantissa of its logarithm. Thus if the number is 31.62 or 3.162 or 0.03162 we enter the table with 3162 and read off the mantissa.

27. To find the logarithm of a number by Table VII.

EXAMPLE 1. Find the logarithm of 16.17.

When seeking the mantissa, we ignore the decimal point. In the left-hand column (headed N for Number), we look for the number 161 formed of the first three digits of 1617 and find it in the twelfth line. Since the fourth digit is 7, we glance along this twelfth line until we reach the entry 2087 in the column headed 7. Hence .2087 is the mantissa of log 16.17. Since the first significant digit 1 lies one place to the left of units' place, the characteristic is 1. Hence log 16.17 = 1.2087, to four decimal places.

EXAMPLE 2. Find log 256.2.

Since our number exceeds 199.9, it occurs in the second part of Table VII and interpolation is necessary. Our number lies between 256 and 257 whose logarithms occur in the table:

$$\left. \begin{array}{l} \log 256 = 2.4082 \\ \log 257 = 2.4099 \end{array} \right\} \; .0017 = \text{difference.}$$

Since 256.2 is two-tenths of the way from 256 toward 257, we add $.2 \times .0017 = .0003$ to log 256 to obtain log 256.2 = 2.4085.

This correction 3 to the final digit may be obtained by inspection from the Proportional Parts tablette at the end of Table VII In the column headed 17 and opposite to the marginal number 2 (for .2), we find the entry 3.

EXERCISES ON FINDING LOGARITHMS

1. Find the logarithms of 56.78, 0.3456, 0.08765.
2. Verify by Table VII that $\log 35 = \log 5 + \log 7$, $\log 2^3 = 3 \log 2$, $\log 2 + \log 5 = 1$, $\log 8 + \log 5 - 2 \log 2 = 1$.
3. Verify that $\log 1849 = 2 \log 43$, $\log 1728 = 3 \log 12$.
4. Given $\sqrt{10} = 3.162$, find log 3162, log 316.2, log 0.3162.

5.* Show that the principle of interpolation is not valid if applied to numbers whose differences are not relatively small, by finding the error in log 200 when its value is interpolated between log 100 and log 300.

28. To find the number with a given logarithm by Table VII.

EXAMPLE. Given $\log N = 2.5000$, find N to four significant digits.

Since the mantissa does not occur in the table, we use the adjacent numbers 4997 and 5011 between which 5000 lies:

$$\left.\begin{array}{l}\log 316 = 2.4997 \\ \log N\ \ = 2.5000 \\ \log 317 = 2.5011\end{array}\right\} \left.\begin{array}{c}3 \\ \\ \end{array}\right\} 14$$

Thus N exceeds 316 by $3/14 = .2$, as may also be seen by inspection of the P. P. tablette for 14, whose entry 3 lies opposite to 2 in the margin. The decimal point must be inserted so that there will be two digits to the left of units' place. Hence $N = 316.2$.

29. Extraction of roots by logarithms. There is one step in the work which needs explanation. To find $\sqrt{N}$, given $N = 0.1631$, we use

$$\log N = \bar{1}.2125, \qquad \log \sqrt{N} = \tfrac{1}{2}(\bar{1}.2125).$$

Just as in the problem to take half of 13 ft., 2 in., we "borrow" 1 ft. from 13 ft. and add 12 in. to 2 in., and see that the answer is 6 ft., 7 in., — so here we "borrow" 1 from the characteristic $\bar{1}$ and add it to the mantissa. Thus

$$\log \sqrt{N} = \tfrac{1}{2}(-2 + 1.2125) = \bar{1}.6063, \quad \sqrt{N} = 0.4039.$$

Similarly,

$$\log \sqrt[3]{N} = \tfrac{1}{3}(-3 + 2.2125) = \bar{1}.7375, \quad \sqrt[3]{N} = 0.5464.$$

EXERCISES ON COMPUTATION BY LOGARITHMS

1. What numbers have the logarithms 2.1516, $\bar{2}.2222$, $\bar{4}.3333$? Compute to four significant figures:

2. $\dfrac{8124 \times 0.00345}{0.00069 \times 87.42}$.   3. $\sqrt[5]{1234}$.   4. $(84.62)^{\frac{2}{3}}$.

5. $\sqrt[3]{45.24} \times \sqrt[7]{1234}$.   6. 2^{20}.   7. $(8.765)^3$.

8. Find the number of digits in 2^{400} and in 25^{100}.

9. Find the radius r of a circle whose area πr^2 is 222.2 square feet, where $\pi = 3.1416$, approximately.

10. Find the radius r of a sphere whose volume is
$$\frac{4}{3}\pi r^3 = 4444 \text{ cubic feet.}$$

11. If interest is compounded annually at 5 per cent a year, $1 amounts to $1.05 at the end of one year, to $(1.05)^2$ dollars at the end of two years, etc. Find the amount on $2760 at the end of 15 years.

12. What sum of money put at compound interest at 6 per cent annually will amount to $2000 at the end of 10 years?

13. The combined area of the eastern states is 451900, that of the central states is 1380400, and that of the western states is 1193300, each in square miles. Find the percentage area of each division.

14. The Mississippi carries about 75×10^8 cubic feet of sediment yearly to the Gulf. How thick a layer would this sediment make if spread uniformly over the central states (Ex. 13) drained by that river? In how many years would the erosion be one foot?

15. How many cubic feet of water are held by a tank 125.2 feet long, 106.3 feet wide and 12.4 feet deep?

16. How many cubic feet of gas are held by a cylindrical tank 52.4 feet high, the radius of the circular base being 63.6 feet?

17. Regarding the earth to be a sphere of radius $r = 3957$ miles, find its volume, circumference, and surface $4\pi r^2$.

18. How many feet per minute does a point on the equator move as a result of the earth's daily rotation (see Ex. 17)?

19. The earth moves about 6×10^8 miles in its yearly revolution about the sun. How far does it move in one hour?

20. The average distance from the center of the earth to the center of the moon is 238900 miles, and the moon revolves about the earth once in 27.32 days. Find the average velocity of the moon in (a) miles per hour and (b) feet per second.

21. The male population of a town is 7646 and the female population is 8534. Find the percentage of each.

22. How much iron is contained in 28.6 grams of pianoforte wire, 99.7 per cent of which is iron?

23. Potassium bromide salt was found by chemical analysis to contain .2463 gram of potassium and .5038 gram of bromine. Find the percentage of each in the salt.

30. Logarithmic scale. The multiplications and divisions which we have learned to perform by use of a table of logarithms can be performed geometrically (but less accurately if the drawing is of moderate size) by use of segments representing log 2, log 3, etc. The following segments (Fig. 22) represent log 2, . . ., log 10 to the same scale, the annexed values of the logarithms to two decimal places having been taken from Table VII:

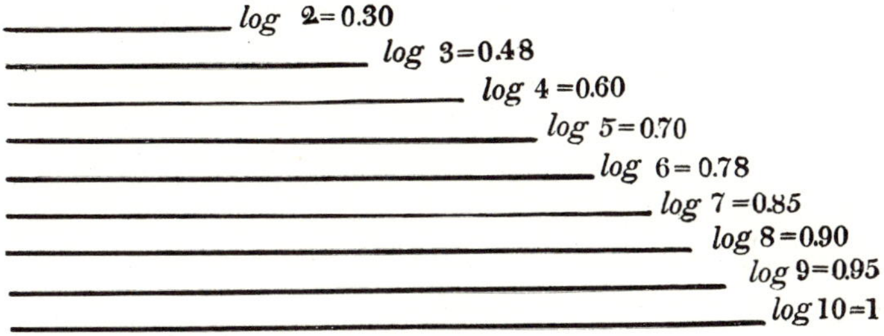

```
_____ log 2 = 0.30
_____ log 3 = 0.48
_____ log 4 = 0.60
_____ log 5 = 0.70
_____ log 6 = 0.78
_____ log 7 = 0.85
_____ log 8 = 0.90
_____ log 9 = 0.95
_____ log 10 = 1
```

Fig. 22

We now transfer these segments to the same line so that their left-hand points coincide, and omit "log" from the labels log 2, log 3, etc., at their right-hand points, thus retaining only the labels 2, 3, etc. We obtain Fig. 23, in which the left-hand point is labeled 1 since log 1 = 0.

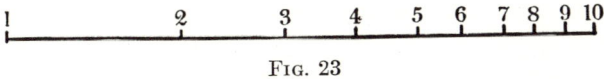

Fig. 23

Such a *logarithmic scale* was proposed by E. Gunter in 1620. It may be used to perform multiplication and division. For example, to multiply 2 by 3, transfer with the dividers or a pair of compasses the segment extending from 1 to 3 to a position starting at 2; the right-hand end of the transferred segment is seen to be at 6, in agreement with the fact that

$$\log 2 + \log 3 = \log 6.$$

Hence multiplication and division can be performed geometrically by means of a logarithmic scale (Fig. 23).

31. Slide rules. It was noticed by W. Oughtred in 1630 that we may dispense with the use of the dividers in Art. 30 by using two like logarithmic scales E and F (Fig. 24), which slide along

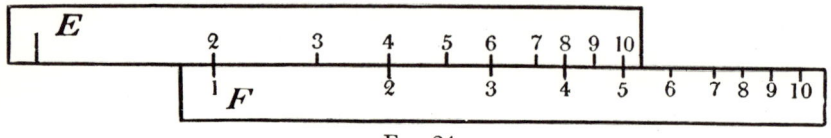

Fig. 24

each other. The process to multiply 2 by 3 now consists in placing scale F so that its point marked 1 is underneath the point marked 2 on scale E; then above the point marked 3 on scale F we find on scale E the required product 6.

To divide 6 by 3, place scale F so that its point 3 falls under point 6 on scale E and read on E the point above 1 on F.

The above pair of logarithmic scales enables us to find the products, when not exceeding 10, of numbers having only one digit, and hence would be of no practical use. But we readily extend its usefulness as follows.

First, by using also log 1.1, log 1.2, ..., log 9.9, we subdivide each main interval in Fig. 23 into ten (unequal) divisions, which are marked by short bars (and every fifth one by a longer bar) and not by numbers (1.1, 1.2, ..., 1.9 for the first main division). Such a modified logarithmic scale is shown in the left half of scale A in Fig. 25, where are omitted the subdivisions of the shorter main divisions.

By using two such modified scales sliding along each other, as the left halves of scales A and B in Fig. 25, we can find the products of numbers each having a units' digit and one decimal place.

Second, we can now readily extend the scale to include all whole numbers not exceeding 100. For example, we obtain a segment representing log 27 = 1 + log 2.7 by adding the length unity of the entire scale to the known segment which represents log 2.7. Thus we have only to annex a copy of our scale at the right of it. At first sight it would appear to be necessary to change the former labels 1, 2, ..., 10 at the main division points to the proper labels 10, 20, ..., 100 on the annexed scale. But such a change in labels is not usually made on slide rules, so that the two halves of scale A in Fig. 25 have the same labels. The label for the point in common to the two halves of scale A is taken to be 1 instead of 10; the final point is labeled 1 instead of 100. Thus the point which is 7 small divisions to the right of the main division 2 of our annexed scale (the right half of scale A) is read 27, while if on the initial scale (the left half of scale A) it is read 2.7.

Scale B (Fig. 25) is exactly like scale A and slides along it. By their use we can multiply numbers each having two significant digits.

While the two like scales A and B serve for multiplication and division, we need a new scale D whose comparison with scale A will enable us to compute squares and square roots. We proceed to show in detail how this is accomplished.

Scales C and D are alike and each is a single logarithmic scale from 1 to 10 whose length equals the combined lengths of the halves of scale A. Hence the logarithm of any number is represented

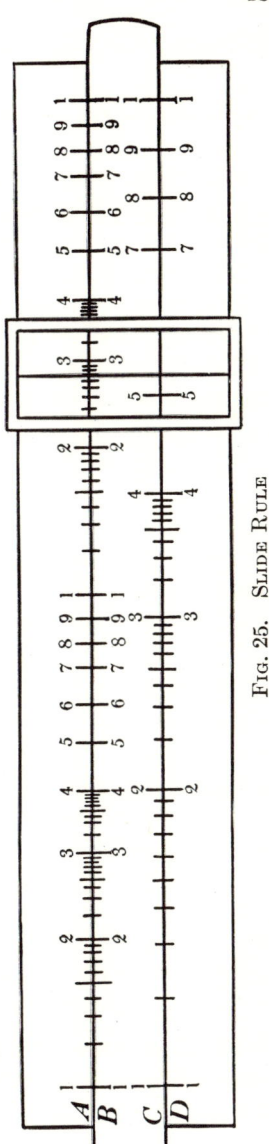

Fig. 25. Slide Rule

on scale D by a segment twice as long as the segment representing the same number on scale A. Thus the number on scale A vertically above any number on scale D is equal to the square of the latter number. Hence the pair of scales A and D serves to find squares and square roots. To facilitate the comparison of scales A and D which are not in direct contact, there is a small movable *runner*, or framed rectangular glass, a fixed vertical line on which connects corresponding numbers of scales A and D.

Scales A and D are on the rule, while B and C are on the slide.

Scales C and D may be used together for multiplication and division just as A and B were used; while giving greater accuracy than the latter, the range of numbers is smaller. To find 6×7 by use of C and D, shift the slide C to the left until its right-hand mark 1 is above 6 on D; the reading on D of the point below 7 on C is 4.2, so that the desired product is 42.

We have now described the slide rule and shown how to use it to perform multiplication, division, squaring, and extraction of square roots. We next indicate the further devices necessary for performing trigonometric computations.

If the slide be entirely withdrawn, its reverse side will usually be found to have along one edge a scale S of logarithmic sines and along the other edge a scale T of logarithmic tangents (Art. 32). To compute $a = c \sin x$, set the beginning point of scale S opposite to c of scale A, and opposite to x on S read a on A (since we have added log sin x to log c). To find $c \cos x$, use $c \sin (90°-x)$. To find $b \tan x$, use scales T and A.

For further details, including descriptions of the more accurate cylindrical slide rules of Thacher and Fuller (which are equivalent to straight rules 720 and 500 inches long), see Raymond's *Plane Surveying*, pp. 179–198. Directions are usually furnished with each slide rule sold.

32. Logarithms of trigonometric functions. Since sin A and tan A are numbers, they have logarithms denoted by log sin A and log tan A, which are read "log sine A" and "log tangent A." For example, by Table I of natural sines, sin 25° 20′ is equal to 0.4279. By Table VII of the logarithms of numbers, log 0.427 = $\bar{1}$.6304, log 0.428 = $\bar{1}$.6314. Hence, by interpolation,

log sin 25° 20′ = log 0.4279 = $\bar{1}$.6313 = 9.6313 — 10.

This result may be read off at once from Table VIII of log sines. Opposite to 25° 20′ occurs the entry 6313, to which is to be prefixed the heading 9. of log sin column. We must remember to annex —10, which is not printed in the table.

The logarithms, to four decimal places, of the sines, tangents, cotangents, and cosines of each acute angle are given in this Table VIII, except that 10 must be subtracted from every entry read from the table.

EXAMPLE. Find log cot 6°12′.

By the table,

log cot 6°10′ = 10.9664 — 10, log cot 6°15′ = 10.9605 — 10.

From the former we subtract the correction $\frac{2}{5} \times 59 = 24$ (which may be read off from the P. P. tablettes for differences of 5′), and obtain

log cot 6°12′ = 0.9640.

EXERCISES ON LOGARITHMS OF TRIGONOMETRIC FUNCTIONS

1. Find log sin 30°13′, log cos 42°57′, log tan 42°57′.
2. Find the acute angles for which

 log sin x = 9.8334 — 10,   log cot y = 0.3362,
 log cos z = 8.7054 — 10,   log tan w = 0.4498.

3. Given log sin A = 9.7480 — 10, find A and log tan A.
4. Given log tan B = 10.0700 — 10, find B and log cos B.
5. Verify that log sin 13° — log cos 13° = log tan 13°. Why is the equation true?
6. Verify that log cos 8°23′ — log sin 8°23′ = log cot 8°23′. Why true?
7.* Verify that log (1 — cos 22°) + log (1 + cos 22°) = 2 log sin 22°. Why true?

CHAPTER V

SOLUTION OF RIGHT TRIANGLES BY LOGARITHMS

33. Results in Chapter II recalled. We saw in Chapter II that we can solve any right triangle if we are given two parts, at least one of which is a side, by using $A + B = 90°$ and two of the four formulas

$$\sin A = \frac{a}{c}, \quad \cos A = \frac{b}{c}, \quad \tan A = \frac{a}{b}, \quad a^2 + b^2 = c^2.$$

Since we there used tables of the natural functions, long multiplications, divisions, and extractions of square roots, were necessary. But this labor may be spared, and hence the possible number of errors reduced, by using logarithms.

34. Solution by logarithms. Since we require no further theory, we are ready to take up an illustrative example.

EXAMPLE. Given angle $A = 55°45'$ and the adjacent side $b = 12.02$, solve the right triangle.

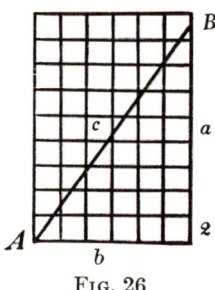

FIG. 26

Solution. Since we need a figure to derive the formulas required in the computation, we draw one to scale on square-ruled paper (Fig. 26) and measure the unknown parts, thus obtaining a rough check on the later computations. By measurement,

$$a = 17.3, \quad c = 21.3, \quad B = 34°,$$

approximately. Next, we make a complete outline which shows all the formulas to be used and also the individual terms of the formulas, leaving blank spaces for the later insertion of their numerical values. Finally we insert the values from the tables and perform the additions, etc. It saves time to look up all the logarithms together. By thus separating the theoretical work of making an outline for the solution from the mechanical work with the tables, we materially reduce the chance of errors.

$$\tan A = \frac{a}{b}, \quad a = b \tan A \qquad \cos A = \frac{b}{c}, \quad c = \frac{b}{\cos A}$$

Ch. V] SOLUTION OF RIGHT TRIANGLES BY LOGARITHMS 49

$$\begin{array}{ll}
\log a = \log b + \log \tan A & \log c = \log b - \log \cos A \\
\log b = 1.0799 & \log b = 1.0799 \\
\log \tan A = 10.1670 - 10 & \log \cos A = 9.7503 - 10 \\
\hline
\log a = 1.2469 & \log c = 1.3296 \\
a = 17.66 & c = 21.36
\end{array}$$

Check: $a^2 = c^2 - b^2 = (c + b)(c - b)$
$c + b = 33.38 \qquad \log(c + b) = 1.5234$
$c - b = 9.34 \qquad \log(c - b) = 0.9703$
$\phantom{c - b = 9.34} \qquad \overline{\log(c^2 - b^2) = 2.4937}$
$\phantom{c - b = 9.34} \qquad \log\sqrt{c^2 - b^2} = 1.2469 = \log a.$

Our check formula is preferable to $\sin A = a/c$, since in employing the latter we would use our values of $\log a$ and $\log c$ and hence not detect possible errors in finding a and c from their logarithms.

Traverse Table VI furnishes a check which is more accurate and quicker to apply than that from a drawing to scale. Thus for $56°$ and $c = 21\tfrac{1}{3}$, we read off opp. leg $a = 17.7$, adj. leg $b = 11.9$.

Before applying the computation check, note whether the computed parts agree approximately with their measured values or those from the traverse table; if not, repeat the construction of the drawing and the measurement of the unknown parts, or the readings from the traverse table, and, if the gross error is not thus detected, look for a gross error in the computation (Art. 36).

35. Given the hypotenuse and a leg. Given the hypotenuse c and a leg b, we saw in Art. 15 that it is best first to find a by means of

(1) $\quad a^2 = (c + b)(c - b)$

and then determine angle A from its tangent.

EXAMPLE. At what greatest distance at sea can a mountain 3 miles high be seen, if the earth is regarded as a sphere of radius 3957 miles?

Solution. In Fig. 27, let C be the point at sea, B the top and F the foot of the mountain, and A the center of the earth. Then BC is tangent

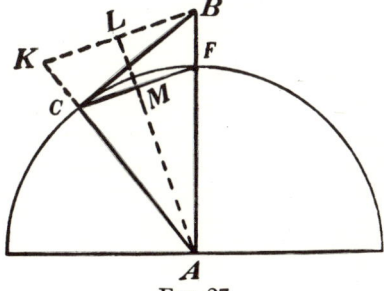

FIG. 27

to the earth and hence is perpendicular to the radius CA. We regard $a = BC$ as the required distance, given that $b = AC = 3957$ and

$$c = BF + FA = 3 + 3957.$$

$c + b = 7917$	$\log (c + b)$	$= 3.8985$
$c - b = 3$	$\log (c - b)$	$= 0.4771$
	$\log a^2$	$= 4.3756$
	$\log a$	$= 2.1878$
	a	$= 154.1$

NOTE. If we regard the chord CF as the required distance, we may compute its length after finding angle A.

$$\tan A = \frac{BC}{AC} = \frac{a}{b}$$

$\log a = 2.1878$
$\log b = 3.5974$
$\log \tan A = 8.5904 - 10$
$A = 2°13.8'.$

Draw AM perpendicular to chord CF. In the right triangle ACM,

$$\sin CAM = \sin \tfrac{1}{2} A = \frac{CM}{b}$$

$\log CM = \log b + \log \sin \tfrac{1}{2} A$
$\log b = 3.5974$
$\log \sin 1°6.9' = 8.2891 - 10$
$\log CM = 1.8865$
$CM = 77.00$
Chord $CF = 154.0.$

Hence the chord is practically of the same length as the tangent CB.

When, as in our example, leg b is only slightly less than the hypotenuse c, the small angle A cannot be accurately determined by $\cos A = b/c$. For instance, if $\log \cos A = 9.9999 - 10$, we cannot tell by Table VIII which of the angles between $50'$ and $1° 40'$ should be taken as A. While we may proceed as in the above example, we readily obtain a formula which gives A at once and with appropriate accuracy (cf. Art. 15).

In Fig. 27 draw BK perpendicular to the bisector AML of angle BAC. Then the right triangles ALB and ALK are equal, and

$$AK = AB = c, \quad CK = AK - AC = c - b.$$

Since angles CBK and $CAL = \frac{1}{2}A$ are both complementary to angle AKB, they are equal. Hence, from the right triangle BCK,

$$\tan \tfrac{1}{2} A = \tan CBK = \frac{CK}{CB} = \frac{c-b}{a} = \sqrt{\frac{(c-b)^2}{(c+b)(c-b)}},$$

by (1). The desired formula is therefore

(2) $$\tan \tfrac{1}{2} A = \sqrt{\frac{c-b}{c+b}}.$$

In the above example, we had

$$\begin{array}{rl} \log (c-b) = & 0.4771 \\ \log (c+b) = & 3.8985 \\ \hline & 2\,|\,\overline{4.5786} \\ \log \tan \tfrac{1}{2}A = & \overline{2}.2893 = 8.2893 - 10 \\ \tfrac{1}{2}A = & 1°6.9'. \end{array}$$

36. Errors of computation. Gross errors may arise by

1. Reading from the figure the wrong ratio as the value of a trigonometric function, and hence starting from a false formula.
2. Solving the formula incorrectly for the unknown part.
3. Passing erroneously to the logarithmic form of the formula.
4. Taking an entry from a wrong column of a table, perhaps using the label at the top instead of the bottom of the column.
5. Failing to omit the characteristic 1 of $\log a = 1.2470$ and erroneously entering the table with 1247, when seeking a.
6. Adding two logarithms when we should subtract.
7. Supplying the wrong characteristic to the logarithm, perhaps failing to subtract 10 from the tabulated logarithm of a trigonometric function. When an answer is in error only in the position of the decimal point, the error was due presumably to the present cause only.

If wide disagreement with the values from the drawing to scale or from the traverse table shows that a gross error still remains undetected, check the additions and subtractions by "casting out nines." To cast out nines from 678, subtract 9 from $6 + 7$ to obtain 4 and subtract 9 from $4 + 8$ to obtain 3. To cast out nines from 406, subtract 9 from $4 + 6$ to obtain 1. Casting out nines from the sum 1084 of 678 and 406, we obtain 4. Since $3 + 1 = 4$, the addition is checked. Similarly, if we desire to check that the subtraction of 406 from 678 yields 272 correctly, we cast out nines from the result to obtain 2 and note than $3 - 1 = 2$.

When the computed values agree approximately with the values measured from the drawing or read from the traverse table (so that gross errors are improbable), the check formula may show that the computed values contain a small error. Such an error is usually due to one of the following causes:

I. Numerical error in interpolation.

II. Adding the correction for interpolation instead of subtracting it or vice versa.

III. Failure to read minutes in the proper line of the table.

Exercises on Solving Right Triangles by Logarithms

Solve by logarithms the right triangles in which the following two parts are given, check by a formula and either by a drawing to scale or by the traverse table.

1. $A = 28°5'$, $c = 1140$.
2. $A = 36°44'$, $a = 97.06$.
3. $a = 2238$, $c = 4295$.
4. $b = 35.89$, $c = 43.27$.
5. $a = 879.0$, $b = 656.3$.
6. $A = 53°30'$, $b = 91.28$.
7. $a = 6.845$, $b = 8.463$.
8. $A = 43°48'$, $c = 147.2$.

9. Find the greatest distance at sea at which a mountain 2 miles high can be seen, taking the earth's radius as 3957 miles.

10. At what distance can the pilot of an aeroplane $\frac{1}{4}$ mile high see an object on the earth?

11. How far has a man rowed from a lighthouse 66 feet high when he observes it disappear on the horizon?

12. How far apart are two ships whose crow's nests are 80 and 95 feet above water and are just visible from each other?

13. What was the slope of a road bed 10000 feet long which, after being made horizontal by leveling, measured 9996 feet?

14. Solve the triangle whose hypotenuse equals the product of a leg by 3.

Ch. V] SOLUTION OF RIGHT TRIANGLES BY LOGARITHMS 53

37. Area($\triangle$) of a right triangle. By geometry, $\triangle = \frac{1}{2} ab$. If the legs a and b are not both given, we may first compute the unknown leg or legs by partially solving the triangle. But as a number computed by logarithms is usually not quite exact in the last decimal place, it is preferable to find the area from the given parts whenever possible.

Given angle A and leg a or hypotenuse c, we may use the first or the second of the following formulas:

$$\triangle = \tfrac{1}{2} a^2 \cot A, \qquad \triangle = \tfrac{1}{2} c^2 \sin A \cos A.$$

To verify these formulas, insert the values from Art. 33:

$$\tfrac{1}{2} a^2 \cot A = \tfrac{1}{2} a^2 \cdot \frac{b}{a} = \tfrac{1}{2} ab, \quad \tfrac{1}{2} c^2 \sin A \cos A = \tfrac{1}{2} c^2 \cdot \frac{a}{c} \cdot \frac{b}{c} = \tfrac{1}{2} ab.$$

Finally, if a and c are given, we must first compute A or b, preferably b (Art. 35).

Exercises on the Area of a Right Triangle

Find the areas of the right triangles in which
1. $a = 14, A = 18°14'$.
2. $a = 12.3, c = 140$.
3. $c = 34, A = 20°6'$.
4. $c = 4.231, A = 86°4'$.
5. Solve the triangle, given $b = 20$, area ($\triangle$) $= 232$.
6. Solve the triangle, given $A = 61°$, area $= 48$.

38. Isosceles triangles and regular polygons. An isosceles triangle is divided into two equal right triangles by the perpendicular $VF = h$ from the vertex V to the base AB, whose length will be designated by s (Fig. 28). The solution of the isosceles triangle is therefore reduced to that of one of its component right triangles.

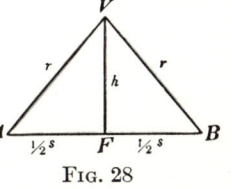

Fig. 28

Consider a regular polygon $ABCD...$ of n sides, each of length s, which is inscribed in a circle with the center V and radius $VA = r$. [In Fig. 29 is shown a regular pentagon $ABCDE$ both inscribed in a circle of radius r and circumscribed about a (dotted) circle of radius h.]

The radii VA, VB, VC, etc., divide the polygon into n equal isosceles triangles VAB, VBC, etc. Since the sum of the n angles AVB, BVC, etc., is 360°, each contains $360/n$ degrees. The half angle AVF therefore contains $180/n$ degrees. Problems on inscribed regular polygons therefore reduce to problems on one of the right triangles in Fig. 28.

Similar remarks hold for a regular polygon circumscribed about a circle of radius h.

A hexagon has 6 sides, an octagon has 8 sides, and a decagon has 10 sides.

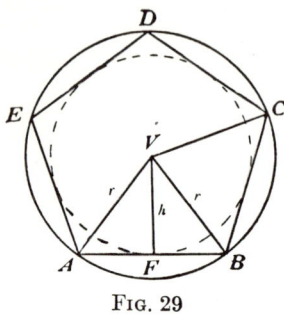

Fig. 29

EXAMPLE. Find the side of a regular pentagon circumscribed about a circle of radius 10.

Solution. We employ Fig. 29 with $h = 10$, ignoring the outer circle. Angle AVF contains $180/5$ degrees. Hence

$$\tan 36° = \tan AVF = \frac{AF}{h}, \quad AF = 10 \tan 36° = 7.265, \quad AB = 14.530.$$

EXERCISES ON ISOSCELES TRIANGLES AND REGULAR POLYGONS

For an isosceles triangle lettered as in Fig. 28, with $V = \angle AVB$ and area $\triangle$:

1. Given $r = 286$, $s = 220$, find A, V, h, $\triangle$.
2. Given $s = 47.04$, $V = 69°49'$, find r, h, $\triangle$.
3. Given $h = 8.4$, $\triangle = 10.92$, find A, V, r, s.
4. Given $s = 42.90$, $V = 121°15'$, find r, h, $\triangle$.
5. Given $r = 30.01$, $A = 52°10'$, find s, h, $\triangle$.
6. Given $\triangle = 54.34$, $h = 14.89$, find A, r, s.

7. A barn is 80 feet wide and 160 feet long, while the pitch of the roof is 45°. Find the length of the rafters and the area of the roof.

8. Find the angle at the center of a circle of radius 90 subtended by a chord of length 132.

9. Find the radius of a circle in which a chord of length 20 subtends an angle 133° at the center.

Ch. V] SOLUTION OF RIGHT TRIANGLES BY LOGARITHMS 55

10. The perimeter p (sum of sides) of a regular polygon of n sides inscribed in a circle of radius r is equal to $2rn \sin (180°/n)$, and its area is equal to $\frac{1}{2}hp$.

11. Find the radius of the circle inscribed in a regular pentagon, the area and perimeter of the pentagon, when the radius of the circumscribed circle is 4 inches.

12. Find the side of a regular decagon inscribed in a circle of radius 100.

13. Find the side of a regular decagon circumscribed about a circle of radius 100.

14. Find the difference between the perimeters of a regular pentagon and a regular hexagon if the area of each is 4800.

15. Find the side, and the radii of the inscribed and circumscribed circles, of a regular octagon whose area is 96.

16. Find the area of the regular octagon formed by cutting off the corners of a square whose side is 100.

17. Find the area of a regular pentagon if its diagonals are each equal to 6.

18. A wedge measures 20 inches along its side, while the angle at the vertex is 20°. Find the width of the base.

19.* A flagpole 24 feet high, standing on a roof which slopes upward at angle 20°, casts a shadow 40 feet long extending perpendicular to the ridge pole of the roof. What is the angle of elevation of the sun?

20.* The base of the great pyramid of Gizeh is a square whose side is 762 feet long and its top is a square whose side is 32 feet long. Each face makes an angle of 51°51' with the horizontal plane. Find the height.

21.* A regular pyramid of altitude 6.079 has a square base whose side is 4.284. Find the angles which the lateral edges and the slant height make with the plane of the base.

39. Problems on heights and distances. Most of the exercises below are slight variations of the example solved and of Ex. 7, for which convenient formulas are supplied.

EXAMPLE. To find the height x of a hill above the horizontal plane through a point P, set up a pole of known length h on the top of the hill and measure the angles of elevation T and B at P of the top and bottom of the pole. Prove that

(3) $$x = \frac{h \tan B}{\tan T - \tan B}.$$

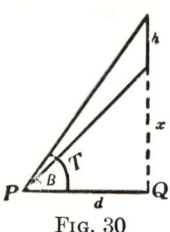

Fig. 30

Solution. Let d be the horizontal distance PQ (Fig. 30) from P to the point Q below the top of the hill. Then

$$\tan B = \frac{x}{d}, \quad \tan T = \frac{x+h}{d}.$$

By division,

$$\frac{\tan B}{\tan T} = \frac{x}{x+h}.$$

Solving for x, we obtain (3).

Note that we must compute the denominator in (3) by use of the table of natural tangents. The rest of the work is performed conveniently by logarithms. An equivalent formula involving only multiplications and divisions, but no subtraction, and hence more suitable for logarithms, will be derived from (3) in Art. 98.

Exercises on Heights and Distances

1. Apply formula (3) when $h = 20$, $T = 42°$, $B = 35°$.

2. From a point of a horizontal plane the angle of elevation of a mountain peak 2 miles above the plane is 64°, and that of a cloud directly over the peak is 67°. How high is the cloud above the peak?

3. From the top of a cliff the angles of depression of the top and bottom of a lighthouse $96\frac{1}{2}$ feet high are observed to be 23°15′ and 24°20′ respectively. How much higher is the cliff than the lighthouse?

4. The angle of elevation of the top of a flagstaff is 36°25′ as measured by a transit whose telescope is 5 feet above the ground, the horizontal distance from the transit to the foot of the flagstaff being 125.4 feet. Find the height of the flagstaff.

5. Find the width BC of a river, given the length 310.4 feet of a line AB along one bank, and granted that an object C on the opposite bank is located so that $ABC = 90°$, $CAB = 50°25′$.

6. A ladder 24 feet long stands at an angle of elevation of 72° against a wall. If the foot of the ladder is drawn away $1\frac{1}{2}$ feet, what is its new angle of elevation and how far down the wall has the top of the ladder moved?

7. To find the height h of a hill above a horizontal plane, measure the angles A and B of elevation of the top of the hill from two points P and Q in our plane such that if the line PQ were extended through Q it would

pass through the foot F of the perpendicular dropped from the top of the hill to our plane. If d is the distance between P and Q, show that

$$h = \frac{d}{\cot A - \cot B}.$$

Hint: Employ the length l of QF.

8. Apply the formula in Ex. 7 when $d = 500$ ft., $A = 30°$, $B = 45°$.

9. From the top of a hill the angles of depression of two consecutive milestones on a straight horizontal road leading to the hill were observed to be 5° and 15°. Find the height of the hill.

Hint: Show that the formula of Ex. 7 may be applied here.

10. The shadow of a tree lengthened 70 feet while the angle of elevation of the sun decreased from 60° to 40°. Find the height of the tree.

11. A tree stands on the bank of a river. The angle of elevation of its top from a point opposite on the other bank is 37°5′, but is 17°3′ from a point 80 feet from that bank in a straight line from the first point. Find the width of the river and the height of the tree.

12. A hill is inclined 38° to the horizon. After walking 600 feet away from the foot of the hill, a man finds that the angle of elevation of a point half way up the hill is 20°. How high is the hill?

13. From two successive positions, d miles apart, of a ship the angles between its direction of sailing and the direction of a rock were found to be $26\frac{1}{2}°$ and 45°. How near is the rock when the ship passes it? Find another pair of equally favorable angles.

14.* From a point on level ground the angles of elevation of the foot and of the top of a flagstaff standing on the roof of a building were found to be 40° and 51° respectively. From a point 150 feet farther away on the ground the angle of elevation of the top of the flagstaff was found to be 33°45′. Find the height of the flagstaff.

15.* The angles of elevation of the top of a tower from the fourth floor of a building and from a point directly below on the second floor were found to be 25°30′ and 35°12′, while the distance between consecutive floors is 12 feet. Find the height of the tower and its horizontal distance from a point of observation in the building.

16.* To an eye 20 inches in front of a mirror, an object appears to be 16 inches back of the mirror, the line of sight making an angle of 33°

with the mirror. What is the distance and direction of the object from the eye?

17.* A man observes that the horizontal angle subtended by a cylindrical gas tank is 12°, and after moving 400 feet directly away from the tank the angle is 8°. What is the radius of the tank?

18.* A man in a balloon observes that the angle of depression of a house due north is 33°. After the balloon drifts horizontally 4 miles due west, the angle is 21°. How high is the balloon?

19.* A hill is due south of one milestone A and is due east of an adjacent milestone B on the same straight horizontal road. At A the angle of elevation of the top of the hill is 40° and at B 27°. How high is the hill?

CHAPTER VI

Navigation: Dead Reckoning

40. Navigation and its subdivisions. Navigation is the science which enables the mariner to determine with sufficient accuracy the position of his ship at any time. The branch of the science which makes use of observations on the sun or stars is called *celestial navigation* or *nautical astronomy*. The branch which makes use only of the measurement of angles and distances between points on the earth is called *terrestrial navigation;* it comprises piloting and dead reckoning. In *piloting*, a ship's position is found from visible objects on the earth or from soundings of the depth of the sea. In *dead reckoning*, which alone is treated in this text, a ship's position at a specified time is computed from the distances and directions which the ship has sailed from the port left or from a place whose position was found by celestial observations.

41. Geographical terms. The earth rotates daily about its axis, which intersects the earth's surface at the north pole P and south pole P'. The earth differs from a sphere by being slightly flattened at the poles. But for the ordinary purposes of navigation the earth is assumed to be a sphere.

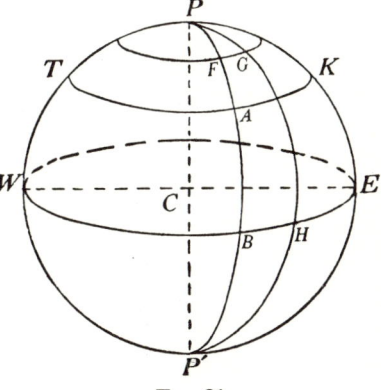

Fig. 31

Meridians are great circles, like $PABP'$ and $PGHP'$, in Fig. 31, in which planes through both poles intersect the earth's surface.

The *equator* $WBHE$ is the intersection of the earth's surface and the plane through the earth's center C perpendicular to the axis PP'. Thus each point B, H, E of the equator is 90° from each pole P and P'.

A *parallel of latitude* is a small circle, like TAK, in which the earth's surface is intersected by a plane perpendicular to the axis.

The *latitude* AB of a place A on the earth's surface is the arc of the meridian intercepted between the place A and the equator. All points on the same parallel of latitude have the same latitude; for example, $AB = KE = TW$. Points between the equator and the north pole P are said to be in *north latitude;* those between it and the south pole P', in *south latitude;* for example, the latitude of A is 40° N. The *difference of latitude* AF of two places A and G is the arc of a meridian included between their parallels of latitude.

The *longitude* of a place A on the earth's surface is the arc BH of the equator intercepted between the meridian of A and the *prime meridian* PGH through Greenwich, England, and is measured by the angle BPH at the pole P. Longitude is reckoned from the prime meridian east or west in degrees up to 180°; for example, the longitude of A is 30° W. The *difference of longitude* of two places is the arc of the equator included between their meridians.

42. Nautical mile. A nautical or sea mile is defined in the United States of America to be 6080.27 feet in length and equal to one-sixtieth part of a degree of a great circle on a sphere whose surface has the same area as the earth's surface. In England a nautical mile is of length 6080 feet. For the purposes of navigation, a nautical mile is assumed to equal one minute of latitude, so that there are 60 nautical miles in a degree of latitude. Throughout this chapter, mile means nautical mile.

A statute mile contains 5280 feet.

43. How distance is measured. The distance sailed by a steamer in a given time is most conveniently determined from the number of revolutions of the screw propeller. It may also be determined by the *patent log;* this instrument carries at the end of a tow line a rotator which if drawn through the water turns about its axis, causing also the tow line to turn, the motion being transmitted to a register aboard ship.

44. Ship's course. The *true course* of a ship is the angle which the ship's track in the water makes with the meridian (true north and south line) through the ship's position.

It may be measured clockwise from north and have any value from 0° to 360°. It is so measured on the new[1] compass card used in the United States Navy, the circular card being numbered clockwise from 0° at north completely around the circumference to 360°, which is again at north. For example, south (or S) is 180°, while west (or W) is 270°.

Or the course may be measured from north or south toward east or west to give an angle not exceeding 90°. For example, if a ship proceeds from O in a direction OA between south and east and making an angle of 75° with the meridian OS (Fig. 32), its course is south 75° east or S 75° E. Similarly, if the ship's track OB is between north and west and makes an angle of 35° with the meridian ON, its course is N 35° W. These two courses when read on the new compass card are 105° and 325°, respectively, being the angle $NOA = 180° - 75°$ and the re-entrant angle $NOB = 360° - 35°$, each read clockwise from N.

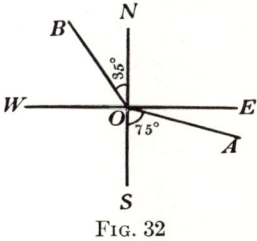

Fig. 32

---

[1]On the old compass card, courses are measured in *points* from N or S toward E or W to give a value from 0 to 8 points = 90°, one point being $11\frac{1}{4}$°. Each of the 32 points and the intermediate half and quarter points has a name. For example, NE$\frac{1}{4}$E is $4\frac{1}{4}$ points from N toward E and thus is N 47°48′45″ E in the second system of the text. No new principle is involved in solving problems expressed in this older, more cumbersome notation, which is avoided here in the interests of simplicity, and since a special traverse table is desirable when working with courses expressed in points.

62 TRIGONOMETRY [Art. 45

We shall postpone to Part II consideration of the various corrections to the reading of the ship's compass, and assume for the present that we know the true course.

PART I. THE SAILINGS (TRUE COURSE ASSUMED)

45. Plane Sailing. Let the distance D sailed from A to B be so short that the curvature of the earth may be neglected. Let the meridian AF through A and the parallel of latitude BF through B intersect at F (Fig. 33). Then AF is the *difference of latitude* of A and B, while FB is called the *departure*. Let angle C be the true course. Then

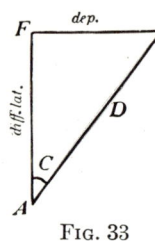

Fig. 33

diff. lat. $= D \cos C$, dep. $= D \sin C$.

EXAMPLE. From latitude 36° N, a ship sails 243 miles S 56° W. Find *lat. in* (i.e., the latitude of the place arrived at) and the departure.

Solution. Divide the distance by 3 to obtain a distance, 81, less than 100. Multiply by 3 the entries in Traverse Table VI which are opposite to distance 81 and above the angle 56°, using the headings at the bottom of the page and retaining only one decimal place. We get dep. = 201.4, diff. lat. = 135.9. Dividing the latter by 60, to convert miles into degrees, we have diff. lat. = 2°16′. Since the ship sailed in a southerly direction, we subtract this from 36° N and get lat. in = 33°44′ N.

In place of the first step in the solution, we may add the entries for the distances 200 and 43 (as in Ex. 1, Art. 17).

EXERCISES ON PLANE SAILING

Find the quantities indicated by question marks, using Table VI for Exs. 1–5, 7, and logarithms for Exs. 6, 8.

Ex.	True Course	Dist.	Dep.	Lat. out	Lat. in
1.	5°	188	?	40° 33′ N	?
2.	124°	488	?	1° 45′ N	?
3.	S 17° W	?	?	40° 17′ N	37° 6′ N
4.	?	360	?	21° 59′ S	24° 49′ S
5.	236°	?	48.2	38° N	?
6.	?	?	289.2 W	20° 48′ N	17° 13′ N

Ch. VI]   NAVIGATION: DEAD RECKONING   63

7. A ship sails a course of 309° for 74 miles from Michigan City. How far north and how far west is it from its port of departure?

8. Ludington is 59 miles east and 142 miles north of Chicago. Find a ship's course and distance from Chicago to Ludington.

46. Unfavorable case. When the departure p and difference of latitude l are given and the course C and distance D are desired, Traverse Table VI is not as convenient as in all other such problems. While logarithms could be used, it is customary in the practice of navigation to employ the traverse table, as in the following solutions.

EXAMPLE 1. Given $p = 82.3$, $l = 34.3$, find C and D.

Solution. Since p is a little more than the double of l, angle C is a little more than 60°. After inspecting Table VI for several such angles, we extract the numbers in the first and third lines below:

C	dis. D	dep. p	lat. l
67°	88	81.0	34.38
67°18'	89.2	82.3	34.3
68°	92	85.3	34.46

We ignore the variation of the given l from the entries l, since an error less than 0.2 of a mile is negligible for the purposes of Plane Sailing. In view of the values of p, the interpolation ratio is 13/43, so that the corrections to C and D are

$$\frac{13}{43} \times 60' = 18', \quad \frac{13}{43} \times 4 = 1.2.$$

The method used in Ex. 1 applies for all distances <100 and all courses between 60° and 90°, an error of 0.2 in l being allowed. For courses between 0° and 30°, we employ entries from the table having the given p, to within 0.2, and interpolate for C, D, l. But for distances <100 and courses between 30° and 60° we may commit an error of 0.3 even though we use the better of the two methods (the first if the course is >45°, and the second if <45°).

When greater accuracy is required, proceed as in Ex. 2.

EXAMPLE 2.[1] Given $p = 63.1$, $l = 68.7$, find C and D.

[1] The instructor may elect to omit this example.

Solution. Evidently C is only a few degrees less than 45°. From the traverse table we read off the first and third lines of the following tablettes:

$C = 42°$

p	l	D
62.90	69.86	94
63.10	70.08	94.30
63.57	70.60	95

$C = 43°$

p	l	D
62.74	67.28	92
63.10	67.67	92.52
63.43	68 02	93

In the middle line of each tablette, we insert the given value of p, and (starting with p instead of l since $C < 45°$) interpolate the values of l and D in the usual manner. We now have the first and third lines of the new tablette:

C	l	D
42°	70.08	94.30
42°34′	68.70	93 28
43°	67.67	92.52

Insert in the middle line the given value of l and interpolate the values of C and D. We have carried the work to two decimal places (although one is enough for navigation) to show the accuracy of the method. In fact, computation by five-place logarithms gives $C = 42°34′0″$, $D = 93.282$.

Exercises on Interpolation

Given the departure p and difference of latitude l, find the course C and distance D by Table VI, allowing errors of 0.2.

1. $p = 14$, $l = 85$.
2. $p = 25$, $l = 90$.
3. $p = 90$, $l = 25$.
4. $p = 85$, $l = 14$.
5. $p = 14.7$, $l = 65.7$.
6. $p = 64.8$, $l = 53$.

47. Traverse Sailing. Let a ship sail a short distance AB on one course and then a second short distance BC on a new course, etc. (Fig. 34), so that the method of Plane Sailing is applicable to each of the sailings.

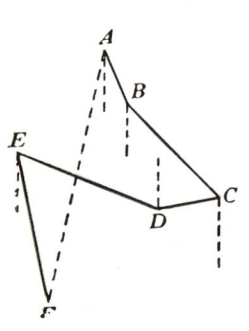

Fig. 34

NAVIGATION: DEAD RECKONING

In four columns we enter the north and south differences of latitude and the east and west departures. By footing up the columns and subtracting the totals, we get the difference of latitude and departure of the final point F reached with respect to the point A of starting, and hence have the combined effect of the successive sailings. We thus speak of the *course and distance made good*, just as if the ship had sailed in a straight line AF from its initial point A to its final point F.

The letters S and E of the course S 22° E tell that the difference of latitude is south and the departure is east.

EXAMPLE. A ship sails the five successive courses and distances in the following table. Find the course and distance made good.

Solution. The courses and distances are shown to scale in Fig. 34.

Courses	Dist.	Diff. lat.		Departure	
		N	S	E	W
S 22° E	15		13.9	5.6	
S 45° E	34		24.0	24.0	
S 79° W	16		3.1		15.7
N 68° W	39	14.6			36.2
S 11° E	40		39.3	7.6	
Made good		14.6	80.3	37.2	51.9
			14.6		37.2
S 12° 36′ W	67.3		65.7		14.7

Hence the effect of the successive sailings is to carry the ship 67.3 miles S 12°36′ W (from A to F in Fig. 34).

EXERCISES ON TRAVERSE SAILING

Given courses C and distances D, find the course and distance made good:

Ex. 1

C	D
80°	25
130°	38
210°	50

Ex. 2

C	D
172°	18
219°	37
205°	56

Ex. 3

C	D
S 25° W	43
S 28° W	39
S 17° W	27

Ex. 4

C	D
N 70° W	21
N 31° E	9
N 20° E	9
S 25° W	30

66 TRIGONOMETRY [Art. 48

5. A ship in lat. 30°20′ S sails 54 miles S 39° E, 90 miles S 56° W, 96 miles S 34° E, 64 miles E, and 36 miles S 28° E. Find the latitude in and course and distance back to the starting point.

6. A ship in lat. 34°40′ N sails 124 miles on course 307°, 32 miles on course 349°, 80 miles on course 273°, 58 miles on course 307°, 60 miles on course 11°, and 28 miles on course 8°. Find the latitude in and the course and distance back to the starting point.

7. The distance PA across an island is 44 miles and A is due north of P. A ship sailed N 25° W from P to a point B and then N 65° E to A. The return trip was made on the opposite side of the island, sailing S 29° E from A to a point F and then S 61° W to P. Find the shorter of the distances sailed going and returning.

48. Parallel Sailing. This term is used when a ship sails on a parallel of latitude. While this is a very special case, the method used solves the important question to find the difference of longitude GH of two places A and B on the same parallel of latitude, given the departure AB (Fig. 35). Let P be the adjacent pole, C the center of the earth, and draw AO and BO perpendicular to PC. Then O is the center of the small circle which gives the parallel of latitude through A and B. Since BO and HC are in the plane of the meridian PBH and are perpendicular to PC, they are parallel lines. Similarly, AO and GC are parallel. Hence the angles AOB and GCH are equal, so that they subtend arcs AB and GH proportional to the radii AO and GC of their circles. Also GC and AC are equal, being radii of the earth. Denote by L the latitude AG of A; it subtends angle ACG, which equals the alternate angle CAO. Hence in

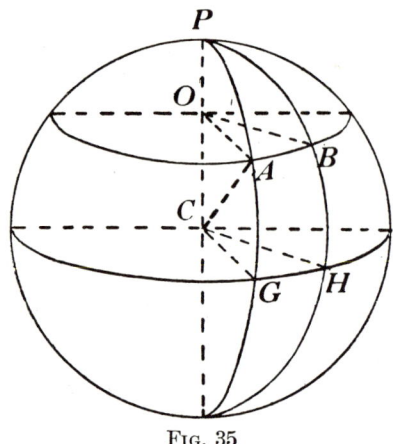

Fig. 35

triangle CAO, angle O is a right angle, and angle CAO equals L. Thus

$$\cos CAO = \frac{AO}{AC}, \text{ or } \cos L = \frac{AO}{GC} = \frac{AB}{GH} = \frac{\text{dep.}}{\text{diff. long.}},$$

(1) $\qquad$ dep. = (diff. long.) $\cos L$.

EXAMPLE 1. A ship in latitude 49° N and longitude 100° W sails due west to a place in longitude 101°35′ W. Find the distance sailed.

Solution. The difference of longitude is 1°35′ or 95 nautical miles. The distance sailed is here the departure and, by (1), equals 95 cos 49°. By Table VI, this product equals 62.33.

EXAMPLE 2. A ship in latitude 38° N sails 71.8 miles due west. Required the difference of longitude D.

Solution. By (1), 71.8 = D cos 38°. By Table VI,
$\qquad$ 71.7 = 91 cos 38°, $\quad$ 72.5 = 92 cos 38°.

Hence the interpolation ratio is .1/.8. Adding 1/8 of 1 to 91, we get D = 91.1 miles or 1°31.1′.

EXERCISES ON PARALLEL SAILING

Find the quantities indicated by question marks.

Ex.	Lat.	Dep.	Long. out	Long. in
1.	52°	?	0°59′ W	2°24′ E
2.	61°25′	?	179°20′ W	176°52′ E
3.	60°	204 E	160° 2′ E	?
4.	51°28′	70.9 E	32° 7′ W	?
5.	34°57′	981 E	?	53°20′ E
6.	?	156 W	25°40′ W	30°54′ W

7. A ship in lat. 40° N, long. 165° W, sails due east until her longitude is 155°30′ W. Find the distance sailed.

8. How far must a ship sail due east in lat. 60° N to change her longitude by 5°?

9. From lat. 30° N, long. 45° W, a ship sails due west 240 miles, then due north 240 miles, and finally due east 240 miles. Find lat. in and long. in.

10. Two ships in lat. 35° N, 150.7 miles apart, sail 300 miles due north. How much closer are they at the end of the run?

11. Two ships A and B steam due west at the same speed, while B changes longitude twice as fast as A. If A is in lat. 20° N and to the southward of B, find B's latitude.

12. In what latitude is the length of a degree of longitude 47 miles?

49. Middle Latitude Sailing. We now abandon the assumption made in Plane Sailing and take into account the curvature of the earth. Let the ship's track be a *rhumb line* (AB in Fig. 36),

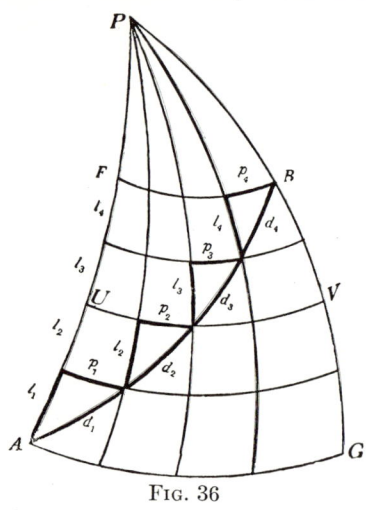

Fig. 36

making the same angle C with all the meridians crossed. By thus keeping the ship on a constant true course, the navigating officer not only simplifies his computations but also is spared the trouble of sending new orders as to the course to the helmsman. The distance between two places A and B is the number of nautical miles in the rhumb line joining them.

In Fig. 36, P represents the north pole, AB the ship's rhumb track, AG and FB the corresponding parallels of latitude, each above the equator, and FAB the constant course C. Divide the distance $D = AB$ into parts $d_1,...,d_4$, each so short that the resulting right triangles having them as hypotenuses may be regarded as plane triangles. Let $p_1,...,p_4$ be the corresponding intercepts on the parallels of latitude, and $l_1,...,l_4$ the corresponding intercepts on the meridians and hence the differences of latitude. Apply to each small triangle the formulas derived in Plane Sailing (Art. 45). First, we get

$l_1 = d_1 \cos C, \ l_2 = d_2 \cos C, \ l_3 = d_3 \cos C, \ l_4 = d_4 \cos C.$

Adding, we have

$AF = (d_1 + d_2 + d_3 + d_4) \cos C = D \cos C$, diff. lat. $= D \cos C$.
Second,
$$p_1 = d_1 \sin C, p_2 = d_2 \sin C, p_3 = d_3 \sin C, p_4 = d_4 \sin C.$$
Hence, on adding, we get $p_1 + p_2 + p_3 + p_4 = D \sin C$. Since the meridians converge toward the pole P, we see that p_1 is less than the corresponding intercept on the parallel AG and greater than that on FB. Hence $p_1 + p_2 + p_3 + p_4$ is less than AG and greater than FB and thus equals the intercept UV made by the meridians PA and PBG on a certain intermediate parallel of latitude. It is assumed that the latter is the parallel half way between FB and AG. Then UV is called the *departure in middle latitude*, i.e., the east and west arc intercepted by the meridians through A and B on the parallel whose latitude is midway between the latitudes of A and B. Hence our second result becomes

$$\text{dep. in middle lat.} = D \sin C.$$

For purposes of computation we may therefore replace our spherical triangle AFB by the plane right triangle AFB (Fig. 33) of Plane Sailing, provided departure in Plane Sailing be replaced by departure in middle latitude. The last replacement is to be made also in applying formula (1) of Parallel Sailing to compute the difference of longitude.

The assumption made concerning UV will not introduce inadmissible errors[1] if the distance sailed is not greater than a day's run, and the ship is not in a large north or south latitude.

EXAMPLE 1. A ship in lat. 42°30′ N, long. 58°51′ W, sails 300 miles S 34° E. Required the latitude and longitude arrived at, using Middle Latitude Sailing.

Solution. By Table VI with course S 34° E and distance 300, we find diff. lat. = 248.7 miles or 4°8.7′ S and dep. in mid. lat. = 167.8 E.

lat. out = 42°30′ N		lat. out = 42°30′
diff. lat. = 4° 8.7′ S		½ diff. lat. = 2° 4.4′
lat. in = 38°21.3′ N		mid. lat. = 40°25.6′

[1] Corrections to be used when the distance is large are given in a table in Bowditch's *American Practical Navigator*, p. 77.

We now apply formula (1) of Parallel Sailing to find diff. long., given dep. = 167.8 and $L = 40°25.6'$. Dividing by 3 to get numbers directly within Table VI, we have dep. = 55.9. From $55.9 = d \cos 40°$, Table VI gives diff. long. $d = 73$. From $55.9 = d \cos 41°$, $d = 74.1$. Adding

$$25.6/60 \times 1.1 = 0.5$$

to the former, we get 73.5. Its product by 3 gives diff. long. = 220.5 miles, or 3° 40.5′ E. This must be subtracted from the given longitude. Hence long in = 55°11′ W.

EXAMPLE 2. A ship in lat. 49°57′ N, long. 15°16′ W, is bound for a port in lat. 47°18′ N, long. 20°10′ W. Find the course and distance to be sailed.

Solution. diff. lat. = 2°39′ S = 159 miles,
diff. long. = 4°54′ W = 294 miles,
mid. lat. = 49°57′ − ½ (2°39′) = 48°37.5′ N = L,
dep. = 294 cos L.

Taking L to be 48° and 49° in turn, we obtain by Table VI the departures 196.7 and 192.9 respectively. By interpolation, dep. = 194.3. Dividing the numbers by 3, we have diff. lat. = 53, dep. = 64.8. The course is thus > 45°. By mental interpolations on lat. in Table VI, we get

C	lat.	dep.	dist.
50°	53	63.2	82.5
51°	53	65.5	84.2

Hence, by interpolation on dep., C = S 50°42′ W, dist. = $83.7 \times 3 = 251.1$

EXERCISES ON MIDDLE LATITUDE SAILING

Find the quantities indicated by question marks.

Ex.	Lat. out	Lat. in	Long. out	Long. in	True course	Dist.
1.	25°35′ N	27°28′ N	60° W	54°55′ W	?	?
2.	32°30′ N	34°10′ N	25°24′ W	29° 8′ W	?	?
3.	46°24′ S	?	178°28′ E	?	S 53°26′ E	278
4.	20°29′ N	?	179°10′ W	?	253°	333
5.	41°38′ N	41°26′ N	59°16′ W	?	101°15′	?
6.	41°19′ N	41°11′ N	57°47′ W	?	?	167
7.	46°28′ N	45°17′ N	22°18′ W	19°39′ W	?	?
8.	36°52′ N	?	75°51′ W	?	N 66° E	175
9.	36°52′ N	38°42.2′ N	75°51′ W	71°51.6′ W	?	?

50. The Mercator chart. A clear understanding of the leading method of making a map of the earth's surface is of great importance not only in navigation but also in geography and other earth sciences. The student will not fail to appreciate the practical nature of this topic.

The earth's surface is mapped on the interior of a rectangle in such a way that the meridians are represented by parallel straight lines perpendicular to the straight line representing the equator, while the parallels of latitude are represented by straight lines parallel to the line representing the equator. Since the earth's meridians converge at the poles and yet have been plotted as parallel lines, there has been an opening out of these meridians, i.e., a stretching of east and west lengths. But we desire that any small figure on the map shall be of the same shape as the corresponding figure on the earth. Hence there must be simultaneously a stretching of north and south lengths. For a very short such vertical length in latitude L, the stretching factor is sec L, when the earth is regarded as a sphere. For, by Art. 48, diff. long. = dep. $\times$ sec L. On a Mercator chart we agreed that the east and west length called departure should be stretched until it becomes equal to the corresponding diff. long. mapped unstretched on the line representing the equator. Hence dep. has been stretched in the ratio sec L, and we agreed to use the same stretching factor for small vertical lines. This argument is valid only for a very short arc, say one minute of arc. Given a longer arc extending from the equator vertically to lat. 5° N, we divide it into 300 arcs each equal to a minute and hence obtain the stretched arc containing sec $1'$ + sec $2'$ + ... + sec $300'$ minutes. It is too laborious to compute such sums without the aid of integral calculus, which leads to a formula convenient for computation.[1]

---

[1] For latitude L the number of nautical miles in the stretched latitude is

$$\frac{r}{.4343} \log \tan (45° + \tfrac{1}{2}L) - r(e^2 \sin L + \tfrac{1}{3}e^4 \sin^3 L + ...),$$

where r is the equatorial radius and e is the eccentricity of the ellipse whose rotation produces the earth's surface.

The resulting stretched latitudes are called *meridional parts* and are given by Table IX.

For example, the meridional parts corresponding to latitude 45° (or 2700′) are 3013.4. But the meridional parts for lat. 1° are 59.6, showing a shrinking and not a stretching, which is explained by the fact that the earth is not a sphere.

By use of Table IX we readily construct a Mercator chart to scale, for example for the region extending from 40° to 55° north latitudes and from 60° to 75° west longitudes (Fig. 37). On a horizontal line representing the parallel of latitude 40° take any convenient segment to represent 5° difference of longitude, and at one of its ends construct an equal segment, and another one at the remote end of the latter. Mark the equally spaced points with the labels 60, 65, 70, 75. Then the vertical lines through these points represent the meridians whose longitudes are 60°, 65°, 70°, 75° W.

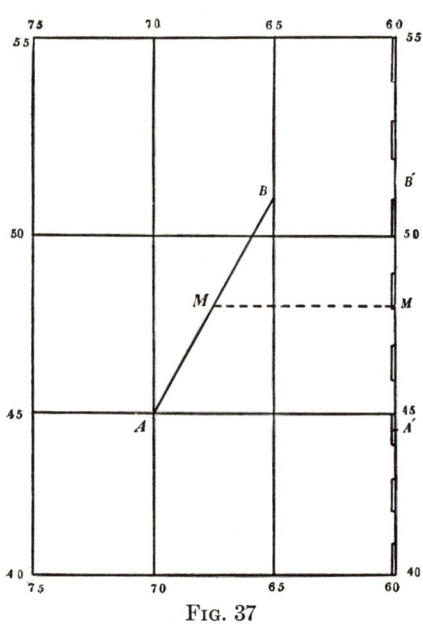

Fig. 37

It remains to locate the horizontal lines which represent the parallels of latitudes 45°, 50°, 55°. This is done by means of Table IX as follows:

$$\begin{aligned}\text{Meridional parts for lat. } 40° &= 2607.6\\ \text{Meridional parts for lat. } 45° &= 3013.4\\ \hline \text{Meridional diff. of lat.} &= 405.8\end{aligned}$$

Divide the last number by the number 300 of minutes in 5°. The quotient 1.35 is the number of units of length in the distance of parallel 45° above parallel 40°. Similarly, the meridional parts for lat. 50° are 3456.5, and $(443.1)/300 = 1.48$ is the distance of parallel 50° above parallel 45°. Likewise, parallel 55° is 1.64 units above parallel 50°.

By employing similarly the meridional parts for each intermediate degree of latitude 41°, 42°,..., we locate the points of division shown on the scale at the right of Fig. 37. For greater distinctness, alternate intervals of one degree are marked by double lines.

51. Angle and distance on a Mercator chart. Any angle on the earth's surface is represented by an equal angle on a Mercator chart. Since the rhumb line on which a ship sails makes the same angle C with all the meridians crossed, it is mapped as a straight line. For this reason Mercator charts are of special importance in navigation.

To find from the chart the length of the rhumb line from place A, in latitude 45° N and longitude 70° W, to place B in latitude 51° N and longitude 65° W, plot A and B on the chart, as in Fig. 37; the straight line AB represents the rhumb line on the earth. Project the middle point M of AB on to the vertical scale at the right of the chart, and measure up and down from the projection M' a distance equal to one-half of AB. The number 6.9 of degrees between the extreme points A' and B', when reduced to miles by multiplication by 60, is the approximate length 414 of the rhumb line.

52. Mercator's Sailing. This method has the advantage that the computations can be conveniently checked graphically on the Mercator chart which shows the ship's position at all times and hence its relation to possible danger places. Further, it involves no assumption restricting its accuracy, such as was made in Middle Latitude Sailing. The latter method is not sufficiently accurate when the distance sailed is more than 500 miles, especially when the course is less than 45° or the ship reaches a high latitude. In these cases Mercator's Sailing should be used.

In Mercator's Sailing we use two plane right triangles each having an angle equal to the ship's course C. One triangle (Fig. 38) is drawn on a Mercator chart and has as legs the difference of

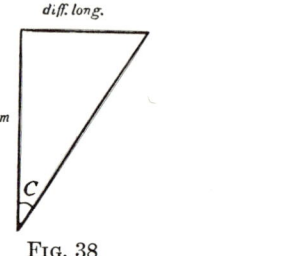

Fig. 38

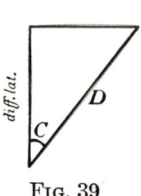

Fig. 39

longitude, and the meridional difference of latitude m corresponding to the actual latitudes of the point sailed from and the point reached. The hypotenuse is not used. The other triangle (Fig. 39) has as hypotenuse the distance D sailed and as vertical leg the difference of actual latitudes; its horizontal leg is not used. This plane triangle is the one which we saw (Art. 49) can be substituted for the spherical triangle on the earth's surface.

For computation by logarithms, we use the formulas

diff. long. = $m \tan C$, diff. lat. = $D \cos C$,

which follow from Fig. 38 and Fig. 39 respectively. To use Table VI, we have only to note that, in Fig. 38, m is the leg adjacent to C and diff. long. is the leg opposite.

EXAMPLE 1. A ship in lat. 42°30′ N and long. 58°51′ W sails 300 miles S 34° E. Find the latitude and longitude arrived at, using Mercator's Sailing.

Solution. By Table VI, diff. lat. = 248.7 miles = 4°8.7′ S.

lat. out = 42°30′ N, whose merid. parts = 2806.4
diff. lat. = 4° 8.7′ S
lat. in = 38°21.3′ N, whose merid. parts = 2480.8
merid. diff. lat. m = 325.6.

NAVIGATION: DEAD RECKONING

Since m exceeds the entries in Table VI, divide it by 4. Then by Table VI with course S 34° E, ¼ m = 81.4 in adj. leg column, read off ¼ diff. long. = 54.9 in opp. leg column. Hence diff. long. = 219.6 miles or 3°40′ E. Thus long. in = 55°11′ W. Cf. Ex. 1, Art. 49.

EXAMPLE 2. A ship sails on a rhumb line from lat. 42°3′ N, long. 70°4′ W to lat. 36°59′ N, long. 25°10′ W. Find the course and distance sailed.

lat. out = 42° 3′ N	merid. parts = 2770.1	long. out = 70° 4′ W
lat. in = 36°59′ N	merid. parts = 2377.3	long. in = 25°10′ W
diff. lat.= 5° 4′ S	m = 392.8	diff. long. = 44°54′ E
= 304′ S		= 2694′ E

Since the numbers are so large, solution by logarithms is preferable:

$$\tan C = \frac{1}{m} \cdot \text{diff. long.} \qquad D = \text{diff. lat.} / \cos C$$

log 2694 = 3.4304	log 304 = 2.4829
log 392.8 = 2.5942	log cos C = 9.1592 − 10
log tan 81°42.2′ = 10.8362 − 10	log D = 3.3237
C = S 81°42.2′ E	dist. = 2107.

EXERCISES ON MERCATOR'S SAILING

1. Construct a Mercator chart of the region from 30° to 50° north latitudes and from 20° to 40° east longitudes. If a ship sails from lat. 30° N, long. 25° E, to lat. 40° N, long. 35° E, find from the chart the course and distance.

In the following exercises, find the quantities indicated by question marks.

Ex.	Lat. out	Long. out	Lat. in	Long. in	True course	Dist.
2.	40° N	70° W	20° S	15° W	?	?
3.	30°22′ N	68°15′ W	43°17′ N	15°18′ W	?	?
4.	10°15′ S	170°10′ E	5°10′ N	81°12′ W	?	?
5.	45°15′ N	35°26′ W	?	?	49°	175
6.	50°48′ N	9°10′ W	?	?	S 41° W	275
7.	37° N	48°20′ W	51°18′ N	?	?	1027
8.	51°15′ N	9°50′ W	37°5′ N	?	214°	?

9. A ship sails from lat. 34°22′ S, long. 18°24′ E, to lat. 52°21′ S, long. 59°18′ W. Find the true course and distance by Middle Latitude and Mercator's Sailings. Which method is more accurate?

10. A ship sails 1022 miles 214° from latitude 51°26′ N, longitude 9°29′ W. Find lat. in and long. in by Middle Latitude and Mercator's Sailings. Which method is more accurate?

PART II. FINDING THE TRUE COURSE; COMPASS CORRECTIONS

53. The mariner's compass. The compass consists of the compass card (Art. 44), one or more magnetic needles firmly attached to the lower surface of the card in a position parallel to the north and south line, and a bowl with a pivot at its center upon which the card turns — the whole being enclosed in the compass box.

The angle between the ship's fore-and-aft line and the magnetic needle equals the arc between the north or south point on the circumference of the card and the point of the latter which is adjacent to a certain mark on the inner surface of the bowl (such that this mark and the pivot of the card are in the same plane with the ship's keel line).

54. Variation and deviation of the compass. The *variation* of the compass at a place is the angle through which the needle is deflected from true north by terrestrial magnetism alone (for details, see Art. 71). Thus, in a ship without any magnetic substance or motors, the needle lies in the *magnetic meridian*, whose angle with the true meridian is the variation of the compass. The true meridian of a place is the great circle passing through it and the earth's poles.

As a modern ship contains considerable iron or other magnetic metal, and carries motors, there is an additional source of error in the ship's compass. The angle which the direction of the needle makes with the magnetic meridian is called the *deviation* of the compass. When the effect of the deviation is to draw the north end of the needle eastward (i.e., to the right) of the magnetic meridian, the deviation is marked E or $+$; in the contrary case, W or $-$. The marking of variation is similar.

55. Leeway. The angle which the ship's heading (fore-and-aft line) makes with her track through the water (as indicated by the ship's wake) is called the *leeway*. It is estimated from various factors including the direction and velocity of the wind. Leeway is marked E or + when the wind turns the ship's head to the right or clockwise, but W or — when the wind turns the ship to the left or counter-clockwise.

56. Courses. The *compass course* of a ship is the angle which the direction of the ship's head makes with the needle as it actually points (as deflected from true north by both variation and deviation), and is measured clockwise from compass north to the direction of the ship's head.

The *true course* of a ship is the angle which the ship's track (not its head) makes with the true meridian, and is measured clockwise from true north to the ship's track.

To find the total correction which must be added algebraically (i.e., with attention to sign) to the compass course to obtain the true course, we have only to combine algebraically the separate corrections for variation, deviation, and leeway. This rule may be proved as in the following Ex. 1.

EXAMPLE 1. The compass course is 45°, variation 8° E, deviation 5° E, and leeway 11° W (due to a wind blowing from southeast). Find the true course.

Solution. From the observer's position O on ship (Fig. 40), let ON represent true north, OM magnetic north (direction of needle deflected by variation only), OC compass north (direction of needle deflected by both variation and deviation), OH the direction of the ship's head, and OT the direction of the ship's track through the water. Here the compass course is $\angle COH = 45°$, and the leeway is $\angle TOH = 11°$, whence the track's course COT by compass is 34°. Adding the deviation $\angle MOC = 5°$ and the variation $\angle NOM = 8°$ to COT, we get the true course $NOT = 47°$.

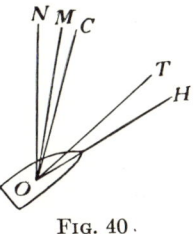

Fig. 40.

Or we may find the total correction $+8° + 5° - 11° = +2°$, add it to the compass course 45°, and obtain the true course 47°.

EXAMPLE 2. The true course is 124°, variation 10° W, deviation 4° E, and leeway 17° W. Find the compass course.

Solution. The total correction is $-10° + 4° - 17° = -23°$. This must be subtracted from the true course to obtain the compass course 147°.

Exercises on Compass Corrections

In each exercise find the unknown course.

Ex.	Compass course	Variation	Deviation	Leeway	True course
1.	11°	10° W	5° E	6° E	?
2.	S 67° E	5° E	3° W	11° W	?
3.	28°	21° E	6° E	11° W	?
4.	?	15° W	6° E	6° E	20°
5.	?	10° E	18°30′ W	8° E	259°
6.	?	15° E	18° E	6° E	S 85° E

7. At a certain place the rate of the Gulf Stream is 4 miles per hour. If a ship heads directly across it at 20 miles per hour, what is the leeway due to the current?

Miscellaneous Exercises on the Sailings

1. From latitude 36° N, a ship sails 81 miles on compass course 230°, the variation being 15° W, deviation 5° E, and leeway 11° W. Find the lat. in and the departure.

2. A ship sails 20° west in lat. 60° N. The variation at the initial point I is 26° W, and deviation 7°40′ W. Find the distance sailed and the compass course at I.

3. From lat. 49° 28.5′ N, long. 13°30′ E, a ship sailed 36 miles on compass course 312°, the variation being $-15°$, and deviation $-7°$. Find lat. in and long. in by Middle Latitude Sailing.

4. From lat. 15°15′ N, long. 45° W, a ship sailed 110.8 miles S $44\frac{1}{2}$° E by compass, the variation being 13° W, and deviation 6°35′ E. Find lat. in and long. in by Middle Latitude Sailing.

5. Find by Mercator's Sailing the compass course and distance from Cape East, New Zealand (lat. 37°50′ S, long. 178°36′ E), to San Francisco

Ch. VI] NAVIGATION: DEAD RECKONING 79

(lat. 37°48′ N, long. 122°24′ W), the variation being 14°20′ E, and deviation 5°40′ E.

57. Dead reckoning. Given several successive short sailings each with a constant course, we find the true courses, then compute the net difference of latitude and net departure as in Traverse Sailing, and finally find the course and distance made good and the position at sea usually by Middle Latitude Sailing (not by Plane Sailing as in the final step in Traverse Sailing), but by Mercator's Sailing if still greater accuracy is needed.

EXAMPLE. A ship sails from a point near Cape Henry lighthouse (lat. 36° 55.6′ N, long. 76° 0.5′ W) on the following series of courses, with variations and deviations of compass and leeway shown. Find the course and distance made good and the position by dead reckoning.

Compass course	Variation	Deviation	Leeway	Total error	True course	Distance	N	S	E	W
28°	6° W	3° E	0	— 3°	25°	1.4	1.3		0 6	
53°	5° W	3° E	3° W	— 5°	48°	27.6	18.5		20.5	
191°	6° W	0	3° E	— 3°	188°	31.5		31.2		4.4
67°	6° W	3° E	5° W	— 8°	59°	14.2	7.3		12.2	
177°	6° W	0	6° E	0	177°	11.0		11.0	0.6	
42°	8° W	3° E	3° W	— 8°	34°	87.0	72.1		48.7	
Made good				53°54′		96.8	99.2	42 2	82 6	4.4
							57 0		78.2	

Diff. lat. 57.0′ N
Lat. out = 36°55.6′ N
Lat. in = 37°52.6′ N
Mid. lat. $L = 37°24.1′$

Dep. 78.2 = $D \cos L$,
D = diff. long. = 98 for $L = 37°$
99.2 for $L = 38°$
98.5 for $L = 37°24′$

Long. in = 76°0.5′ — 1°38.5′ = 74°22′ W.

EXERCISES ON DEAD RECKONING

1. From lat. 48°20.5′ N, long. 10°10′ W, a ship sailed 22.2 miles on compass course 257°, variation — 20°, deviation — 3°; thence 216.5 miles on compass course 232°, variation — 20°, deviation — 1°. Find lat. in and long. in.

2. From lat. 49°40.5′ N, long. 15° W, a ship sailed the courses

Compass C.	Dev.	Var.	Dist.
N 76° W	4° W	17° W	60
N 7½° E	5° W	18° W	30
N 34½° E	3½° W	18° W	97.6
S 67½° W	0	18° W	3.7

Find lat. in and long. in.

3. At noon a ship was in lat. 49°15′ N, long. 24°15′ W.

Time	Comp. C	Dev.	Var.	Speed
noon	N 69° W	4°20′ W	16°40′ W	20
3 P.M.	N 68° W	4°20′ W	17°40′ W	20
6 P.M.	N 23° E	4°20′ W	18°40′ W	21
1 A.M.	S 66° E	5°20′ E	18°40′ W	20
3:30 A.M.	S 67° E	5°20′ E	17°40′ W	20

The speed is in knots, a knot being 1 nautical mile per hour. Find the ship's position at 7:00 A.M.

4. At 8:00 P.M. a ship was in lat. 50°8′ N, long. 16° W, and was steaming 35° at 20 knots; at midnight, true course 300°; at 5:00 A.M., true course 204°; at 8:00 A.M., true course 132°, new speed 22 knots. Find the position at noon.

5. At noon, a ship in lat. 48°23.5′ N, long. 10°32.8′ W, was steaming 354°40′ at 25 knots, deviation 5°10′ W. At 7:00 P.M. it altered its (compass) course to 96°20′, deviation 3°40′ E. Constant variation 17° W. Find its position at midnight.

6. Took departure, Cape Henry lighthouse bearing 293° (see Art. 61) by ship's compass, distant 10 miles, deviation $+3°$, variation $-6°$. Thence ran as follows:

Compass courses	Dist.	Dev.	Var.	Leeway
73°	60	$+3°$	$-6°$	$+3°$
118°	20	$+6°$	$-6°$	$+3°$
160°	10	$+3°$	$-6°$	$+3°$
319°	10	$-6°$	$-6°$	$-3°$
26°	28	$+3°$	$-6°$	$-3°$

Find the course and distance made good from the lighthouse, and the position by dead reckoning.

Hint: Since the true bearing of the lighthouse is 290°, the true departure course is 110° and distance 10.

7. At noon a ship was in lat. 48°22′ N, long. 70°50′ E, steaming S 63° E by compass, speed 20 knots, deviation 5°30′ E. At midnight, the course was N 81° E, speed 20 knots, deviation 2° E. At 6:00 A.M., course N 6° E, speed 21 knots, deviation 5° W. Constant variation 1° W. A current was setting E (by magnetic compass) with velocity 1 knot from noon until 6:00 A.M. Find the position at noon. (Treat current as an additional course.)

CHAPTER VII

LAND SURVEYING

58. Branch of surveying treated. *Land surveying* treats of the determination of the lengths and directions of the boundary lines and the area of a tract of land, as well as the accurate representation of the boundary lines on a map. In *plane surveying*, which alone is considered here, the curvature of the earth is ignored and the part surveyed is regarded as a plane.

No discussion will be given here of the following further branches of surveying: *geodetic surveying*, in which the curvature of the earth is taken into account; *leveling*, in which the relative elevations of points are determined; *topographic surveying*, which combines the methods of leveling and horizontal location, and treats of the construction of contour maps; *mine*, *marine*, and *railroad surveying*.

The object of the present chapter is merely to define and illustrate the terms used in the elements of land surveying, to describe the instruments employed, without discussing their adjustments, and to treat in detail the application of plane trigonometry to the balancing of land surveys and the computing of areas.

59. Chains, tapes, area. A Gunter's chain is 66 feet long and is composed of 100 links connected by small rings. Since there are 5280 feet in a (statute) mile, there are 80 chains in a mile. Since a square mile contains 640 acres, an acre is equal to 10 square chains. Hence an acre contains $10 \times 66^2 = 43560$ square feet.

Instead of a Gunter's chain, it is now customary to use the more accurate steel tapes. When the number of acres in a field is desired, it is convenient to use a steel tape 66 (or 33) feet in length, graduated to feet and tenths of a foot on one side and to links on the reverse side. In city surveying and often in farm surveying, use is made of steel tapes 50 or 100 feet in length, graduated to feet and tenths of a foot and often also to hundredths of a foot.

Since the distances measured are assumed to be horizontal (cf. Art. 60), it is necessary in the case of sloping ground to elevate one end of the chain or tape.

By the area of a tract of land is meant the area of its projection on a horizontal plane. Hence if a piece of hilly ground were completely leveled, its area would remain the same.

60. Course. By a *course IT* is meant any one of the horizontal straight lines AB extending from the vertical line through the initial point I to the vertical line through the terminal point T. The vertical plane through I and T intersects the ground in an irregular curve ICT (Fig. 41). The course from I to T is not this curve, but is a horizontal straight line AB which is a horizontal projection of the curve.

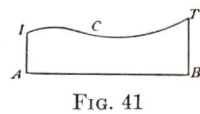

Fig. 41

The distance between I and T, in the sense used in surveying, is AB. In brief, we ·do not employ the actual lines, distances, and areas on the ground, but rather their horizontal projections.

61. True bearing. A true north and south line is called a *true meridian*. The *true bearing* of a course IT is the angle which it makes with the true meridian through the initial point I of the course, and is measured from the north or south point toward the east or west point to give an angle not exceeding 90°. For example, if (Fig. 42) we start from the initial point I and measure in the direction IA proceeding between the north and east points and making an angle of 55° with the meridian IN, the bearing of IA is N 55° E and is read "north 55° east." For the course IB, which proceeds between the north and west points

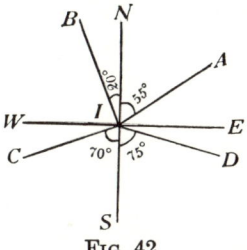

Fig. 42

and makes an angle of 20° with the meridian, the bearing is N 20° W. Similarly, the bearings of the courses IC and ID are S 70° W and S 75° E respectively.

We postpone to Part II the description of the surveyor's compass and transit and the measurement of certain angles by them from which the true bearings of courses are easily found.

Part I. Balancing a Survey, Area (True Bearings Assumed)

62. Latitude and departure. Given a course IT of length D and true bearing B, as N 55° E in Fig. 43 or S 55° W in Fig. 44, draw the perpendicular TF to the true meridian through I. Then IF is called the *latitude* and FT the *departure* of the course IT. We have

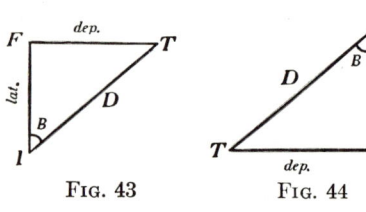

Fig. 43 Fig. 44

$$\text{lat.} = D \cos B,$$
$$\text{dep.} = D \sin B.$$

According as T is north (Fig. 43) or south (Fig. 44) of I, the latitude of the course IT is called north or south. According as T is east (Fig. 43) or west (Fig. 44) of I, the departure of the course IT is called east or west. The letters N and E of a bearing N 55° E tell that the latitude is north and the departure is east.

Given two of the four quantities B, D, lat., dep., we can find the remaining two by Traverse Table VI with sufficient accuracy for ordinary farm surveying. But for city surveying the work should be done by logarithms and checked against gross errors by the traverse table, perhaps omitting interpolations.

63. Balancing a survey. All measurements involve errors. Hence before attempting to find the area of a tract of land, we must adjust the measurements recorded in the field notes of a survey by making such corrections as will properly distribute

LAND SURVEYING

the errors of measurement. This adjustment of the errors is known as *balancing the survey*.

Consider the following survey of a triangular field (Fig. 45), in which the data in the first three columns are taken from the field notes of the survey, while the entries in the next four columns have been read off from the traverse table:

Course	Bearing	Dist.	Lat.		Dep.		Balance	
			N	S	E	W	Lat.	Dep.
AB	N 60°10' E	26	12.94		22.56		+13.02	+22.56
BC	S 18° 5' W	31.2		29.66		9.68	−29.56	− 9.69
CA	N 38° W	20.9	16.47			12.87	+16.54	−12.87
Sum of Dist. =		78.1	29.41	29.66	22.56	22.55		
				29.41		22.55		
	Error in Lat. =			0.25	0.01	= error in Dep.		

We have added the north latitudes, then the south latitudes, etc. If the survey had been exact (which is not to be expected in view of errors of measurement in the field), the sum of the north latitudes would have been equal to the sum of the south latitudes. In our example, the latter sum exceeds the former by 0.25, which is called the error in latitude. This error is distributed among the individual latitudes in proportion to the lengths of the courses, the proportionate parts of the error 0.25 being

$$\frac{26}{78.1} \times .25 = .08, \qquad \frac{31.2}{78.1} \times .25 = .10, \qquad \frac{20.9}{78.1} \times .25 = .07.$$

The partial errors in the north latitudes are here to be added to them, while the partial error in the south latitude is to be subtracted from it. The corrected latitudes are entered in the first of the columns headed "Balance"; to the north latitudes prefix the sign +, and to the south latitudes the sign −, thus enabling us to put all of them in a single column. Moreover, these signs are needed in the further problem to find the area of the field. Similarly we obtain the corrected departures and prefix the sign + to the east departures and the sign − to the west departures.

The bearings and distances are now inconsistent with the balanced latitudes and departures and should be corrected. Thus for the first course we have the legs 13.02 and 22.56 of a right triangle and require the hypotenuse and an acute angle, which may be most readily found by logarithms (but also from the traverse table by double interpolation, Art. 46).

If a map of the field is made by plotting the courses in turn, the final point, which should coincide with the initial point, lies at a distance from it, called the error of closure. It is equal to the hypotenuse of a right triangle whose legs are the errors in latitude and departure. These were .25 and .01 in our example, so that the error of closure is .25. The ratio of this to the perimeter 78.1 is approximately 1/312, which is too large a relative error, even for farm surveying for which the relative error should be $< 1/500$ and preferably $< 1/2000$.

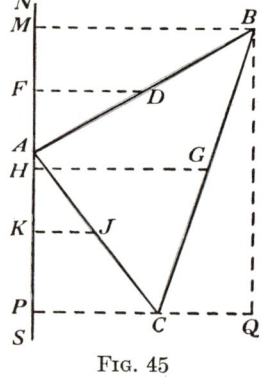

Fig. 45

64. Double meridian distances. Select the meridian which passes through that one of the stations which is farthest west. In our example this is the initial station A (Fig. 45). The *meridian distance* (called also longitude) of a course AB is the distance FD of its mid-point D from the meridian NAS. Likewise HG and KJ are the meridian distances of BC and CA. We have

$2FD = MB$, $2HG = MB + PC = MB + MB + (-QC)$,
$2KJ = PC = MB - QC = MB + PC + (-QC) + (-PC)$.

Hence, *the double meridian distance of the first course is equal to its departure; the double meridian distance of any new course is equal to the algebraic sum* [1] *of the double meridian distance and departure of the preceding course together with the departure of the course itself.*

65. Area of a field. The area of triangle ABC in Fig. 45 is evidently obtained by subtracting triangles ABM and ACP from the trapezoid $MBCP$. Hence the algebraic sum of the

---

[1] By the algebraic sum of 10, 2, and -5 is meant 7.

latter two triangles and the negative of the trapezoid is equal to the negative of ABC. As the sign before the area obtained for the field is of no interest and is changed by passing around the field in the reverse sense, it is ignored. The double areas of the three auxiliary figures are found by the following multiplications:

Course	Lat.	Double mer. dist.	Double area	
AB	$+AM$	$2FD$	$2ABM$	
BC	$-PM$	$2HG$	$-2MBCP$	Alg. sum
CA	$+PA$	$2KJ$	$2PAC$	$= -2ABC$

Hence, *if we multiply the latitude of each course by its double meridian distance, paying attention to their signs, and divide the algebraic sum of these products by 2, we obtain the area of the closed field.*

We shall now illustrate the rules given in the last two sections by performing the computations necessary to find the area of the triangle in Arts. 63, 64 obtained after balancing its survey.

Course	Lat.	Dep.	Double mer. dist.	Double area	
AB	$+13.02$	$+22.56$	$+22.56$	$13.02 \times 22.56 =$	$+293.73$
			$+22.56$		
			-9.69		
BC	-29.56	-9.69	$+35.43$	$-29.56 \times 35.43 =$	-1047.30
			-9.69		
			-12.87		
CA	$+16.54$	-12.87	$+12.87$	$16.54 \times 12.87 =$	$+212.87$

$$+506.60 \quad +506.60$$
$$2)\overline{540.70}$$
$$270.35$$

As a check, the double meridian distance $+12.87$ for CA is the negative of its departure. If the given distances are in chains, the area is 27.035 acres.

66. Plotting. To plot our triangular field on square-ruled paper, choose a vertical ruled line to represent the meridian NS through the most westerly station A. To represent A take the intersection of NS with any horizontal line of the ruling. We locate stations B and C by means of their balanced latitudes and departures. On AN lay off AM (Fig. 45) to contain 13.02 units and on the perpendicular at M lay off MB to contain 22.56 units, thus plotting B. By adding algebraically the latitude $-$ 29.56 and departure $-$ 9.69 of C with respect to B to the latitude 13.02 and departure 22.56 respectively of B with respect to A, we obtain the latitude $-$ 16.54 and departure $+$ 12.87 of C with respect to A. Hence we lay off AP downwards of length 16.54 and on the perpendicular at P lay off PC to the right to contain 12.87 units, thus plotting C.

Exercises on Balancing Surveys and Finding Area

Balance each of the following surveys, plot, and find the area in acres. Use logarithms for Exs. 5, 6.

1.

Course	Bearing	Chains
AB	N10°E	6.50
BC	S72°15′E	7.35
CA	S63°W	9.15

2.

Course	Bearing	Chains
AB	N15°E	9.6
BC	S10°40′E	7.2
CA	S60°5′W	4.4

3.

Course	Bearing	Chains
AB	S45°30′E	8.61
BC	S29°15′W	12.48
CD	N58°10′W	13.89
DA	N51°10′E	15.15

4.

Course	Bearing	Chains
AB	S60°10′E	13.0
BC	S38°W	10.45
CA	N18°5′W	15.6

5.

Course	Bearing	Chains
AB	S21°15′E	24.68
BC	N72°15′W	25.84
CD	N9°30′W	13.36
DA	N84°E	18.08

6.

Course	Bearing	Chains
AB	S64°E	5.40
BC	S21°30′W	9.60
CD	N74°45′W	4.43
DA	N16°30′E	10.52

PART II. SURVEYING INSTRUMENTS; FINDING TRUE BEARINGS

67. Verniers. There is a simple device, called a vernier, which increases the accuracy of measurements made by instruments used in surveying, astronomy, physics, etc.

The *vernier* (invented in 1631 by Pierre Vernier) is a short attachment which slides along the side of a scale, enabling us to measure portions of the scale smaller than the least divisions on the scale.

Consider a scale S graduated to feet and tenths of a foot. Let 9 small divisions (each .1 of a foot) of the scale have together the

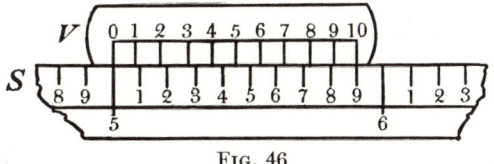

Fig. 46

same length as 10 divisions on the vernier V. Hence each division on the vernier is equal to .9/10 of a foot. Thus a small division of the scale exceeds a division on the vernier by .1 — .09 = .01 of a foot. The reading in Fig. 46 is 5 feet. We always seek the reading on the scale S of the point exactly opposite to the

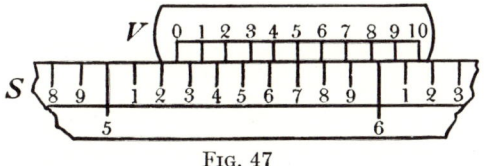

Fig. 47

zero of the vernier. Let the vernier move to the right until 1 on the vernier becomes exactly opposite to 1 on the scale, so that the vernier has moved .01 of a foot; then the reading of the point opposite to 0 is 5.01 feet. In Fig. 47, 5 on the vernier is exactly opposite to a division point on the scale, while 0 is opposite to a point P between divisions 2 and 3; whence the reading at P is 5.25.

Such a vernier is attached to a leveling-rod.

The present form of the vernier is called a *direct vernier* since the markings 1, 2, 3, ... on it proceed in the same direction as the markings on the scale.

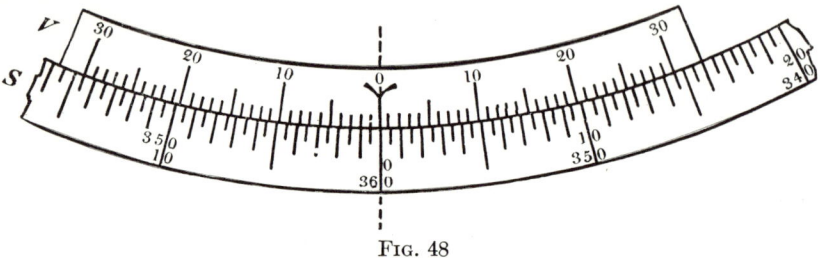

Fig. 48

We next describe a type of *double vernier* for reading angles. Let S (Fig. 48) represent a portion of a circular scale graduated to half degrees from 0° to 360° in each direction; let 29 of these small divisions of the scale have together the same length as 30 small divisions on the vernier V.

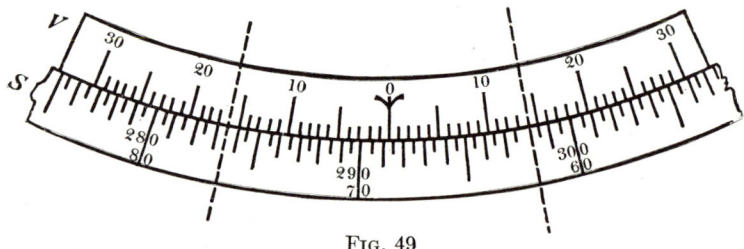

Fig. 49

Each small division of the scale exceeds a division on the vernier by $30' - \frac{29}{30} \times 30' = 1'$, so that readings may be made to minutes. Next, let the vernier take the new position shown in Fig. 49.

Ch. VII] LAND SURVEYING 91

We read from the zero of the scale S to the zero of the vernier V, then in the same direction along the vernier until we reach coincident lines (marked dotted); add the reading of the vernier to the reading of the scale. Thus, if we use the lower markings on the scale S, which increase to the left, we add the reading 16′ of the left half of the vernier to the reading 68°30′ of the scale to obtain the angle 68°46′. But when using the upper markings on the scale, we add the reading 14′ of the right half of the vernier to the reading 291° of the scale to obtain the angle 291°14′.

Exercises on Verniers

1. The least count (i.e., smallest reading) by any direct single vernier is found by dividing the value of the smallest division of the scale by the number n of divisions on the vernier, if these n divisions cover $n-1$ smallest divisions of the scale.

2. On a scale whose smallest division is equal to 20 minutes, 59 divisions cover 60 divisions on the vernier. Show that the least count is 20 seconds.

3. Construct a retrograde vernier whose markings 0, 1, 2, ..., proceed in the opposite direction from the markings on the scale, and such that 11 small divisions (each 0.1 of a foot) of the scale have together the same length as 10 divisions on the vernier. What least length can be read by its use?

68. Surveyor's compass. A surveyor's vernier compass (Fig. 50) consists of a horizontal brass plate which supports at its center a compass circle and a magnetic needle, a vertical sight vane at each end, two spirit levels (Art. 4) placed at right angles to each other, a vernier (the rôle of which is explained at the end of Art. 71), and a tripod or Jacob's staff on which the instrument is supported.

Each *sight vane* has long narrow slits terminated by larger circular holes through which the object to be sighted is more readily found. The observer always looks through the sight vane adjacent to the south point of the compass circle toward the sight vane adjacent to the north point. The latter vane has graduations for the rough measurement of vertical angles.

The brass head, by which the compass is attached to the tripod, has a ball-and-socket joint to give a universal motion, thus en-

Fig. 50. The Surveyor's Compass.

abling the surveyor to *level the instrument,* i.e., to bring the main plate into a horizontal plane. This will be the case when the bubble in each of the two spirit levels is at the middle, provided the levels have been properly adjusted.

The *compass circle* is graduated to half degrees from 0° to 90° each way from the north and south points N and S. When the face of an ordinary pocket compass or a mariner's compass is viewed from above, the point 90° to the right of N is marked E, and the point 90° to the left of N is marked W. But on a surveyor's compass, these markings E and W are interchanged

(Fig. 51), with the result that, if the plane of the sight vanes is directed toward true east, the north end of the needle points to the mark E on the compass circle.

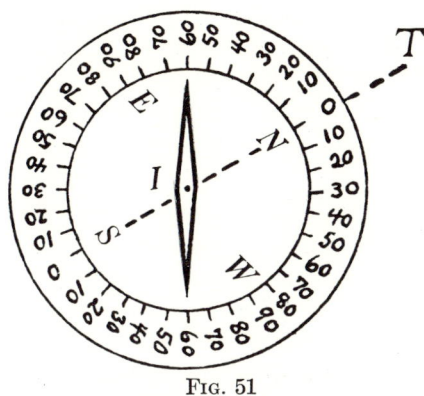

Fig. 51

The needle is unreliable and often, as in city surveying, local attraction renders it practically useless. In any case the compass cannot be read closer than 5 or 10 minutes. Hence, except for rough work for which speed rather than accuracy is the main requirement, the compass has been displaced by the transit (Art. 72). But since the compass was the instrument in general use before the introduction of the transit, it is especially adapted to retracing old surveys. Also, owing to the relations of a new survey of farm lands to old official surveys with a compass, and to the fact that the transit usually carries a compass box for use in checking, the surveyor must understand the simple principles of the compass.

69. Bearing with respect to any course. We may select any course AB as the reference course. The *bearing* of a course IT with respect to AB is the angle between them which is measured from B or A toward the right (clockwise) or left to give an angle not exceeding 90°. In the case of true bearing (Art. 61), the reference line was a true meridian. Also here a bearing is written N 60° E if IT lies 60° to the right of IB (Fig. 52).

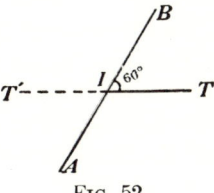

Fig. 52

94   TRIGONOMETRY   [Art. 70

The bearing of the reverse course TI (or IT') is S 60° W and is called the *reverse bearing* of the given course IT.

70. Magnetic bearing. When the reference line is the local magnetic meridian, determined by the magnetic needle at rest, a bearing is called the *magnetic bearing*. Thus the magnetic bearing of a course IT is the angle which it makes with the magnetic meridian through I, and is measured from the north or south point of the magnetic needle toward east or west to give an angle not exceeding 90°.

To find the magnetic bearing of a course IT (Fig. 51), place the compass so that its center is vertically above I, level it, and sight toward T (or a point vertically above or below T); read the number of degrees between the north end of the needle and the nearest zero mark. Thus, in Fig. 51, the bearing is N 60° E. As a check, take a back sight toward I upon arriving at T; the bearing of the reverse course[1] TI should be S 60° W.

71. Magnetic declination. The earth acts like a large, but irregular, magnet whose two magnetic poles[2] are somewhat remote from the north and south geographical poles N and S of the earth. Hence the north point of a compass needle will not in general point true north, viz., toward N. The angle which the needle makes with the true meridian (north and south line of the place) is called the *magnetic declination* or *variation* of the compass at the given place and the given time. If the needle makes an angle of 8° with the true meridian, the declination is 8° E or 8° W according as the north end of the needle points east or west of the true meridian.

Besides the small change in the declination during the day, there is the more important *secular variation*, which is a change in the

[1] When the point N of the compass card, with its center at T, is directed toward I, the new figure is like Fig. 51, but with interchanges of N with S, E with W, I with T. The beginner should draw the new figure.

[2] The north magnetic pole is in latitude 70° N, longitude $96\frac{3}{4}$° W, approximately; the south magnetic pole is in latitude $73\frac{1}{2}$° S, longitude $147\frac{1}{2}$° E, approximately.

same direction for a period of years, followed by a change in the opposite direction, with a period of about two and a half centuries before the declination returns to its initial value. Thus the declination was 8°30' W at Philadelphia in 1700; it diminished until it reached the minimum 1°30' W in 1800, and then increased to 7°45' W in 1915.

Variation charts for different regions of the earth are published about every fifth year and show curves passing through the places where the variation is the same; the charts give also the yearly change at any place.

The only use made of the *vernier* on a compass is to set it so that the compass readings will give the true bearings of lines (without requiring subsequent correction for the declination). To do this let the observer stand at the south end of the instrument and turn the vernier to the right or left, according as the variation is west or east, and through an angle equal to the variation.

EXAMPLE. Given the magnetic bearing N 40° E and the magnetic declination 10° E, find the true bearing.

Solution. In Fig. 53, *IN* represents the true meridian, *IM* the magnetic meridian (containing the north point of the needle *IM*), and *IT* the course. Hence the true bearing is N 50° E.

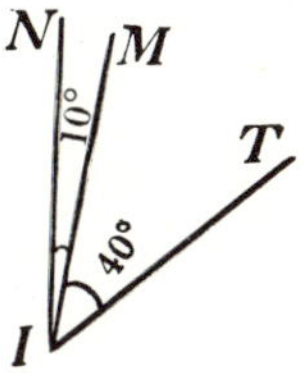

FIG. 53

EXERCISES ON BEARINGS AND SURVEYS BY COMPASS

1. Given the magnetic bearing N 78° E and the magnetic declination 6° W, find the true bearing.

2. Given the true bearing N 80°15' W and the variation of the needle 13° E, find the magnetic bearing.

3. Given the true bearing S 20° W and magnetic bearing S 2° E, find the variation of the needle.

4. The magnetic declination is 10°20' W. Find the magnetic bearings of the cardinal points, viz., true N, true E, S, W.

5. A course of an old survey had the magnetic bearing N 20° E. By a recent survey it has the magnetic bearing N 17°40' E. Given that the present magnetic declination is 6°30' W, find the declination at the time of the old survey.

6. Given the following magnetic bearings of two courses from the same point, find the angle between them:

(a) N 35° E and S 42° W.
(b) S 80° E and N 65° E.
(c) N 35° E and N 87° W.

7. Using the bearings in the table in Art. 63, find the bearings of BC and CA with respect to AB as the reference course.

Balance the following surveys and find the area in acres.

8.

Course	Magnetic bearing	Chains
AB	N35°25'E	5.29
BC	S 25°25'E	7.02
CA	N71°30'W	6.41

Magnetic declination 10° E

9.

Course	Magnetic bearing	Chains
AB	S54°E	10.80
BC	S31°30'W	19.20
CD	N64°45'W	8.86
DA	N26°30'E	21.04

Magnetic declination 10° W

72. Surveyor's transit. This instrument (Fig. 54) is the most important one used in land surveying. It enables us to measure directly the angle between two courses to minutes, often to 30 or 20 seconds, while with a compass it is necessary to measure the magnetic bearing of each course and the compass reads only to within 5 or 10 minutes. The principle of the transit is the same as that of the telescopes used in astronomy.

The transit has a *telescope* which revolves in a vertical plane perpendicular to the horizontal supporting axis. The axis rests in bearings at the top of two standards which are rigidly attached to a horizontal circular plate, so that if the telescope is turned sidewise (horizontally), the plate must turn with it. This plate is called the *upper* or *vernier plate* and carries a vernier,[1] two spirit levels placed at right angles to each other, and a graduated compass circle. Just below the vernier plate is another horizontal

---

[1] Often two verniers placed diametrically opposite to each other, both being read to eliminate the error due to the imperfect centering of the graduated circle.

Fig. 54. The Surveyor's Transit

circular plate, called the *lower plate* or the *limb* of the instrument; it has on its outer edge the graduated circle.

Each plate has its own separate motion controlled by a set screw and a tangent screw, as will be described in detail. The two plates may be rotated independently of one another, or may be clamped together by means of a set screw, which is not attached to the lower plate, although it appears to be so in Fig. 54. In fact, when the set screw is loose, the upper plate can revolve, taking the screw with it. When the screw is set, the upper plate is virtually clamped to the lower, but in such a manner that the upper plate may be rotated slowly relatively to the lower plate by turning the tangent screw, which operates at right angles to the set screw.

> For example, the zero of the vernier may be brought approximately opposite to the zero of the limb and, after the set screw is tightened, the zero of the vernier may be brought exactly opposite to the zero of the limb by slowly turning the tangent screw. In the same manner, without disturbing the limb, we may point the telescope approximately and then exactly on an object.

At the bottom of Fig. 54 is shown the *leveling head,* composed of a central cylinder and a small circular plate separated by four vertical leveling screws which are used to level the transit. The limb may be clamped to the leveling head by means of a set screw and then rotated slowly by use of the lower tangent screw.

Similarly, the movement of the telescope in a vertical plane is controlled by a set screw (working upon the supporting axis of the telescope) and a tangent screw. The axis of the telescope usually carries a large *vertical circle* or arc with a vernier attached to read vertical angles to minutes. Just underneath the telescope is attached a long spirit level used to level the telescope when finding the difference of elevation of two stations or when running horizontal courses.

Within the telescope are two fine perpendicular *cross wires* whose intersection and the optical center of the object glass determine the *line of collimation*. This line indicates the point toward which the telescope is pointed.

The telescope may possess a pair of horizontal *stadia wires* fastened to movable slides so adjusted that the wires subtend say one foot on a graduated stadia rod standing 100 feet away, and hence subtend three feet on a rod 300 feet away, etc. With the stadia wires we can therefore rapidly measure distances approximately, which is especially useful over rough ground.[1]

73. Measuring angles with a transit. To measure a *horizontal angle ABC*, place the transit over the vertex B of the angle, level the transit, and set the zero of the vernier exactly opposite to the zero of the limb. Bring the line of collimation to bear approximately on A, clamp the lower plate to the leveling head and make the line of collimation bear exactly on A by means of the lower tangent screw. Unclamp the upper plate and turn it until the line of collimation bears approximately on C, clamp, and make the line of collimation bear exactly on C by means of the upper tangent screw. Then angle ABC is the arc over which the zero of the vernier has passed and can be read by observing the point on the limb at which the zero of the vernier stops. If it stops exactly opposite to a graduation mark of the limb, the angle is read without using the vernier. But usually it stops between graduation marks and then the vernier reading tells how far it has passed beyond the last mark (cf. Art. 67).

To measure the *angle of elevation* or *depression* of an object relative to the horizontal plane (Art. 5), make the line of collimation horizontal (as shown by the level bulb attached to the telescope), whence the vertical circle or arc reads zero if in proper adjustment. Then sight approximately at the object, tighten the set screw, and, by turning the tangent screw, bring the line of collimation exactly on the object. Then read the vertical circle.

74. Traverse. A series of connected courses $AB, BC, CD, \ldots$ is called a *traverse*. It is called *closed* if it returns to the starting point. Thus a survey of a field is a closed traverse.

In a traverse with a transit four main types of angles are used: direct angle, deflection angle, azimuth, and bearing. The first three types will be defined in turn. The fourth type has been defined above.

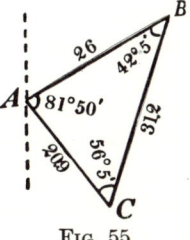

Fig. 55

[1] For details, see Tracy's *Plane Surveying*, 1914, pp. 300–317.

75. Direct angle. The *direct angle* between two consecutive courses AB and BC is the angle ABC measured in a specified direction (right or left) and may have any value up to 360°. In a closed traverse we may employ only interior angles as in Fig. 55, or only exterior angles (that at B in Fig. 55 being 317°55′).

76. Deflection angle. It is often convenient to use the *deflection angle* which a course makes with the preceding course reversed, the angle being measured from the latter to the right or left to give a result less than 180°. Thus, in Fig. 56, the deflection angle at B is $A'BC$ and is read to the right from BA'; that at C is $B'CD$ and is read to the left from CB'.

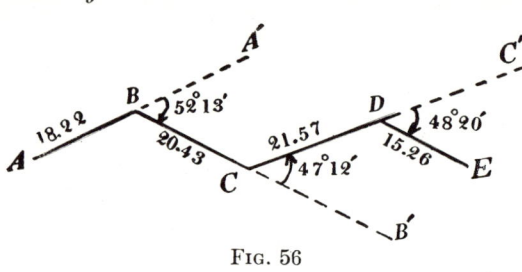

Fig. 56

77. Azimuth. The angle which a course makes with a chosen reference line (such as the magnetic meridian) is the *azimuth* of the course; it may have any value up to 360° and is read clockwise from a chosen end of the reference line (such as north on the magnetic meridian). In Fig. 57, the azimuth of BC with respect to the meridian BN is 205°, and that of AB is 47°.

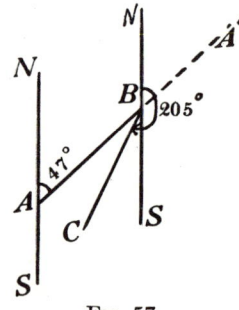

Fig. 57

EXERCISES ON THE FOUR TYPES OF ANGLES

1. Given the bearing N 60°10′ E of the first course AB in Fig. 55, calculate the bearings of BC and CA. Check that the sum of the three angles at the right of the meridian through A is 180°.

2. Given the bearing N 70°25′ E of the first course AB in Fig. 56, calculate the bearings of the remaining three courses.

3. In a triangular field ABC, the interior angles are $A = 42°5′$, $B = 81°50′$, $C = 56°5′$, and the bearing of AB is S 60°10′ E. Find the bearings of BC and CA.

4. Given the true bearings N 60°10′ E, S 18°5′ W, N 38° W of courses AB, BC, CA, find the azimuths of these courses with respect to the reference lines (i) true meridian, and (ii) AB.

5. In the second column of the following table are given the azimuths of the courses with respect to course AB. Given also the magnetic bearing N 30° W of AB, verify the entries in the last two columns:

Course	Azimuth with AB	Bearing with AB	Magnetic Bearing
AB	0°	N	N 30° W
BC	94°	S 86° E	N 64° E
CD	174°	S 6° E	S 36° E
DA	256°	S 76° W	S 46° W

6. Given the last column in Ex. 5, derive the azimuths with AB.

7. Given the bearings with AB in Ex. 5, derive the azimuths with AB.

78. Balancing a transit survey. If we have measured the interior angles of a field of n sides, their sum should be equal to $2(n-2)$ right angles; any error is distributed equally among the n angles. When deflection angles are used, the difference between the sum of those measured to the right (R) and the sum of those measured to the left (L) should always be equal to 360°, as the reader may prove by means of the sum of the interior angles and the relation between any interior angle and the corresponding deflection angle. If, for example, the difference is 360°2′30″ and if there are three R's and two L's, subtract 30″ from each R and add 30″ to each L; or we may compute the interior angles and distribute any error in their sum equally among the angles.

From the angles so adjusted we compute the bearings and then the latitudes and departures by logarithms, and balance the survey as in Art. 63, and compute the area.

Exercises on Balancing Surveys and Finding Area

Balance and find the area of the following surveys. In Exs. 3, 4, 5 assume that AB is a true meridian. In Ex. 6, use as the meridian a line not a course.

1.

Course	Azimuth	Chains
AB	252°45′	8.20
BC	163°45′	12.05
CD	113°55′	9.80
DA	346°05′	18.50

2.

Course	Azimuth	Chains
AB	0°	9.60
BC	154°20′	7.20
CA	225°05′	4.40

3.

Course	Deflection angle	Feet
AB	86°31′ R	335.05
BC	10°13′ L	464.98
CD	124°53′ R	483.72
DE	76°03′ R	616.53
EA	82°46′ R	242.84

4.

Course	Direct angle	Feet
AB	$ABC = 44°24.5′$	265.8
BC	$BCD = 107°55′$	391
CD	$CDA = 83°52.5′$	141.7
DA	$DAB = 123°48′$	250

5.

Course	Direct angle	Feet
AB	$ABC = 132°12′$	678.53
BC	$BCD = 89°32′53″$	137.47
CD	$CDA = 90°25′27″$	502.98
DA	$DAB = 47°50′$	589.35

6.

Course	Direct angle	Feet
AB	$ABC = 89°52′40″$	399.91
BC	$BCD = 90°15′47″$	432.28
CD	$CDA = 89°41′33″$	400.30
DA	$DAB = 90°10′$	433.26

CHAPTER VIII

TRIGONOMETRIC FUNCTIONS OF ANY ANGLE

79. Rectangular coördinates. The reader became familiar in Chapter VI with the idea of locating a point on the earth's surface by means of its latitude and longitude, the former being its distance north or south of the equator, and the latter being the arc on the equator which is intercepted between its meridian and a fixed meridian, as that through Greenwich. Similarly, in defining the two rectangular coördinates of a point P in a plane, we employ (Fig. 58) a horizontal line $X'X$ (which plays the rôle of the equator) and a vertical line $Y'Y$ (which plays the rôle of the meridian of Greenwich).

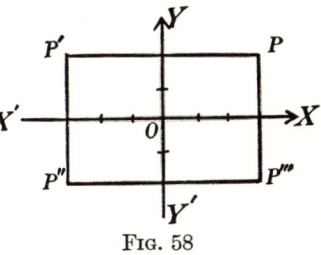

FIG. 58

If to the distance of a point P from $X'X$ we prefix the sign $+$ or $-$, according as P is above or below $X'X$, we obtain a positive or negative number y which is called the *ordinate* of P (and plays the rôle of latitude, north or south). Likewise, if to the distance of P from $Y'Y$ we prefix the sign $+$ or $-$, according as P is to the right or left of $Y'Y$, we obtain a positive or negative number x which is called the *abscissa* of P (and plays the rôle of longitude, east or west).

The abscissa x and ordinate y are together called the *(rectangular) coördinates* of P. The point P is designated by (x, y).

In Fig. 58, the coördinates of P are $x = +3$, $y = +2$, whence P is $(3, 2)$; those of P' are $x = -3$, $y = +2$, whence P' is $(-3, 2)$. Similarly, P'' is $(-3, -2)$, and P''' is $(3, -2)$.

As a further illustration of the signs of coördinates, we recall from Art. 63 that it is convenient in surveying to mark north latitudes $+$, south latitudes $-$, east departures $+$, and west departures $-$.

The line $X'X$ is called the *x-axis* (less often, the *axis of abscissas*), and $Y'Y$ the *y-axis*. Their point of intersection O is called the *origin* (or *origin of coördinates*).

To *plot a point* is to locate it with reference to the axes by means of its coördinates. For example, if we plot the point ($-3, 2$), we obtain P' in Fig. 58. The work of plotting points is simplified by the use of square-ruled paper (called also rectangular coördinate paper), which has been used in the earlier chapters in drawing right triangles to scale.

80. Radius vector. The distance OP is called the *radius vector* of the point P, and denoted by r. By its definition, r is a positive number. Since OP is the hypotenuse of a right triangle whose base is of length x or $-x$, and vertical side is of length y or $-y$, we see that $x^2 + y^2 = r^2$, so that

$r = +\sqrt{x^2+y^2}$ is the radius vector of the point (x, y).

Exercises on Rectangular Coördinates

On square-ruled paper choose as the origin a convenient intersection of two rulings. After inspecting the size of the coördinates of the points to be plotted, select the number of units which shall be represented by a small (or a large) division of the ruled paper, and mark the number along one such division.

1. Plot the points $(3, 4)$, $(3, -4)$, $(-3, 4)$, $(-3, -4)$, $(4, 3)$, $(4, -3)$, $(-4, 3)$, $(-4, -3)$, $(5, 0)$, $(-5, 0)$, $(0, 5)$, $(0, -5)$, $(1, \sqrt{24})$, $(2, \sqrt{21})$. What is the radius vector of each point? On what circle do all the points lie?

2. Plot the points $(\pm 33, \pm 56)$, $(\pm 56, \pm 33)$, $(\pm 16, \pm 63)$, $(\pm 63, \pm 16)$, $(\pm 25, \pm 60)$, $(\pm 60, \pm 25)$, $(\pm 39, \pm 52)$, $(\pm 52, \pm 39)$, $(\pm 65, 0)$, $(0, \pm 65)$, using all combinations of signs. What is the radius vector of each point? On what circle do all the points lie?

3. Plot the points $(-2, -3)$, $(-1, -1)$, $(0, 1)$, $(1, 3)$, $(2, 5)$. Do they appear to lie on a straight line?

4. Find y so that $(0, -200)$, $(1, y)$, $(2, 400)$ shall lie on a straight line.

81. Generalized notion of angle. We have been concerned mainly with right triangles, no one of whose angles exceeds 90°. We shall soon consider oblique triangles, no one of whose angles exceeds 180°. But we learned in navigation to employ angles of any size up to 360°. Likewise in surveying, where we distinguished between the clockwise and counter-clockwise directions in which angles may be measured, starting for example from the north point. These remarks and especially the rotation of the telescope of a transit in the act of measuring an angle prepare us for the following general notion of angle:

An angle may be considered as generated by the rotation of a straight line which first coincides with the initial side of the angle and then rotates about the vertex of the angle until finally it coincides with the terminal side of the angle. An angle is called **positive** *if the rotation is counter-clockwise,* **negative** *if the rotation is clockwise.*

For example, in Figs. 59–61 are shown three angles *IOT* whose directions of rotation are indicated by curved arrows. In Fig. 59, the positive angle 320°

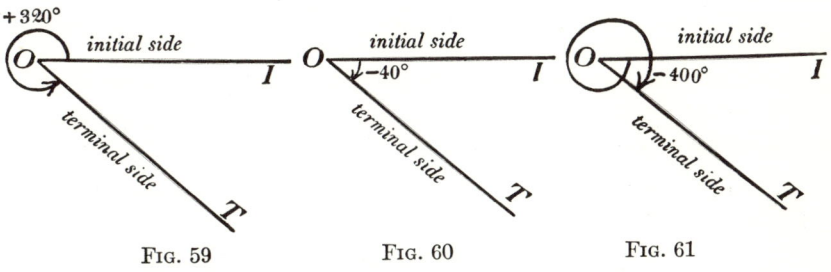

FIG. 59   FIG. 60   FIG. 61

is generated by counter-clockwise rotation from the initial side *OI* to the terminal side *OT*. In Fig. 60, the negative angle — 40° is generated by clockwise rotation. In Fig. 61, there has been a complete revolution clockwise through 360° followed by a further rotation clockwise through 40°, the combined result being the negative angle — 400°.

82. Trigonometric position of an angle; the four quadrants.

When, as in Figs. 59–61, an angle IOT is placed so that its initial side OI is horizontal and is drawn toward the right from O, the angle is said to be in its *trigonometric position*.

The horizontal line $X'X$ and the vertical line $Y'Y$, which intersect at O, divide the plane into four parts, called *quadrants*, which are numbered as in Fig. 62. If a line whose initial position is OX rotates counter-clockwise about O, it passes in turn over the first, second, third, and fourth quadrants. In any one of its positions, the rotating line is the terminal side of an angle having OX as initial side; this angle is said to be in the quadrant which contains the terminal side. For example, the angles in Figs. 59–61 are all in the fourth quadrant, while angle 120° in its trigonometric position (Fig. 65) is in the second quadrant.

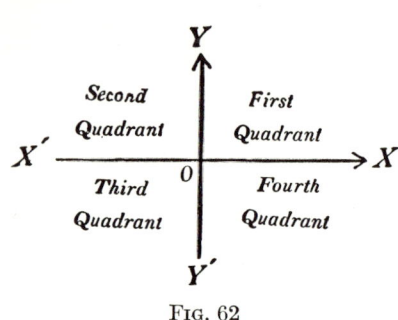

Fig. 62

Exercises on the Quadrants and Trigonometric Position

1. Name the quadrants of the following angles when placed in their trigonometric positions: 230°, —120°, — 300°, 950°, —1000°.

2. Give two positive and two negative angles in their trigonometric positions whose terminal sides bisect $\angle X'OY'$.

3. Name the quadrants in which lie the plots of the points (3, — 4), (—3, 4), (— 3, — 4). What least positive angles in their trigonometric positions have these points on their terminal sides?

4. What angle does the minute hand of a clock describe in 2 hours and 20 minutes? The hour hand?

5. What angle is described by a spoke of a bicycle wheel, 3 feet in diameter, when the bicycle travels 100 feet?

Ch. VIII] FUNCTIONS OF ANY ANGLE

83. Trigonometric functions of any angle. The six trigonometric functions of any acute angle were defined in Art. 7. We shall now define the six trigonometric functions of any angle A, with the exception of certain of the functions of $0°$, $\pm 90°$, $\pm 180°$, or any multiple of $90°$.

Place the angle A in its trigonometric position XOT (so that its initial side is the horizontal line OX extending to the right from

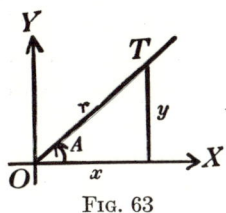
Fig. 63

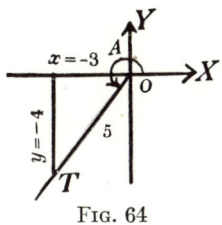
Fig. 64

the origin O of a system of rectangular coördinates). Select any point T, other than O, on the terminal side of angle A. Let x be the abscissa of T, y its ordinate, and r its radius vector. Not only for the cases of the angles A shown in Figs. 63, 64, but for an angle A of any size and any sign, we make the following definitions:

$$\sin A = \frac{y}{r}, \qquad \cos A = \frac{x}{r}, \qquad \tan A = \frac{y}{x} \text{ (if } x \neq 0\text{)},$$

$$\csc A = \frac{r}{y} \text{ (if } y \neq 0\text{)}, \ \sec A = \frac{r}{x} \text{ (if } x \neq 0\text{)}, \ \cot A = \frac{x}{y} \text{ (if } y \neq 0\text{)}.$$

Or in words, the *sine* is the ratio of the ordinate to the radius vector, ..., the *cotangent* is the ratio of the abscissa to the ordinate provided the ordinate is not zero.

These ratios are the same, no matter what point T is selected. The values of the six functions depend only on the angle A.

For the case of an acute angle (Fig. 63), these definitions agree with those given in Art. 7, where r was called the hypotenuse, x the adjacent side, and y the opposite side.

When A is equal to 0°, 90°, 180°, or any multiple of 90°, one of the numbers x and y is zero and cannot be used as a divisor. It was therefore necessary in our definition of tan A as y/x to exclude the cases in which $x = 0$. No definition is given of the tangent of 90°, 270°, or of any odd multiple of 90°; the tangent is said to be *undefined* for these angles. Accordingly we avoid the symbols tan 90°, tan 270°, and similarly csc 0°, cot 0°, sec 90°, csc 180°, cot 180°, sec 270°, together with the symbols obtained by increasing or decreasing these angles by multiples of 360°. The fact that there exists no entirely satisfactory definition of these excluded symbols will become evident when we have studied the graphs of the functions (Arts. 107–8).

Angles — 340°, 20°, 380° and 740° have the same terminal side when placed in their trigonometric positions, and hence by definition have the same sines, the same cosines, etc. So always, the trigonometric functions of angles which differ by any multiple of 360° have the same values.

EXAMPLE 1. Find the trigonometric functions of angle 120°.

Solution. Place angle 120° in its trigonometric position XOT (Fig. 65). For convenience take $OT = r = 2$. Since $\angle BOT = 60°$, we complete the equilateral triangle OTB, and see that OC and TC are of lengths 1 and $\sqrt{3}$ respectively. Hence $x = -1$, $y = +\sqrt{3}$, so that

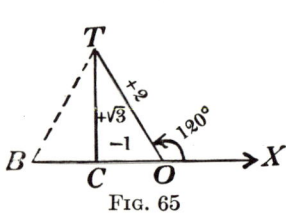

Fig. 65

$$\sin 120° = \frac{\sqrt{3}}{2}, \quad \cos 120° = \frac{-1}{2},$$

$$\tan 120° = \frac{\sqrt{3}}{-1} = -\sqrt{3}.$$

EXAMPLE 2. Given tan $A = 4/3$, find sin A and cos A.

Solution. The ratio of the ordinate y to the abscissa x is 4/3. Since it is a question of a ratio and not of actual lengths, we may take $x = \pm 3$ to avoid fractions. First, let $x = +3$. Then

$$y = +4, \ r^2 = 3^2 + 4^2, \ r = 5,$$

and angle A is in the first quadrant (as in Fig. 63). Thus sin $A = 4/5$,

Ch. VIII]   FUNCTIONS OF ANY ANGLE   109

$\cos A = 3/5$. Second, let $x = -3$. Then $y = -4$, $r = 5$, and angle A is in the third quadrant (Fig. 64). Hence $\sin A = -4/5$, $\cos A = -3/5$. Thus there are two sets of answers.

Exercises on the Definitions of the Trigonometric Functions

1. Prove that, for an angle in the second quadrant, the sine and cosecant are positive and the remaining four functions are negative. For an angle in the third quadrant, the tangent and cotangent alone are positive. For an angle in the fourth quadrant, the cosine and secant alone are positive.

2. By noting their relations to 45°, 30°, 60° (Figs. 10, 11), find in terms of radicals the sine, cosine, and tangent of 135°, 150°, 210°, 225°, 240°, 300°, 315°, 330°.

3. Using the results in Ex. 2, find the sines and cosines of $-210°$, 495°, $-495°$, $-60°$, $-390°$.

4. By using the present letters y, x, r in place of the letters a, b, c of Art. 10, extend the proofs given there of

(1) $\sin^2 A + \cos^2 A = 1$, (2) $\tan A = \dfrac{\sin A}{\cos A}$, (3) $\cot A = \dfrac{\cos A}{\sin A}$,

(4) $\sec^2 A = 1 + \tan^2 A$, (5) $\csc^2 A = 1 + \cot^2 A$

to any angle A, with exception in case of (2) and (4) of angles A which are odd multiples of 90° (whence $x = 0$), and in case of (3) and (5) of angles which are even multiples of 90° (whence $y = 0$), since in the excepted cases the formula involves either a function which is undefined or a fraction whose denominator is zero.

5. Which of the formulas in Ex. 4 determines the value of a new function when $\tan A = 4/3$? How do we then get $\cos A$? Why is it better to use (2) rather than (1) when finding $\sin A$? Compare your answers with those found geometrically in Ex. 2 of the text above these exercises.

Find both geometrically and by means of the formulas in Ex. 4 the remaining functions of angle A, when it is given that

6. $\tan A = -\dfrac{1}{3}$.   7. $\sin A = \dfrac{5}{13}$.   8. $\cos A = -\dfrac{3}{5}$.

9. $\tan A = \dfrac{2}{3}$ with A in the third quadrant.

10. $\sin A = -\frac{2}{3}$ with A in the fourth quadrant.

11. $\sec A = 2$, with $\tan A$ negative.

By considering angles which approach 0° or 90°, show that

12. $\sin 0° = 0$, $\cos 0° = 1$, $\tan 0° = 0$, $\sec 0° = 1$.

13. $\sin 90° = 1$, $\cos 90° = 0$, $\cot 90° = 0$, $\csc 90° = 1$.

84. Trigonometric identities. An equality like $\sin^2 A + \cos^2 A = 1$ which is true of all angles A is called an *identity*. The same term is applied also to an equality (like $\tan A = \sin A/\cos A$ in Ex. 4 above) which is true for all those angles A for which both members have a meaning, i.e., for which the functions involved are defined and the denominators are not zero. Apart from the additional task of listing such exceptional angles, if any, the work of proving an identity is the same as in Art. 11.

Exercises on Identities

Prove the following identities, stating[1] the exceptional values, if any, for which either member is undefined.

1. $(\sin A + \cos A)^2 + (\sin A - \cos A)^2 = 2$.
2. $\sin^2 A (\csc^2 A - 1) = \cos^2 A$.
3. $\sin^2 A + \tan^2 A \sin^2 A = \tan^2 A$.
4. $\sin^2 A \sec^2 A = \sec^2 A - 1$.
5. $(1 + \tan B)^2 + (1 - \tan B)^2 = 2 \sec^2 B$.
6. $\sin B + \cos B \cot B = \csc B$.
7. $\cos^4 C - \sin^4 C = 2 \cos^2 C - 1$.
8. $\sin C \tan^2 C \cot^3 C = \cos C$.
9. $\dfrac{\sin \alpha}{1 + \cos \alpha} = \dfrac{1 - \cos \alpha}{\sin \alpha}$.
10. $\dfrac{\sin \alpha}{1 - \cot \alpha} + \dfrac{\cos \alpha}{1 - \tan \alpha} = \sin \alpha + \cos \alpha$.
11. $\dfrac{\sin y + \tan y}{\csc y + \cot y} = \sin y \tan y$.

[1] The instructor may omit this requirement in some of the exercises assigned.

12. $(\cot y + \csc y)^2 = \dfrac{1 + \cos y}{1 - \cos y}$.

13. $\dfrac{(\sec \theta + \csc \theta)^2}{\sec^2 \theta + \csc^2 \theta} = 1 + 2 \sin \theta \cos \theta$.

14. $\sec \theta - \tan \theta = \dfrac{\cos \theta}{1 + \sin \theta}$.

15. $(1 + \tan A)(1 + \cot A) \sin A \cos A = (\sin A + \cos A)^2$.

16. $(\sin A + \sec A)^2 + (\cos A + \csc A)^2 = (1 + \sec A \csc A)^2$.

17. $(\sin B + \cos B)(\tan B + \cot B) = \sec B + \csc B$.

18. $(1 + \sin C + \cos C)^2 = 2(1 + \sin C)(1 + \cos C)$.

19. $(1 - \sec x - \tan x)(1 - \csc x - \cot x) = 2$.

20. $(1 + \tan \theta + \sec \theta)(1 + \tan \theta - \sec \theta) = 2 \tan \theta$.

85. Reduction of the trigonometric functions of any angle to functions of an acute angle. Since our tables of the values of the trigonometric functions give directly only functions of acute angles, we seek formulas, like $\cos 130° = -\cos 50°$, which express the functions of any angle in terms of functions of acute angles.

First, if A is any acute angle or any angle between 90° and 180°, we shall prove the formulas

(1) $\begin{cases} \sin A = \sin(180° - A), & \csc A = \csc(180° - A), \\ \cos A = -\cos(180° - A), & \sec A = -\sec(180° - A), \\ \tan A = -\tan(180° - A), & \cot A = -\cot(180° - A), \end{cases}$

which enable us to express the functions of obtuse angles in terms of functions of acute angles. If A is acute, write B for $180° - A$. But if A is between 90° and 180°, write B for A. In either case, B is an angle between 90° and 180°. Place B in its trigonometric position XOT (Fig. 66) and for convenience take the radius vector OT to be of unit length. Construct $\angle XOT'$ equal to $\angle X'OT = 180° - B$, and take $OT' = OT$. Draw the perpendiculars $T'X$ and TX'. The right

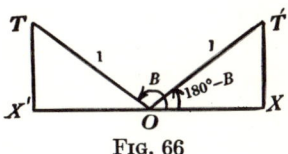

Fig. 66

triangles $T'OX$ and TOX' have equal hypotenuses and equal angles at O, and hence are equal. Thus $T'X = TX'$, $OX = OX'$. By the definitions of the trigonometric functions,

$$\sin B = TX' = T'X = \sin(180°-B),$$
$$\cos B = -OX' = -OX = -\cos(180°-B).$$

Also,

$$\tan B = \frac{\sin B}{\cos B} = \frac{\sin(180°-B)}{-\cos(180°-B)} = -\tan(180°-B).$$

Whether B is equal to A or to $180° - A$, the three formulas just proved are the same as the three formulas in the first column of (1). Taking reciprocals, we get those in the second column; for example,

$$\csc A = \frac{1}{\sin A} = \frac{1}{\sin(180°-A)} = \csc(180°-A).$$

When $A = 90°$, its tangent and secant are undefined (Art. 83), while the four formulas (1) which do not involve these two functions are true, since $\cos 90° = \cot 90° = 0$. Hence formulas (1) hold for every angle between $0°$ and $180°$ for which the functions involved are defined.

Second, we shall prove the identities

(2) $\begin{cases} \sin A = -\sin(360°-A), & \csc A = -\csc(360°-A), \\ \cos A = \cos(360°-A), & \sec A = \sec(360°-A), \\ \tan A = -\tan(360°-A), & \cot A = -\cot(360°-A), \end{cases}$

which enable us to express the trigonometric functions of any angle A between $180°$ and $360°$ in terms of those of $360° - A$, which is an angle between $0°$ and $180°$. If the latter angle is between $90°$ and $180°$, we saw that by means of formulas (1) we can pass to functions of an acute angle, which are given by the tables.

If A is between $0°$ and $180°$, write B for $360° - A$. But if A is between $180°$ and $360°$, write B for A. In either case, B is an angle between $180°$ and $360°$. Place B in its trigonometric position XOT (Fig. 67 if $B<270°$, Fig. 68 if $B>270°$).

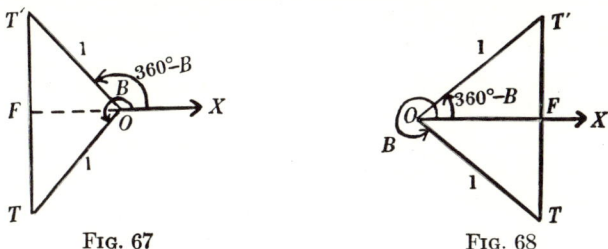

Fig. 67   Fig. 68

Take the radius vector OT to be of unit length. Draw the perpendicular TF to OX and produce it to T', where $T'F = TF$. Since the right triangles OTF and $OT'F$ are equal, $\angle TOF = \angle T'OF$. In Fig. 68, $\angle TOF + B = 360°$, whence $\angle T'OF = 360° - B$. In Fig. 67,

$$B = 180° + \angle FOT, \quad \angle XOT' = 180° - \angle T'OF;$$

adding, we get $B + \angle XOT' = 360°$. Hence, in either figure, $\angle XOT' = 360° - B$. By the definitions of the trigonometric functions,

$\sin B = -FT = -FT' = -\sin(360° - B)$ (Fig. 67 or Fig. 68),
$\cos B = -OF = +\cos(360° - B)$ (Fig. 67),
$\cos B = +OF = +\cos(360° - B)$ (Fig. 68).

Then, if $B \neq 270°$,

$$\tan B = \frac{\sin B}{\cos B} = \frac{-\sin(360° - B)}{\cos(360° - B)} = -\tan(360° - B).$$

The proof of these formulas holds true also in the limiting cases $B = 180°$, $B = 360°$. We have now proved the three formulas in the first column of (2), with exception of the tangent formula when $A = 90°$ or $270°$. From these formulas, by taking reciprocals, we obtain the three in the last column of (2), with exception only of angles for which the functions involved are undefined. Hence formulas (2) are identities.

Since angles $360° - A$ and $-A$ have the same terminal side and hence the same trigonometric functions, formulas (2) imply

(3) $\sin(-A) = -\sin A, \cos(-A) = \cos A, \tan(-A) = -\tan A.$

EXAMPLE. Express the functions of 580° in terms of functions of an acute angle.

Solution. Since $580° = 220° + 360°$, the functions of 580° are the same as the functions of 220°. By (2), for $A = 220°$, we have
$$\sin 220° = -\sin 140°, \quad \cos 220° = \cos 140°, \quad \tan 220° = -\tan 140°.$$
By (1), for $A = 140°$, we get
$$\sin 140° = \sin 40°, \quad \cos 140° = -\cos 40°, \quad \tan 140° = -\tan 40°.$$
Hence
$$\sin 580° = -\sin 40°, \quad \cos 580° = -\cos 40°, \quad \tan 580° = \tan 40°.$$

Exercises on Reduction to Acute Angles

Express as a function of an acute angle and find from the table of natural functions:

1. $\cos 510°$.   2. $\tan 525°$.   3. $\sin(-165°)$.   4. $\tan 975°$.
5. $\tan(-30°)$.   6. $\sec(-60°)$.   7. $\cot 800°$.   8. $\csc 525°$.

Using the table of logarithms of the trigonometric functions, find

9. $\log \cos 285°20'$.   10. $\log \tan(-120°15')$.   11. $\log \sin 484°10'$.

12. Why is there no meaning for $\log \cos 150°$, $\log \sin 225°$, $\log \tan 300°$?

13.* Show that (1) are identities by proving them also for angles A between 180° and 360°.

Hint: Let $A = 360° - \alpha$, so that (1) and (2) are true when A is replaced by α, and (3) when A is replaced by $180° - \alpha$.

14.* By replacing A by $180° + A$ in (2) and then using (1), prove that
$$\sin(180° + A) = -\sin A, \quad \cos(180° + A) = -\cos A,$$
$$\tan(180° + A) = \tan A.$$
Then by use of a table of natural functions, find $\sin 200°$, $\cos 200°$, $\tan 200°$.

CHAPTER IX

SOLUTION OF OBLIQUE TRIANGLES

86. Altitude and area of any triangle. Select any angle A of any triangle ABC and place the triangle so that angle A is in its trigonometric position (Fig. 69 if A is acute, Fig. 70 if A is obtuse, Fig. 71 if A is a right angle).

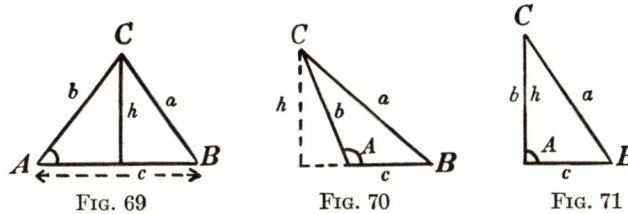

FIG. 69   FIG. 70   FIG. 71

Denote the altitude on AB by h, the side AC by b, and the base AB by c. In each figure, $\sin A = h/b$. Hence $h = b \sin A$.

Since the area of a triangle is equal to one-half the product of its base c by its altitude h, it is equal to $\tfrac{1}{2}bc \sin A$. *The area of any triangle is equal to one-half the product of any two sides multiplied by the sine of the included angle.*

87. Law of sines. *The sides of any triangle are proportional to the sines of the opposite angles.* If the sides are a, b, c, and the opposite angles are A, B, C, respectively, then

(1) $\qquad \dfrac{a}{b} = \dfrac{\sin A}{\sin B}, \quad \dfrac{a}{c} = \dfrac{\sin A}{\sin C}, \quad \dfrac{b}{c} = \dfrac{\sin B}{\sin C}.$

It will be sufficient to prove only the first formula (1), provided we agree that a and b denote *any* two sides of any triangle. By Art. 86, $h = b \sin A$ and, by applying the same result to angle B, we have $h = a \sin B$. Thus $b \sin A = a \sin B$, and hence we obtain the desired first formula (1).

We shall see that formulas (1) enable us to solve a triangle if we are given a side and two angles, or two sides and the angle opposite to one of them. A suitable check formula is furnished by any one of the formulas (5), (6), (7) of Art. 88.

88. Law of tangents. Given two sides a, b and the included angle C, we cannot solve the triangle by use of the law of sines, since each formula (1) contains two unknowns. We proceed to prove a formula suitable for this purpose.

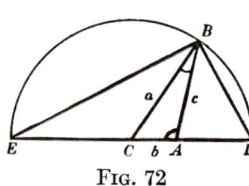

Fig. 72

Let ABC be a triangle in which the side $BC = a$ is greater than the side $AC = b$ (Fig. 72). With center C and radius CB describe a semicircle meeting AC produced in D and E. Join B with D and E. Then
$$EA = EC + b = a + b,$$
$$AD = CD - b = a - b.$$

Since $\angle CBD = \angle CDB$ and $\angle CBD + \angle CDB = 180° - C = A + B$, we have
$$\angle ADB = \angle CDB = \tfrac{1}{2}(A+B),$$
$$\angle ABD = \angle CBD - \angle B = \tfrac{1}{2}(A+B) - B = \tfrac{1}{2}(A-B).$$

Since $\angle EBD$ is inscribed in a semicircle, it is a right angle. Hence, by Art. 12,

$\angle AEB = 90° - \angle ADB = 90° - \tfrac{1}{2}(A+B)$, $\sin AEB = \cos \tfrac{1}{2}(A+B)$,
$\angle EBA = 90° - \angle ABD = 90° - \tfrac{1}{2}(A-B)$, $\sin EBA = \cos \tfrac{1}{2}(A-B)$.

Applying the law of sines to triangle ABD, we get

(2) $\quad \dfrac{a-b}{c} = \dfrac{AD}{AB} = \dfrac{\sin ABD}{\sin ADB} = \dfrac{\sin \tfrac{1}{2}(A-B)}{\sin \tfrac{1}{2}(A+B)}.$

Similarly, applying the law of sines to triangle EAB, we get

(3) $\quad \dfrac{a+b}{c} = \dfrac{EA}{AB} = \dfrac{\sin EBA}{\sin AEB} = \dfrac{\cos \tfrac{1}{2}(A-B)}{\cos \tfrac{1}{2}(A+B)}.$

Hence by division of (2) by (3),

Ch. IX]   SOLUTION OF OBLIQUE TRIANGLES   117

(4) $$\frac{a-b}{a+b} = \frac{\tan \tfrac{1}{2}(A-B)}{\tan \tfrac{1}{2}(A+B)},$$

which is called the *law of tangents*.

Since $\tfrac{1}{2}(A+B) = 90° - \tfrac{1}{2}C$, we may write (2), (3), (4) in the convenient form

(5) $$\frac{a-b}{c} = \frac{\sin \tfrac{1}{2}(A-B)}{\cos \tfrac{1}{2}C},$$

(6) $$\frac{a+b}{c} = \frac{\cos \tfrac{1}{2}(A-B)}{\sin \tfrac{1}{2}C},$$

(7) $$\frac{a-b}{a+b} = \frac{\tan \tfrac{1}{2}(A-B)}{\cot \tfrac{1}{2}C}.$$

Formulas (5) and (6) are known as Mollweide's equations.

EXAMPLE 1. Given $a = 789$, $B = 70°00'$, $C = 63°53'$, solve the triangle.

Solution. $A = 180° - B - C = 110° - 63°53' = 46°7'$. Solving the first two formulas (1) for b and c, we get

$$b = \frac{a \sin B}{\sin A} \qquad\qquad c = \frac{a \sin C}{\sin A}$$

$\log b = \log a + \log \sin B - \log \sin A$ $\qquad \log c = \log a + \log \sin C - \log \sin A$

$\log a = 2.8971$ $\qquad\qquad\qquad\qquad\qquad \log a - \log \sin A = 3.0393$
$\log \sin A = 9.8578 - 10$ $\qquad\qquad\qquad\quad \log \sin C = 9.9532 - 10$
$\qquad\quad\; 3.0393$ $\qquad\qquad\qquad\qquad\qquad\quad \log c = 2.9925$
$\log \sin B = 9.9730 - 10$ $\qquad\qquad\qquad\qquad\; c = 982.8$
$\log b = 3.0123$
$\quad\; b = 1028.7$

Check by the formula derived from (6) by interchanging a and c:

$$c+b = \frac{a \cos \tfrac{1}{2}(C-B)}{\sin \tfrac{1}{2}A} = \frac{a \cos \tfrac{1}{2}(B-C)}{\sin \tfrac{1}{2}A}$$

$B - C = 6°7'$ $\qquad\qquad\qquad\qquad \log a = 2.8971$
$\tfrac{1}{2}(B-C) = 3°3.5'$ $\qquad\qquad\quad \log \cos \tfrac{1}{2}(B-C) = 9.9994 - 10$
$\tfrac{1}{2}A = 23°3.5'$ $\qquad\qquad\qquad\qquad\qquad\qquad\quad 2.8965$
$c+b = 2011.5$ $\qquad\qquad\qquad\quad \log \sin \tfrac{1}{2}A = 9.5929 - 10$
$\qquad\qquad\qquad\qquad\qquad\quad \log (c+b) = 3.3036$
$\qquad\qquad\qquad\qquad\qquad\qquad\; c+b = 2011.8$

The values of b and $c+b$ should be abridged to four significant digits, and then the check is exact to four digits.

EXAMPLE 2. Given two sides $a = 38.56$, $b = 25.69$, and the included angle $C = 59°55'$, solve the triangle.

Solution. $\frac{1}{2}C = 29°57.5'$, $\frac{1}{2}(A + B) = 90° - \frac{1}{2}C = 60°2.5'$. If we can find $\frac{1}{2}(A - B)$, we can get A and B by addition and subtraction. From (7), we get

$$\tan \tfrac{1}{2}(A - B) = \frac{a-b}{a+b} \cdot \cot \tfrac{1}{2}C$$

$a - b = 12.87$
$a + b = 64.25$

$\log(a-b) = 1.1096$
$\log(a+b) = 1.8079$
$\ 9.3017 - 10$
$\log \cot \tfrac{1}{2}C = 10.2393 - 10$
$\log \tan \tfrac{1}{2}(A-B) = \ 9.5410 - 10$

$\tfrac{1}{2}(A - B) = 19°\ 9.8'$
$\tfrac{1}{2}(A + B) = 60°\ 2.5'$
Adding, $A = 79°12.3'$
Subtracting, $B = 40°52.7'$

To find c, use the last formula (1), which gives

$$c = \frac{b \sin C}{\sin B}, \quad \log c = \log b + \log \sin C - \log \sin B$$

$\log b = 1.4097$
$\log \sin C = 9.9372 - 10$
1.3469
$\log \sin B = 9.8159 - 10$
$\log c = 1.5310$
$c = 33.96$

Check by the second formula (1), which gives

$\log a - \log c = \log \sin A - \log \sin C$

$\log a = 1.5862$ $\log \sin A = 9.9922 - 10$
$\log c = 1.5310$ $\log \sin C = 9.9372 - 10$
$.0552$ $.0550$

Exercises on Oblique Triangles

Solve and check the following triangles, given:

1. $a = 111.4$, $A = 65°48'$, $B = 37°24'$.
2. $b = 890$, $B = 26°00'$, $A = 52°20'$.
3. $a = 364.2$, $A = 54°21'$, $C = 68°15'$.
4. $c = 43.09$, $B = 43°25'$, $A = 104°32'$.
5. $a = 148.0$, $b = 255.5$, $C = 62°32'$.

6. $a = 193.8$, $b = 287.3$, $C = 52°21'$.
7. $a = 156.0$, $c = 190.5$, $B = 56°30'$.
8. $b = 1048$, $c = 909.9$, $A = 56°28'$.

9. From a ship, a lighthouse was observed to bear N 56° W; after the ship had sailed 6 miles due east, the lighthouse bore N 67° W. Find the distance from the lighthouse to the ship in each position.

10. Two observers 7 miles apart on a plain, and facing each other, find that the angles of elevation of a balloon in the same vertical plane with themselves are 60° and 75°. Find the distance of the balloon from each observer and its height.

11. At one place on a road running due north an observer sees that a house is northeast. After walking north 2 miles, he sees that the house is S 30° E. How far is the house from the road?

12. Find the distance of a fort F from a battery B if a point C is located such that BC is 800 yards and angles FBC and BCF are 60° and 65°32'.

13. Find the height of a hill above a horizontal plane from one point of which the angle of elevation of the top of the hill is 11°28', while, after walking 1000 yards toward the top up an incline of 3°25', a man finds the angle of elevation of the top to be 21°30'.

14. To find the distance between two objects A and B, separated by a swamp, a station C was chosen, and the distances $AC = 4604$ ft. and $BC = 6422$ ft., and angle $ACB = 78°44'$, were measured. Find the distance AB.

15. It is planned to tunnel through a mountain from A to B, points both visible from C. If $AC = 179.1$ yards, $BC = 360.1$ yards, and $\angle ACB = 36°24'$, how long will the tunnel be?

16. Two ships start at the same time from the same place; one steams due west at the rate of 20.88 miles per hour, and the other steams southwest at the rate of 15.42 miles per hour. How far apart are they at the end of two hours?

17. The area of a parallelogram is 147684 square feet and the diagonals are 544 and 668 feet. Find the angles and sides.

18. Two adjacent sides of a parallelogram are 34.49 and 20.26 and their included angle is 118°44'. Find the two diagonals.

19. The two diagonals of a parallelogram are 100 and 120 and form the angle 130°42'. Find the sides.

120   TRIGONOMETRY   [Art. 88

20. Two ships have wireless apparatus with a range of 1000 miles. One is 446 miles S 40° E, and the other is 804 miles S 61°40′ W from a certain port. Can the ships communicate directly with each other?

21. Find the distance between two pumping stations P and Q in Lake Michigan, given the distance 536 yards between two points A and B on shore and the angles $BAQ = 40°16′$, $QAP = 57°40′$, $ABP = 42°22′$, $PBQ = 71°7′$.

22. Find the distance between two objects C and D not visible from each other, given the segments $AD = 756$ and $DB = 562$ of a line AB through D such that $\angle DAC = 47°29′$ and $\angle DBC = 57°45′$.

23.* A steamer 20 miles south of a harbor sees a ship sail from it N 55° E at the rate of 13.5 miles per hour. In what direction and at what rate must the steamer travel in order to overtake the ship in 2 hours?

24.* A ship is 4.31 miles due west of a tug and is moving 17 miles per hour in the direction S 59°40′ E. Find the direction and time the tug must travel at 11 miles per hour to overtake the ship as soon as possible.

25.* From a captive balloon 4000 feet high the angles of depression of two ships, one due north and the other northwest, are 11°40′ and 14°30′. Find the distance between the ships and the direction from the first ship to the second.

26.* From the top T of a hill, let TC be the perpendicular to the horizontal plane containing the points A, B, C. If the angle TBC of elevation is 10°43′, and the horizontal angles ABC and CAB are 41°24′ and 96°28′ respectively, while the length of AB is 1560 yards, find the height TC of the hill.

27.* At a point in a horizontal plane a tower subtends the angle A, and a flagstaff of height f standing on top of it subtends the angle B. Show that the height of the tower is

$$\frac{f \sin A \, \cos(A+B)}{\sin B},$$

and find the height when $A = 20°30′$, $B = 6°10′$, $f = 50$ feet.

28.* By means of a transit at the top T of a hill the angles of depression of two successive milestones A and B in the horizontal valley are found to be 38° and 28°, and the horizontal projection AFB of angle ATB is 106°. Find the height of the hill above the valley.

29.* To find the distance d from the center E of the earth to the center M of the moon, a station P is chosen in north latitude 45° and a station P' in south latitude 55° such that P' is in the plane EPM, which is perpendicular to the plane of the equator. The radius EP produced makes an angle of 55°20′ with PM, while EP' produced makes an angle of 46°10′ with $P'M$. Find d, given the earth's radius to be 3957 miles.

Hint: Use the latitudes only to find $\angle PEP' = 45° + 55°$.

89. Solution of a triangle, given two sides a, b, and the angle A opposite to one of them.

Geometric discussion.[1] Construct angle DAE equal to A, and on its arm AD lay off AC equal to b. Draw the perpendicular CF from C to the other arm AE. Describe an arc with C as center and a as radius.

Case 1. If A is an acute angle and $a < CF$, the arc (1 in Fig. 73) does not intersect AE, and the triangle is impossible.

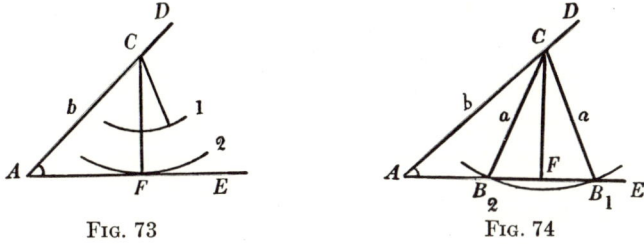

FIG. 73   FIG. 74

Case 2. If A is an acute angle and $a = CF$, the arc (2 in Fig. 73) is tangent to AE at F, and the required triangle is the right triangle ACF.

Case 3. If A is an acute angle and $b > a > CF$, the arc cuts AE at two points B_1 and B_2, both to the right of A (Fig. 74), and there are two triangles AB_1C and AB_2C which have the given parts a, b, A.

Case 4. If $a > b$, the arc cuts AE at a point B to the right of A and at a point B' to the left of A (Fig. 75 or Fig. 76). The

---
[1] The instructor may omit this and assign only the trigonometric solution. If time must be saved, he may omit both and assign Ex. 3.

triangle $AB'C$ is excluded since it does not contain angle A, but contains its supplement. The only solution is triangle ABC.

Case 5. If A is an acute angle and $a = b$, the single solution is the isosceles triangle ABC in Fig. 75 with B' and A coincident.

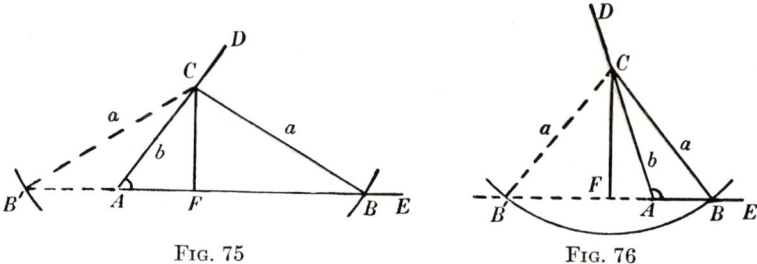

Fig. 75   Fig. 76

Case 6. If A is an obtuse angle and $a = b$, there is no proper triangle (Fig. 76 with B and A coincident).

Case 7. If A is an obtuse angle and $a < b$, the arc cuts AE at two points each to the left of A or fails to cut AE, so that there is no solution. This is also evident since $a < b$ implies $A < B$, whence B and A are both obtuse, contrary to $A + B + C = 180°$.

These results may be summarized as follows:

There is no solution if angle A is acute and $a < CF$, or if A is obtuse and $a \leq b$. There are two solutions if A is acute and $b > a > CF$. There is one and only one solution in the remaining cases.

Trigonometric solution. The law of sines enables us to detect easily the cases in which the triangle is impossible and to solve the triangle or two triangles if the problem is possible, as well as to obtain anew the criteria found by the above geometric discussion.

Write h for the altitude $CF = b \sin A$ (Art. 86). By the law of sines,

$$\sin B = \frac{b \sin A}{a} = \frac{h}{a}.$$

Case 1. If $a<h$, h/a exceeds unity and hence cannot be equal to sin B. Thus the triangle is impossible.

Case 2. If $a = h$, sin $B = 1$ and $B = 90°$. Then if A is acute, a single triangle exists and it is a right triangle.

Cases 3-7. Let $a>h$. Then h/a is a positive number <1 and we can find from a table of natural or logarithmic sines a single acute angle B_1 for which sin $B_1 = h/a$. Then (Art. 85) $B_2 = 180° - B_1$ is the obtuse angle for which

$$\sin B_2 = \sin B_1 = h/a.$$

Hence the possible values of our angle B are B_1 and B_2.

First, let A be an obtuse angle. The triangle cannot contain a second obtuse angle B_2. If $a \leqq b$ (Cases 6, 7), then $A \leqq B$, whereas the obtuse angle A exceeds the acute angle $B = B_1$. Hence must $a>b$ (Case 4, Fig. 76), and then a single triangle exists. For it, C and c are determined by

(8) $$C = 180° - A - B, \quad c = \frac{a \sin C}{\sin A}.$$

Second, let A be an acute angle. If $a \geqq b$, then $A \geqq B$, so that B is an acute angle, and the oblique angle B_2 is not a value of B. For the single triangle (Cases 4, 5, Fig. 75) with $B = B_1$, we may compute C and c by means of (8). Finally, if $a<b$ (Case 3), then $A<B_1$ by Fig. 74 or by

$$\sin A < \frac{b \sin A}{a} = \sin B_1.$$

Since A and B_1 are each $<90°$, $C_1 = 180° - A - B_1$ is positive, and A, B_1 and C_1 are angles of one triangle. There is here another solution, viz., the triangle with the angles

$$A, \quad B_2 = 180° - B_1, \quad C_2 = B_1 - A.$$

For each triangle, the third side c_1 or c_2 is found by the law of sines (8). Hence only in Case 3 are there two solutions.

EXAMPLE 1. Find the number of triangles having $A = 30°$, $a = 2$, $b = 6$. There is no solution since $b \sin A = 6 \times \frac{1}{2} = 3$ and $a<3$.

EXAMPLE 2. Given $a = 46.73$, $b = 79.80$, $A = 23°20'$, solve the triangle or triangles, and check.

Solution. $h = b \sin A$.

$\log h = \log b + \log \sin A$
$\log b = 1.9020$
$\log \sin A = 9.5978 - 10$
$\log h = 1.4998$
$\log a = 1.6696$

$b > a > h$, two solutions

$\sin B = \dfrac{h}{a}$

$\log \sin B = \log h - \log a$
$= 9.8302 - 10$
$B_1 = 42°33.6'$
$B_2 = 180° - B_1 = 137°26.4'$
$B_1 + A = 65°53.6'$
$B_2 + A = 160°46.4'$
$C = 180° - (B + A)$
$C_1 = 114°6.4'$
$C_2 = 19°13.6'$

$c = \dfrac{a}{\sin A} \cdot \sin C$
$\log c = D + \log \sin C$
$D = \log a - \log \sin A$
$\log a = 1.6696$
$\log \sin A = 9.5978 - 10$
$D = 2.0718$
$\log \sin C_1 = 9.9604 - 10$
$\log c_1 = 2.0322$
$c_1 = 107.70$

$D = 2.0718$
$\log \sin C_2 = 9.5176 - 10$
$\log c_2 = 1.5894$
$c_2 = 38.85$

Check by (6): $a + b = \dfrac{c \cos \frac{1}{2}(B-A)}{\sin \frac{1}{2}C}$

$C_2 = B_1 - A = 19°13.6'$
$\frac{1}{2}C_2 = \frac{1}{2}(B_1 - A) = 9°36.8'$
$\log c_1 = 2.0322$
$\log \cos \frac{1}{2}(B_1 - A) = 9.9939 - 10$
$\phantom{\log \cos \frac{1}{2}(B_1 - A) =} 2.0261$
$\log \sin \frac{1}{2}C_1 = 9.9239 - 10$
$\phantom{\log \sin \frac{1}{2}C_1 =} 2.1022$

$C_1 = B_2 - A = 114°6.4$
$\frac{1}{2}C_1 = \frac{1}{2}(B_2 - A) = 57°3.2'$
$\log c_2 = 1.5894$
$\log \cos \frac{1}{2}(B_2 - A) = 9.7355 - 10$
$\phantom{\log \cos \frac{1}{2}(B_2 - A) =} 1.3249$
$\log \sin \frac{1}{2}C_2 = 9.2227 - 10$
$\phantom{\log \sin \frac{1}{2}C_2 =} 2.1022$

$\log (a + b) = \log 126.53 = 2.1022$

Note. This method of solving and checking the triangles is not only a long one, but is liable to introduce too large an error when angle B_1 exceeds 70°. For, when finding B_1 by our table from its log sine, we may make an error of more than 1', and the final part of our solution may involve an accumulation of appreciable errors. For example, given $a = 13.54$, $b = 16.08$, $A = 52°24'$, the above method yields

$B_1 = 70°14'$, $C_1 = 57°22'$, $C_2 = 17°50'$, $c_1 = 14.39$, $c_2 = 5.234$,

whereas the values obtained by use of six-place tables are

Ch. IX] SOLUTION OF OBLIQUE TRIANGLES

$B_1 = 70°12'21.4''$, $C_1 = 57°23'38.6''$, $C_2 = 17°48'21.4''$, $c_1 = 14.3963$, $c_2 = 5.22594$.

Thus the former value of c_2 presents too large an error, due to an accumulation of several small errors. It is preferable to proceed as in Ex. 3. Moreover, it is desirable that the student bear in mind that every oblique triangle can be solved by solving component right triangles.

EXAMPLE 3. Given $a = 13.54$, $b = 16.08$, $A = 52°24'$, solve the triangle or triangles.

Solution. We solve the two component right triangles ACF and CFB_1 in Fig. 74 by the method given in Art. 35.

$h = CF = b \sin A$
$\log b = 1.2063$
$\log \sin A = 9.8989 - 10$
$\log h = 1.1052$
$h = 12.74$

$AF = b \cos A$
$\log b = 1.2063$
$\log \cos A = 9.7854 - 10$
$\log AF = 0.9917$
$AF = 9.810$

$c_1 = AF + FB_1 = 14.396$
$c_2 = AF - FB_1 = 5.224$.

$\overline{FB_1}^2 = (a+h)(a-h)$
$a + h = 26.28$
$a - h = 0.80$
$\log (a+h) = 1.4197$
$\log (a-h) = \bar{1}.9031$
$2)1.3228$
$\log FB_1 = 0.6614$
$FB_1 = 4.586$

$\cos B_1 = FB_1/a$
$\log a = 1.1316$
$\log \cos B_1 = 9.5298 - 10$
$B_1 = 70°12.2'$
$C_1 = 57°23.8'$
$B_2 = 180° - B_1 = 109°47.8'$
$C_2 = 17°48.2'$.

Only two significant figures are reliable in view of $a - h = 0.80$.

To solve this Ex. 3 by the traverse table, we employ triangles I and II obtained by mental interpolations between triangles with hypotenuses 16 and 17, and triangles III and IV obtained by interpolations between triangles with the hypotenuses 13 and 14:

hyp. = 16.08

Triangle	A	opp.	adj.
I	52°	12.67	9.90
ACF	52°24'	12.74	9.81
II	53°	12.84	9.68

hyp. = 13.54

Triangle	B_1	opp.	adj.
III	70°	12.73	4.63
CFB_1	70°9'	12.74	4.60
IV	71°	12.80	4.41

Hence $AF = 9.81$, $FB_1 = 4.60$, $B_1 = 70°9'$, $c_1 = 14.41$, $c_2 = 5.21$.

126 TRIGONOMETRY [Art. 90

Exercises on Solving Triangles, Given Two Sides and the Angle Opposite to One Side

Find the number of triangles having
1. $A = 30°, b = 10, a = 15$.   2. $A = 30°, b = 10, a = 8$.
3. $A = 30°, b = 10, a = 5$.   4. $A = 30°, b = 10, a = 4$.
5. $B = 37°23', a = 9.1, b = 7.5$.   6. $B = 61°16', a = 12.75, b = 9.512$.

Using Table VI, solve the triangles having
7. $a = 9, b = 10, A = 55°$.   8. $a = 120, b = 100, A = 50°$.
9. $a = 42, b = 67, A = 52°$.   10. $a = 36, b = 38, A = 16°$.

Solve by logarithms and check the triangles having
11. $a = 311, b = 374, A = 27°18'$.   12. $a = 75.64, b = 82.66, A = 50°16'$.
13. $a = 7082, b = 8034, A = 61°27'$.   14. $a = 342, b = 214, A = 31°53'$.

15. A ship is 1190 feet from the nearer of two buoys which are 970 feet apart. The angle at the ship made by the lines to the buoys is $38°36'$. How far is the ship from the farther buoy?

16. The two faces of an embankment measure 145.5 ft. and 252.0 ft., and the angle of inclination of the second face is $12°15'$. Find that of the first face and the width of the embankment at its base.

17. Solve Exs. 2 and 7 of Art. 88 by using only right triangles.

90. Law of cosines. *In any triangle the square of any side is equal to the sum of the squares of the remaining two sides diminished by double the product of those two sides multiplied by the cosine of their included angle.* Or, if the initial side be called a,

(9) $\qquad a^2 = b^2 + c^2 - 2bc \cos A.$

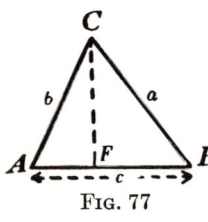

Fig. 77

Drop a perpendicular CF from the vertex C to the base AB or the base produced. If A and B are each $\leq 90°$, F falls within AB (Fig. 77) or at A or B, so that $c = AB = BF + AF$. But $\cos B = BF/a$, $\cos A = AF/b$. Hence $BF = a \cos B$, $AF = b \cos A$, and

(10) $\qquad c = a \cos B + b \cos A.$

Next, let A, for example, be an obtuse angle. Then F falls on AB produced (Fig. 78), so that $c = AB = BF - AF$. But

$\cos B = BF/a$, $\cos A = -AF/b$. Hence $BF = a \cos B$, $AF = -b \cos A$, and

$$c = a \cos B - (-b \cos A),$$

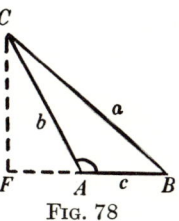
Fig. 78

so that (10) again holds true. We have now proved that *any chosen side of any triangle is equal to the sum of the products obtained by multiplying each remaining side by the cosine of the angle which it makes with the chosen side.*

Hence, when the chosen side is a or b, we have

(11) $a = b \cos C + c \cos B$, $b = a \cos C + c \cos A$.

Multiply equation (10) by c and the two equations (11) by $-a$ and b, respectively, and add. We get

(12) $c^2 - a^2 + b^2 = 2bc \cos A.$

Transposing terms, we have (9).

The law of cosines (9) is merely a combination of two theorems in geometry: The square of the side opposite an acute [or obtuse] angle is equal to the sum of the squares of the remaining two sides diminished [or increased] by double the product of one of those sides by the projection of the other upon it. Thus

$$a^2 = b^2 + c^2 - 2c \cdot AF \quad (A \text{ acute, Fig. 77}),$$
$$a^2 = b^2 + c^2 + 2c \cdot AF \quad (A \text{ obtuse, Fig. 78}).$$

We saw that, in the first case, $AF = b \cos A$, while, in the second case, $AF = -b \cos A$. Thus each of the two different geometric formulas leads to the same trigonometric formula (9).

Formula (9) may be used to compute a when b, c, A are given, or to compute A when a, b, c are given, since it may be written in the form (12) and hence in the form

(13) $$\cos A = \frac{b^2 + c^2 - a^2}{2bc}.$$

But, as these formulas are not adapted to logarithms, computation by them is unnecessarily laborious unless b and c in (9) and a, b, c in (13) are numbers with only one or two significant digits. Formulas adapted to logarithmic computation are given in Arts. 88, 93.

The importance of (9) is due mainly to its being employed frequently in proofs of theorems in pure and applied mathematics.

Exercises on the Law of Cosines

1. Using the law of cosines, write the two further equations of type (9), and from them deduce two of type (13).

Hence solve the triangles in which

2. $a = 2, b = 3, c = 4$.
3. $a = 7, b = 8, c = 9$.
4. $a = 2, b = 3, C = 30°$.
5. $b = 11, c = 10, A = 35°24'$.

6. The two diagonals of a parallelogram are 6 and 8, and their included angle is 60°. Find the sides.

7. Find the inclination of the face of an embankment if a ladder 26 feet long rests 10 feet from the foot of the embankment and reaches 23 feet up its face.

8. From the crossing, at an angle of 54°, of two railroads the distances to two bridges over the same river are 4 and 6 miles. How far apart are the bridges?

9. Two towns A and B are 15 and 20 miles distant from C, while angle ACB is 27°30'. Two men start at the same instant from C and walk at the same rate. One walks to A and then toward B. The other walks to B and then toward A. How far from A do they meet?

10. Divide each member of (10) by $b \sin A$ and replace a/b by its value given by the law of sines. Hence show that

$$\cot B = \frac{c}{b \sin A} - \cot A.$$

By this formula compute B, given $b = 8, c = 12, A = 30°$.

11.* The plane ABC of a side of a hill is inclined 30° to the horizontal plane ABD and intersects the latter in an east and west line AB. A tree standing at A had its upper part broken at a point 12 feet above the ground by a WSW wind (i.e., blowing from S $67\frac{1}{2}°$ W), and the top of the broken tree now rests on the ground 40 feet from A. Find the height of the tree.

91. Area ($\triangle$) of a triangle in terms of its sides.[1]
By Art. 86, $\triangle = \frac{1}{2}bc \sin A$, $\triangle^2 = \frac{1}{4}b^2c^2 \sin^2 A = \frac{1}{4}b^2c^2(1 - \cos^2 A)$.

We shall evaluate the two factors $1 + \cos A$, $1 - \cos A$. By (13),

$$1 + \cos A = \frac{(b+c)^2 - a^2}{2bc}, \quad 1 - \cos A = \frac{a^2 - (b-c)^2}{2bc}.$$

[1] The instructor may assume this result from geometry.

Hence
$$\Delta^2 = \tfrac{1}{16}[(b+c)^2 - a^2][a^2 - (b-c)^2]$$
$$= \tfrac{1}{16}(b+c+a)(b+c-a)(a+b-c)(a-b+c).$$

This result becomes much simpler if we employ the abbreviation s for the *semi-perimeter* (half of the sum of the sides). Then

$$a+b+c = 2s, \quad b+c-a = b+c+a-2a = 2(s-a),$$
$$a+b-c = 2(s-c), \quad a-b+c = 2(s-b).$$

Thus we obtain Heron of Alexandria's formula

(14) $$\Delta = \sqrt{s(s-a)(s-b)(s-c)}.$$

For example, if $a = 13$, $b = 14$, $c = 15$, then
$$a+b+c = 42, \ s = 21, \ s-a = 8, \ s-b = 7, \ s-c = 6,$$
$$\Delta = \sqrt{21 \cdot 8 \cdot 7 \cdot 6} = \sqrt{2^4 \cdot 3^2 \cdot 7^2} = 2^2 \cdot 3 \cdot 7 = 84.$$

92. Radius of the inscribed circle. Let O be the center and r the radius of the circle inscribed in the triangle ABC (Fig. 79). Then the three triangles AOB, AOC, BOC, which together make up triangle ABC, have equal altitudes $OF = OE = OD = r$. Hence the area Δ of triangle ABC is equal to

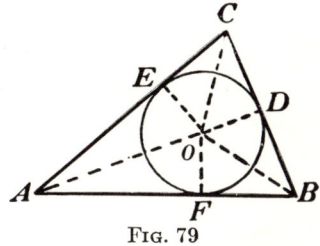

Fig. 79

$$\Delta = \tfrac{1}{2}cr + \tfrac{1}{2}br + \tfrac{1}{2}ar = \tfrac{1}{2}(a+b+c)r = sr,$$

where s is the semi-perimeter of the triangle ABC, as in Art. 91. Employing the value (14) of Δ, we get

(15) $$r = \sqrt{\frac{(s-a)(s-b)(s-c)}{s}},$$

which determines the radius of the inscribed circle in terms of the sides of the triangle. For the example at the end of Art. 91, we have $r = 4$.

93. To compute the angles of a triangle, given the sides. In Fig. 79, the lengths AF and AE of the tangents from A to the

circle are equal by geometry. Similarly, $BF = BD$, $CE = CD$. Hence the perimeter of the triangle is
$$2s = 2AF + 2BF + 2CD.$$
But $AF + BF = c$. Thus $s = c + CD$. In this manner we get
$$CD = s - c, \quad BF = s - b, \quad AF = s - a.$$

Since the center O of the inscribed circle is the point of intersection of the bisectors of the angles of the triangle,
$$\angle OAF = \tfrac{1}{2}A, \quad \angle OBF = \tfrac{1}{2}B, \quad \angle OCD = \tfrac{1}{2}C.$$

In the right triangle OAF, side OF is the radius r of the inscribed circle. Hence

(16) $\quad \tan \tfrac{1}{2} A = \dfrac{r}{s-a}, \quad \tan \tfrac{1}{2} B = \dfrac{r}{s-b}, \quad \tan \tfrac{1}{2} C = \dfrac{r}{s-c}.$

These three equations are usually called the *half-angle formulas*; in conjunction with (15), they furnish the best method of computing by logarithms the angles of a triangle whose sides are given.

EXAMPLE. Given $a = 104$, $b = 114$, $c = 141$, find angles A, B, C.
Solution. Use formulas (15), (16), and $2s = a + b + c$.

$2s = 359$
$s = 179.5$
$s - a = 75.5$
$s - b = 65.5$
$s - c = 38.5$
$\overline{4s - 2s = 359.0}$
(check)

$\log r = 1.5128$
$\log (s - a) = 1.8779$
$\overline{\log \tan \tfrac{1}{2} A = 9.6349 - 10}$
$\tfrac{1}{2} A = 23°20'$
$A = 46°40'$

$\log (s - a) = 1.8779$
$\log (s - b) = 1.8162$
$\log (s - c) = 1.5855$
$\overline{ 5.2796}$
$\log s = 2.2541$
$\log r^2 = 3.0255$
$\log r = 1.5128$
$\log (s - c) = 1.5855$
$\overline{\log \tan \tfrac{1}{2} C = 9.9273 - 10}$
$\tfrac{1}{2} C = 40°13.6'$
$C = 80°27.2'$

$\log r = 1.5128$
$\log (s - b) = 1.8162$
$\overline{\log \tan \tfrac{1}{2} B = 9.6966 - 10}$
$\tfrac{1}{2} B = 26°26.5'$
$B = 52°53'$

Check: $A + B + C = 180°0.2'$.

Ch. IX]   SOLUTION OF OBLIQUE TRIANGLES   131

EXERCISES ON TRIANGLES WITH GIVEN SIDES

Find the areas and angles of the triangles whose sides are
1. $a = 2, b = 3, c = 4$.
2. $a = 51.38, b = 68.56, c = 60.35$.
3. $a = 146, b = 164, c = 182$.
4. $a = 12.66, b = 17.00, c = 15.70$.

Without using logarithms, find the areas of the triangles whose sides are
5. 25, 52, 63.   6. 35, 84, 91.

7. A pole 26 feet long rests 12 feet from the base of an embankment and reaches 16 feet up its face. Find the slope of the embankment.

8. Two islands, which are 6 miles apart, are 9 and 12 miles distant respectively from a boat. What angle is subtended by the islands at the boat?

9. Two circles are drawn with radii 14 and 16 inches and with centers 20 inches apart. Find the length of their common chord.

10. What is the radius of the largest circular track that can be made within a triangular field whose sides are 253.1, 344.3 and 462.1 yards long?

11. Given $AB = 18.64$, $BC = 21.30$, $CA = 34.30$, take a point P in the prolongation through A of AB such that $\angle APC = 15°35'$. Find PC.

12. Three circles of radii 9, 11, and 13 are tangent externally. Find the angles of the triangle formed by joining their centers.

13.* Show by Fig. 79 that $\overline{AO}^2 = bc\,(s-a)/s$ and hence that

$$\sin \tfrac{1}{2}A = \sqrt{\frac{(s-b)(s-c)}{bc}}, \quad \cos \tfrac{1}{2}A = \sqrt{\frac{s(s-a)}{bc}}.$$

By means of one of these formulas find the least angle of the triangle whose sides are 13, 14, 15.

14.* Find the sides of a triangle which contains in its interior three circles each of diameter 20 feet and has each side tangent to two of the circles, given the distances between the centers of the circles to be 91, 82, and 73 feet.

EXERCISES ON RESULTANTS AND COMPONENTS OF FORCES INVOLVING OBLIQUE TRIANGLES
(For definitions and principles, see Arts. 18–21.)

1. Two forces of 3 and 5 pounds have a resultant force of 6 pounds. Find the angles made by the resultant with each component.

2. The angle between the directions of two forces of 466.8 and 687.4 pounds acting on a point is 30°45′. Find their resultant force and the angle it makes with the direction of the smaller given force.

3. Two forces of 120 and 150 pounds have a resultant of 225 pounds. Find the angle between the directions of the two forces.

4. A force of 513 pounds is resolved into two components which make angles of 34°38′ and 92°8′ respectively with the direction of the given force. Find the component forces.

5. A force of 50 pounds is resolved into two components, one of which is 24.4 pounds and makes an angle of 25° with the resolved force. Find the other component and its angle with the resolved force.

6. A train is moving N 54° W at 36 miles per hour and the wind is blowing from northeast at 40 miles per hour. What direction and velocity does the wind appear to have to a passenger?

7. A ship is steaming 20 miles per hour S 10° W and leaves a trail of smoke in the direction N 35° E. If the wind is from the north, what is its velocity?

8. A passenger walks approximately southeast 4 miles an hour across the deck at right angles to the length of the ship, which is steaming N 35° E at 20 miles per hour in a current moving S 50° E at 5 miles per hour. Find the velocity and direction of the motion of the passenger.

9. An aeroplane is flying S 67° W at a speed which would carry it 75 miles per hour in still air. A wind blows from northwest at 28 miles per hour. Find the ground-speed and the ground-course.

10.* Two aeroplanes fly in opposite directions at 60 miles per hour around a triangular field which is 20 miles on each side. A wind of 40 miles per hour blows down one side. For each aeroplane find the time of flight along each side, and compare the total times.

11.* A man can row his boat 6 miles per hour in still water. After rowing 2 hours in a straight line in a river, running due south, he reached a place 15 miles southeast from his starting point. Find the velocity of the current (a) if his course was south of east and (b) if his course was north of east.

CHAPTER X

RELATIONS BETWEEN FUNCTIONS OF SEVERAL ANGLES

94. The addition theorem for sine.[1] If A and B are any two angles,

(1) $\qquad \sin(A + B) = \sin A \cos B + \cos A \sin B.$

Case 1. Let A and B be any positive angles whose sum is less than 180°. At the ends of any convenient segment AB, lay off angles equal to A and B, thus determining a triangle ABC. Denote its sides by a, b, c. By the law of sines (Art. 87), if we divide each side by the sine of its opposite angle, we obtain the same quotient q. Hence

$$a = q \sin A, \quad b = q \sin B, \quad c = q \sin C.$$

By formula (1) of Art. 85, $\sin C = \sin(180° - C) = \sin(A + B)$. Using formula (10) of Art. 90, we have

$$q \sin(A + B) = c = a \cos B + b \cos A$$
$$= q \sin A \cos B + q \sin B \cos A.$$

Dividing each member by q, we obtain (1). Also, (1) is true if $A = 0$ or $B = 0$ since $\sin 0° = 0$, $\cos 0° = 1$. Hence (1) is proved for $A + B < 180°$, $A \geq 0$, $B \geq 0$.

Case 2. Let A and B be angles each ≥ 0 and $\leq 180°$, whose sum is greater than 180°. Then $\alpha = 180° - A$ and $\beta = 180° - B$ are angles ≥ 0 whose sum $360° - (A + B)$ is less than 180°. Hence, by Case 1,

(1') $\qquad \sin(\alpha + \beta) = \sin \alpha \cos \beta + \cos \alpha \sin \beta.$

Substitute for α and β their values and apply (1) and (2) of Art. 85. Thus

---

[1] To economize time, the instructor may prefer to assign only Case 1. However the other cases involve only straightforward applications of earlier formulas and afford excellent practice with them.

$\sin \alpha = \sin(180° - A) = \sin A$, $\cos \alpha = \cos(180° - A) = -\cos A$,
$\sin \beta = \sin(180° - B) = \sin B$, $\cos \beta = \cos(180° - B) = -\cos B$,
$\sin(\alpha + \beta) = \sin[360° - (A+B)] = -\sin(A+B)$.

Hence (1') becomes
$$-\sin(A+B) = \sin A (-\cos B) - \cos A \sin B,$$
which proves (1) for the present case.

Case 3. Let A and B be angles ≥ 0 whose sum is equal to 180°. Since
$$\cos B = \cos(180° - A) = -\cos A,\ \sin B = \sin(180° - A) = \sin A,$$
the right member of (1) is zero, while the left member is $\sin 180° = 0$.

We have now proved (1) when A and B are any angles each ≥ 0 and $\leq 180°$.

Case 4. Let $180° \leq A \leq 360°$, $0 \leq B \leq 180°$. Then $A = 180° + a$, where $0 \leq a \leq 180°$. Thus (1) holds for angles a and B:

(1'') $\sin(a + B) = \sin a \cos B + \cos a \sin B$.

For $B = 180°$, this reduces to $\sin(a + 180°) = -\sin a$, or $\sin A = -\sin a$, since $\cos 180° = -1$, $\sin 180° = 0$. Thus to prove that

(2) $\sin(x + 180°) = -\sin x$ (for every angle x),

it remains to prove it when $180° < x \leq 360°$. Then $x = a + 180°$, where $0 < a \leq 180°$, so that $\sin x = -\sin a$, as just proved. But
$$\sin(x + 180°) = \sin(a + 360°) = \sin a.$$
This completes the proof of (2). Taking $x = a + B$, we have
$$\sin(A + B) = -\sin(a + B).$$
Finally, by (2) and (1) of Art. 85, we have
$$\cos A = \cos(360° - A) = \cos(180° - a) = -\cos a.$$
Hence (1'') becomes
$$-\sin(A + B) = -\sin A \cos B - \cos A \sin B,$$
which proves (1) for the present case.

Ch. X]   FUNCTIONS OF SEVERAL ANGLES   135

Case 5. Let $180° \leq A \leq 360°$, $180° \leq B \leq 360°$. Let $A = 180° + \alpha$, $B = 180° + \beta$. Then (1) holds for angles α and β which are each ≥ 0 and $\leq 180°$:

$$\sin(\alpha + \beta) = \sin \alpha \cos \beta + \cos \alpha \sin \beta.$$

By the results in Case 4, the right member is equal to

$$(-\sin A)(-\cos B) + (-\cos A)(-\sin B).$$

Also, $\sin(\alpha + \beta) = \sin(A + B - 360°) = \sin(A + B)$. Hence (1) is proved.

We have now proved (1) for all angles ≥ 0 which do not exceed 360°. If to such an angle we add a suitably chosen multiple of 360°, we obtain any assigned angle. But any function of the latter is equal to the same function of the former. Hence (1) is true for arbitrary angles A and B.

95. Functions of A + 90°. In formula (1) take $B = 90°$. Since $\sin 90° = 1$, $\cos 90° = 0$, we obtain

(3) $\sin(A + 90°) = \cos A$ (for every angle A).

Let x be any angle, and take $A = x + 90°$ in (3). Thus

$$\cos(x + 90°) = \sin(x + 180°) = -\sin x,$$

by (2). Writing A for x for uniformity, we have

(4) $\cos(A + 90°) = -\sin A$ (for every angle A).

From (3) and (4) we get, by division when $\sin A \neq 0$,

(5) $\tan(A + 90°) = -\cot A$ (for A not a multiple of 180°).

Passing to reciprocals, we have

(6) $\csc(A + 90°) = \sec A$, $\cot(A + 90°) = -\tan A$
      (A not an odd multiple of 90°),

(7) $\sec(A + 90°) = -\csc A$ (A not a multiple of 180°).

It is seen that formulas (3) – (7) are true for all angles except those for which the functions entering are undefined, and hence are identities.

96. The addition theorem for cosine. *If A and B are any angles,*
(8) $\qquad \cos(A + B) = \cos A \cos B - \sin A \sin B.$

For proof, apply the addition theorem for sine to the angles $A + 90°, B$:

$\sin(\overline{A + 90°} + B) = \sin(A + 90°)\cos B + \cos(A + 90°)\sin B.$

In view of (3) and (4), this reduces to (8).

97. The subtraction theorems for sine and cosine. *If A and B are any angles,*
(9) $\qquad \sin(A - B) = \sin A \cos B - \cos A \sin B,$
(10) $\qquad \cos(A - B) = \cos A \cos B + \sin A \sin B.$

For proof, apply the addition theorems for sine and cosine to the angles A and $-B$:

$\sin[A + (-B)] = \sin A \cos(-B) + \cos A \sin(-B),$
$\cos[A + (-B)] = \cos A \cos(-B) - \sin A \sin(-B).$

These reduce to (9) and (10) since $\sin(-B) = -\sin B$, $\cos(-B) = \cos B$ by formulas (3) of Art. 85.

EXERCISES ON THE ADDITION AND SUBTRACTION THEOREMS FOR SINE AND COSINE

Express in terms of radicals the sines and cosines of
1. $15° = 45° - 30°.$ 2. $75°.$ 3. $105°.$ 4. $120°.$
5. Given $\sin A = \dfrac{5}{13}$, $\sin B = \dfrac{3}{5}$, where A and B are acute angles, find $\cos(A - B)$ and $\sin(A + B)$.

Prove that the following relations are identities, stating[1] the exceptional values, if any, for which either member is undefined:
6. $\sin(60° + B) - \sin(60° - B) = \sin B.$
7. $\sin(A + B)\sin(A - B) = \sin^2 A - \sin^2 B = \cos^2 B - \cos^2 A.$
8. $\cos(A + B)\cos(A - B) = \cos^2 A - \sin^2 B = \cos^2 B - \sin^2 A.$
9. $\sin(x + y + z) = \sin x \cos y \cos z + \cos x \sin y \cos z$
$\qquad\qquad\qquad\qquad + \cos x \cos y \sin z - \sin x \sin y \sin z.$

[1] The instructor may omit this requirement.

FUNCTIONS OF SEVERAL ANGLES

10. $\sin(A+B)\cos B - \cos(A+B)\sin B = \sin A$.
11. $\cos^2 C + \cos^2(C+60°) + \cos^2(C-60°) = \dfrac{3}{2}$.
12. $\sin(90°-x) = \cos x$, $\cos(90°-x) = \sin x$, $\tan(90°-x) = \cot x$, $\csc(90°-x) = \sec x$, $\sec(90°-x) = \csc x$, $\cot(90°-x) = \tan x$.
13. $\sin(180°+x) = -\sin x$, $\quad \cos(180°+x) = -\cos x$,
    $\tan(180°+x) = \tan x$, $\quad \csc(180°+x) = -\csc x$,
    $\sec(180°+x) = -\sec x$, $\quad \cot(180°+x) = \cot x$.
14. $\sin(270° \pm x) = -\cos x$, $\quad \cos(270° \pm x) = \pm\sin x$,
    $\tan(270° \pm x) = \mp\cot x$, $\quad \csc(270° \pm x) = -\sec x$,
    $\sec(270° \pm x) = \pm\csc x$, $\quad \cot(270° \pm x) = \mp\tan x$.

15. By Exs. 12–14 and Arts. 85, 95, prove that any function of $180° \pm x$, $x - 180°$, or $360° \pm x$ is equal to $\pm$ the same function of x; while any function of $90° \pm x$, $x - 90°$, $270° \pm x$, or $x - 270°$ is equal to $\pm$ the co-function of x (defined in Art. 12). Each such formula holds for every angle x for which its members are defined, so that the proper sign may be determined by selecting any convenient angle x, for example a positive acute angle. Hence this summary furnishes a useful aid to the memory.

98. Heights and distances. Several earlier formulas may be converted into formulas more convenient for logarithmic computation by replacing $\tan x$ by $\sin x/\cos x$, or $\cot x$ by $\cos x/\sin x$, and then applying the addition or subtraction theorem for sine.

Exercises on Heights and Distances

1. Show that formula (3) of Art. 39 is equivalent to
$$x = \frac{h \sin B \cos T}{\sin(T-B)}.$$
Give another proof by applying the law of sines to the triangle containing angle $T-B$ (Fig. 30). Use this formula to solve Exs. 1–6 of Art. 39.

2. Show that the formula in Ex. 7, Art. 39, is equivalent to
$$h = \frac{d \sin A \sin B}{\sin(B-A)}.$$
Use this formula to solve Exs. 8–12 of Art. 39.

3. Show that the formula in Ex. 14 of Art. 8 is equivalent to

$$h = \frac{l \sin \alpha \sin \beta}{\sqrt{\sin(\alpha+\beta)\sin(\alpha-\beta)}}.$$

Hence find h, given $\alpha = 60°2'$, $\beta = 45°3'$, $l = 2.01$.

4.* To find the height h of an object above a horizontal plane, measure its angle A of elevation at a point of that plane and its angle B of elevation at a point directly above the first point and at a distance d from it. Prove that

$$(h-d)\cot B = h \cot A, \quad h = \frac{d \cot B}{\cot B - \cot A} = \frac{d \sin A \cos B}{\sin(A-B)}.$$

Find h, given $A = 25°40'$, $B = 23°10'$, $d = 60$ ft.

5.* From a point which is f feet above the surface of a pond, the angle of elevation of the top of a tree standing at an edge of the pond is A, while the angle of depression of the reflection of the top in the water is B. If h is the height of the tree and d its horizontal distance from the point of observation, show that

$$(h-f)\cot A = d = (h+f)\cot B,$$
$$h = \frac{f(\cot A + \cot B)}{\cot A - \cot B} = \frac{f \sin(B+A)}{\sin(B-A)}.$$

Given $f = 40$, $A = 41°12'$, $B = 58°43'$, find h and d.

99. The addition and subtraction theorems for tangent and cotangent. *If A and B are any angles such that neither A nor B nor $A + B$ is an odd multiple of $90°$,*

(11) $$\tan(A+B) = \frac{\tan A + \tan B}{1 - \tan A \tan B}.$$

The exceptional values are those for which one of the three tangents is undefined. We have

$$\tan(A+B) = \frac{\sin(A+B)}{\cos(A+B)} = \frac{\sin A \cos B + \cos A \sin B}{\cos A \cos B - \sin A \sin B}.$$

Divide both numerator and denominator by $\cos A \cos B$, which is not zero in view of the restrictions on A and B. Thus

$$\tan(A+B) = \frac{\dfrac{\sin A \cos B}{\cos A \cos B} + \dfrac{\cos A \sin B}{\cos A \cos B}}{1 - \dfrac{\sin A \sin B}{\cos A \cos B}} = \frac{\dfrac{\sin A}{\cos A} + \dfrac{\sin B}{\cos B}}{1 - \dfrac{\sin A}{\cos A} \cdot \dfrac{\sin B}{\cos B}},$$

which proves formula (11).

Similarly, if $\sin(A+B)$, $\sin A$, $\sin B$ are not zero,

$$\frac{\cos(A+B)}{\sin(A+B)} = \frac{\dfrac{\cos A \cos B}{\sin A \sin B} - \dfrac{\sin A \sin B}{\sin A \sin B}}{\dfrac{\sin A \cos B}{\sin A \sin B} + \dfrac{\cos A \sin B}{\sin A \sin B}}$$

gives

(12) $$\cot(A+B) = \frac{\cot A \cot B - 1}{\cot A + \cot B},$$

if neither A nor B nor $A+B$ is a multiple of 180°.

Applying formulas (11) and (12) to the angles A and $-B$, we have

$$\tan[A+(-B)] = \frac{\tan A + \tan(-B)}{1 - \tan A \tan(-B)},$$

$$\cot[A+(-B)] = \frac{\cot A \cot(-B) - 1}{\cot A + \cot(-B)}.$$

By (3) of Art. 85, $\tan(-B) = -\tan B$, whence

$$\cot(-B) = -\cot B.$$

Thus

(13)
$$\tan(A-B) = \frac{\tan A - \tan B}{1 + \tan A \tan B},$$

$$\cot(A-B) = \frac{\cot A \cot B + 1}{\cot B - \cot A}.$$

Exercises on the Addition Theorem for Tangents

1. Prove formula (13) by the method used to prove (11) and (12).

2. Find tan 75° and tan 15° in terms of square roots, using formulas (11) and (13) and the functions of 30° and 45°.

3. Find cot 75° and cot 15°, using (12) and (13). Check by Ex. 2.

4. Given $\tan A = \frac{1}{2}$, $\tan B = \frac{1}{4}$, find $\tan(A+B)$ and $\tan(A-B)$.

5. The slope (Art. 6) of a roof of a house is 2/5. Find its (smaller) angle of inclination with the ground if the slope of the ground is 0.1.

6. The tangent of the angle of inclination of a roof with the ground is 2/5. If the slope of the roof is 1, what is the slope of the ground?

Prove the following identities:

7. $\tan(45° + x) = \dfrac{1 + \tan x}{1 - \tan x}$.

8. $\cot(45° + x) = \dfrac{\cot x - 1}{\cot x + 1}$.

9. $\cot(x - 45°) = \dfrac{1 + \cot x}{1 - \cot x}$.

10. $\dfrac{\sin(A+B)}{\sin(A-B)} = \dfrac{\tan A + \tan B}{\tan A - \tan B}$.

11. $\dfrac{\cos(A-B)}{\cos(A+B)} = \dfrac{1 + \tan A \tan B}{1 - \tan A \tan B}$.

12. $\dfrac{\tan(A-B) + \tan B}{1 - \tan(A-B) \tan B} = \tan A$.

13. $\dfrac{\sin(A+B)}{\cos A \cos B} = \tan A + \tan B$.

14. $\dfrac{\cos(A-B)}{\cos A \sin B} = \tan A + \cot B$.

15. Prove formula (12) by taking the reciprocals of the members of (11) and afterwards verifying (12) when A or $A + B$ is 90° or 270°.

If A, B, C are angles of a triangle, prove that

16.* $\tan A + \tan B + \tan C = \tan A \tan B \tan C$.

17.* $\tan \frac{1}{2}A \tan \frac{1}{2}B + \tan \frac{1}{2}A \tan \frac{1}{2}C + \tan \frac{1}{2}B \tan \frac{1}{2}C = 1$.

18.* $\cot \frac{1}{2}A + \cot \frac{1}{2}B + \cot \frac{1}{2}C = \cot \frac{1}{2}A \cot \frac{1}{2}B \cot \frac{1}{2}C$.

100. Functions of double angles. By the addition theorems for sine and cosine, we have

$\sin(A + A) = \sin A \cos A + \cos A \sin A = 2 \sin A \cos A$,
$\cos(A + A) = \cos A \cos A - \sin A \sin A = \cos^2 A - \sin^2 A$.
Hence

(14) $\sin 2A = 2 \sin A \cos A$, $\cos 2A = \cos^2 A - \sin^2 A$.

We may replace $\cos^2 A$ by $1 - \sin^2 A$, or $\sin^2 A$ by $1 - \cos^2 A$. Hence

(15) $\cos 2A = 1 - 2 \sin^2 A$, $\cos 2A = 2 \cos^2 A - 1$.

Formulas (14) and (15) should be memorized.

Taking $B = A$ in (11) and (12), we get

(16) $\quad \tan 2A = \dfrac{2 \tan A}{1 - \tan^2 A}, \quad \cot 2A = \dfrac{\cot^2 A - 1}{2 \cot A}.$

101. Functions of multiple angles. We may express $\sin 3A$ and $\cos 4A$ in terms of $\sin A$ without introducing square roots.

$$\begin{aligned}\sin(A + 2A) &= \sin A \cos 2A + \cos A \sin 2A \\ &= \sin A (\cos^2 A - \sin^2 A) + \cos A (2 \sin A \cos A) \\ &= 3 \sin A \cos^2 A - \sin^3 A \\ &= 3 \sin A (1 - \sin^2 A) - \sin^3 A,\end{aligned}$$

(17) $\quad\quad\quad \sin 3A = 3 \sin A - 4 \sin^3 A.$

In the first formula (15) we may replace A by $2A$ and obtain

$$\begin{aligned}\cos 4A &= 1 - 2 \sin^2 2A = 1 - 2(2 \sin A \cos A)^2 \\ &= 1 - 8 \sin^2 A \cos^2 A = 1 - 8 \sin^2 A (1 - \sin^2 A),\end{aligned}$$

(18) $\quad\quad\quad \cos 4A = 1 - 8 \sin^2 A + 8 \sin^4 A.$

Exercises on Functions of Multiple Angles

1. Prove formulas (16) from (14) by division.
2. Given $\sin A = 3/5$, with A acute, find $\sin 2A$, $\cos 2A$, $\tan 2A$.
3. Given $\tan A = r/s$, find $\sin 2A$, $\cos 2A$, $\tan 2A$.
4. Express $\cos 3A$ in terms of $\cos A$.
5. Express $\tan 3A$ and $\tan 4A$ in terms of $\tan A$.
6. Express $\cos 4A$ in terms of $\cos A$.

Prove the identities

7. $\sin 2A = \dfrac{2 \tan A}{1 + \tan^2 A}.$
8. $\cos 2A = \dfrac{1 - \tan^2 A}{1 + \tan^2 A}.$
9. $\tan^2(45° - A) = \dfrac{1 - \sin 2A}{1 + \sin 2A}.$
10. $\dfrac{\cot x + 1}{\cot x - 1} = \dfrac{\sin 2x + 1}{\cos 2x}.$
11. $\tan(45° + A) - \tan(45° - A) = 2 \tan 2A.$
12. $\tan x + \cot x = 2 \csc 2x.$
13. $(\sin x + \cos x)^2 = 1 + \sin 2x.$
14. $\cot x - \tan x = 2 \cot 2x.$
15. $\dfrac{\sin 2B}{1 + \cos 2B} = \tan B.$
16. $\dfrac{\sin 2C}{1 - \cos 2C} = \cot C.$
17. $\dfrac{1 - \sin 2y}{1 + \sin 2y} = \left(\dfrac{\tan y - 1}{\tan y + 1}\right)^2.$
18. $\dfrac{\sin^3 z + \cos^3 z}{\sin z + \cos z} = 1 - \tfrac{1}{2} \sin 2z.$

19. $1 + \tan a \tan 2a = \sec 2a$.
20. $\cos^4 \beta - \sin^4 \beta = \cos 2\beta$.
21. $\tan \theta + \cot 2\theta = \csc 2\theta$.
22. $\tan \delta + \tan \delta \sec 2\delta = \tan 2\delta$.
23. $\dfrac{\cos x + \sin x}{\cos x - \sin x} = \tan 2x + \sec 2x$.
24. $\dfrac{1 - \cos 2A + \sin 2A}{1 + \cos 2A + \sin 2A} = \tan A$.
25. $\sin 2x \tan 2x = \dfrac{4 \tan^2 x}{1 - \tan^4 x}$.
26. $\dfrac{\sin 2x - \sin x}{1 - \cos x + \cos 2x} = \tan x$.
27. $\tan(45° + x) + \tan(45° - x) = 2 \sec 2x$.
28. $3 \sin 2x - \sin 6x = 32 \sin^3 x \cos^3 x$.
29. $\tan 3x - \tan x = 2 \sin x \sec 3x$.
30. $\tan A + \tan(A + 60°) + \tan(A - 60°) = 3 \tan 3A$.
31. $\sin 3x = 4 \sin x \sin(60° + x) \sin(60° - x)$; deduce
$$\sin 20° \sin 40° \sin 60° \sin 80° = \dfrac{3}{16}.$$

By a mere change of notation of (14) and (15), prove that

32. $\sin x = 2 \sin \dfrac{x}{2} \cos \dfrac{x}{2}$.
33. $\cos \dfrac{x}{3} = 1 - 2 \sin^2 \dfrac{x}{6}$.
34. $\sin 6x = 2 \sin 3x \cos 3x$.
35. $\cos 8x = 2 \cos^2 4x - 1$.
36.* Express $\sin 5A$ in terms of $\sin A$.
37.* Express $\cos 5A$ in terms of $\cos A$.
38.* Why is $\cos 3 \cdot 18° = \sin 2 \cdot 18°$? Use (14) and Ex. 4, cancel the factor $\cos 18°$, and then replace $\cos^2 18°$ by $1 - \sin^2 18°$. Solve the resulting quadratic equation for $\sin 18°$. Hence obtain a construction of the regular pentagon.
39.* Express $\sin 3A + \cos 3A$ in terms of $d = \cos A - \sin A$.
40.* The angle of elevation of the top of a tree from a point 30 yards from its foot is three times as great as the angle of elevation from a point 150 yards from its foot. Express the height in terms of a square root.

102. Trajectories. Practical applications of functions of the double angle are furnished by problems concerning the *trajectory* (or path of flight) of a projectile (or bullet) fired at a velocity of v feet per second from a gun having a as its angle of elevation.

Fig. 80 shows the trajectory when $v = 2000$, $a = 25°$. In the plane of the trajectory, take the gun as the origin O, the horizontal line through O as the x-axis, and the vertical line through O as the y-axis. The component of the velocity v in the direction of

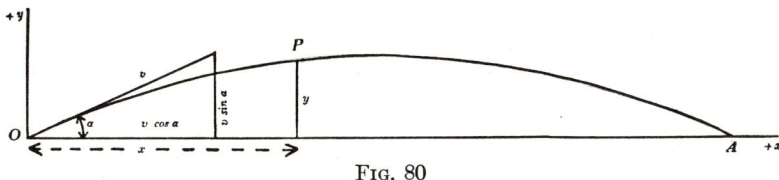

Fig. 80

the x-axis (Art. 21) is $v \cos a$. Hence if the projectile reaches the point P after t seconds, the abscissa of P is equal to $t(v \cos a)$ feet. The component of the velocity v in the direction of the y-axis is $v \sin a$. But under the action of gravity, a body, starting at rest, falls in t seconds a distance of $\frac{1}{2} gt^2$ feet, where g is approximately equal to 32. Hence the coördinates of P are

(19) $\qquad x = vt \cos a, \quad y = vt \sin a - \frac{1}{2} gt^2.$

To find the *horizontal range* $r = OA$, we seek the value r of x for $y = 0$, when the projectile P has reached the point A in the x-axis. From $y = 0$, we get

$$v \sin a = \tfrac{1}{2} gt.$$

Inserting the resulting value of t into the first equation (19), we see that the value of x is

$$r = \frac{v^2}{g}(2 \sin a \cos a) = \frac{v^2}{g} \sin 2a.$$

Exercises on Trajectories

1. Draw the graph of the trajectory when $a = 30°$ and $v = 2000$ ft. per second, by assigning various convenient values to t. Measure the horizontal range.
2. For a and v as in Ex. 1, compute the horizontal range.
3. Given $v = 1600$, $r = 61280$, find the two angles a.
4. What is the maximum range for a given velocity?

5. An athlete puts (throws) the shot from a position 6 ft. above the ground, at an angle of elevation of 45°. If the horizontal range is 48 ft., find the velocity.

Hint: Use formulas (19) with $y = -6$.

6. Given $v = 2000$, $x = 5000$, $y = 8260$, find t and a.

103. Functions of half angles. We shall write formulas (15) in other forms, which the student need not memorize or make use of in the exercises below. In (15) take $2A = x$; we get

$$\cos x = 1 - 2\sin^2 \frac{x}{2}, \quad \cos x = 2\cos^2 \frac{x}{2} - 1.$$

Transposing terms, dividing by 2, and extracting square roots, we obtain

$$(20) \quad \sin \frac{x}{2} = \pm \sqrt{\frac{1-\cos x}{2}}, \quad \cos \frac{x}{2} = \pm \sqrt{\frac{1+\cos x}{2}}.$$

When x is given, these equations enable us to find the sine and cosine of $\frac{1}{2}x$. If $0 < x < 180°$, $\frac{1}{2}x$ is an acute angle and its functions are positive; hence the $+$ sign must be chosen in both equations (20). If $360° < x < 540°$, $\frac{1}{2}x$ is in the third quadrant and its sine and cosine are negative; hence the $-$ sign must be chosen in both equations (20). The signs always depend upon the quadrant of $\frac{1}{2}x$.

From (20) we get, by division,

$$(21) \quad \tan \frac{x}{2} = \pm \sqrt{\frac{1-\cos x}{1+\cos x}}, \quad \cot \frac{x}{2} = \pm \sqrt{\frac{1+\cos x}{1-\cos x}}.$$

In each the sign is determined by the quadrant of $\frac{1}{2}x$.

When x is an acute angle, the first formula (21) was proved geometrically in Art. 35.

EXAMPLE. Given $\cos 45° = \frac{1}{2}\sqrt{2}$, find the sine and cosine of $22\frac{1}{2}°$.

Solution. By (15),

$$\tfrac{1}{2}\sqrt{2} = \cos 45° = 1 - 2\sin^2 22\tfrac{1}{2}° = 2\cos^2 22\tfrac{1}{2}° - 1.$$

Transposing terms and dividing by 2, we get

$$\sin^2 22\tfrac{1}{2}° = \frac{1-\tfrac{1}{2}\sqrt{2}}{2} = \frac{2-\sqrt{2}}{4}, \quad \cos^2 22\tfrac{1}{2}° = \frac{2+\sqrt{2}}{4}.$$

FUNCTIONS OF SEVERAL ANGLES

Since $22\frac{1}{2}°$ is an acute angle, its functions are positive and
$$\sin 22\frac{1}{2}° = \tfrac{1}{2}\sqrt{2-\sqrt{2}}, \quad \cos 22\frac{1}{2}° = \tfrac{1}{2}\sqrt{2+\sqrt{2}}.$$

Exercises on Functions of Half Angles

1. Given $\cos 30° = \tfrac{1}{2}\sqrt{3}$, find $\sin 15°$, $\cos 15°$, $\tan 15°$ in terms of square roots.
2. Given $\cos 150° = -\tfrac{1}{2}\sqrt{3}$, find $\sin 75°$, $\cos 75°$, $\tan 75°$ exactly.
3. Find the sine and cosine of $7\frac{1}{2}°$.

Prove the identities

4. $\tan \dfrac{x}{2} = \dfrac{1-\cos x}{\sin x}.$
5. $\cot \dfrac{x}{2} = \dfrac{1+\cos x}{\sin x}.$
6. $1 + \tan x \tan \tfrac{1}{2} x = \sec x.$
7. $\csc x - \cot x = \tan \tfrac{1}{2} x.$
8. $\sec A + \tan A = \tan (45° + \tfrac{1}{2} A).$
9. $1 + \cot A \cot \tfrac{1}{2} A = \csc A \cot \tfrac{1}{2} A.$
10. $\dfrac{\cos x}{1-\sin x} = \dfrac{1+\tan\tfrac{1}{2}x}{1-\tan\tfrac{1}{2}x}.$
11. $\dfrac{1+\sin x+\cos x}{1+\sin x-\cos x} = \cot \tfrac{1}{2} x.$
12. $\tan \tfrac{1}{2} A + 2 \sin^2 \tfrac{1}{2} A \cot A = \sin A.$

13. A balloon rose vertically at a point whose horizontal distance is 2400 yards from an observer who found the angle of elevation to be 15° when he first sighted the balloon, and 30° at a later time. Find an exact expression for the distance the balloon rose between the two observations.

14.* From the values of $1 + \cos A$ and $1 - \cos A$ in Art. 91, prove that
$$\cos \tfrac{1}{2} A = \sqrt{\frac{s(s-a)}{bc}}, \quad \sin \tfrac{1}{2} A = \sqrt{\frac{(s-b)(s-c)}{bc}}, \quad \tan \tfrac{1}{2} A = \sqrt{\frac{(s-b)(s-c)}{s(s-a)}},$$
where $s = \tfrac{1}{2}(a + b + c)$.

15.* Express the six functions of x in terms of $t = \tan \tfrac{1}{2} x$.

16.* Given the functions of 18° (Ex. 38 of Art. 101), how can we find the functions of 12°, 6°, 3°?

104. Sum or difference of two sines or two cosines expressed as a product.[1]

We employ formulas (1) and (9), viz.,
$$\sin (A + B) = \sin A \cos B + \cos A \sin B,$$
$$\sin (A - B) = \sin A \cos B - \cos A \sin B.$$

---
[1] The instructor who omits Art. 104 should omit Example 2 and Exercises 23–30 of Art. 105.

By addition and subtraction, we get
$$\sin(A+B) + \sin(A-B) = 2\sin A \cos B,$$
$$\sin(A+B) - \sin(A-B) = 2\cos A \sin B.$$
Write x for $A+B$ and y for $A-B$. Then
$$A = \tfrac{1}{2}(x+y), \quad B = \tfrac{1}{2}(x-y),$$
and the preceding two equations become

(22) $\quad \sin x + \sin y = 2 \sin \tfrac{1}{2}(x+y) \cos \tfrac{1}{2}(x-y),$

(23) $\quad \sin x - \sin y = 2 \cos \tfrac{1}{2}(x+y) \sin \tfrac{1}{2}(x-y).$

If we start with the expansions (8) and (10) of $\cos(A+B)$ and $\cos(A-B)$, and proceed in the same manner, we will get

(24) $\quad \cos x + \cos y = 2 \cos \tfrac{1}{2}(x+y) \cos \tfrac{1}{2}(x-y),$

(25) $\quad \cos x - \cos y = -2 \sin \tfrac{1}{2}(x+y) \sin \tfrac{1}{2}(x-y).$

Exercises on Expressing Sums as Products

1. Carry out the indicated steps leading to (24) and (25).

Express as products the following sums or differences:

2. $\sin x + \sin 3x.$ 3. $\cos x - \cos 3x.$ 4. $\sin 7C + \sin 3C.$

5. $\cos 5B + \cos 9B.$

6. $\sin 5A + \cos 3A = \sin 5A + \sin(90° - 3A).$

Prove the identities

7. $\dfrac{\sin 6A + \sin 4A}{\cos 6A + \cos 4A} = \tan 5A.$ 8. $\dfrac{\sin 7A - \sin 5A}{\cos 7A + \cos 5A} = \tan A.$

9. $\dfrac{\sin A + \sin B}{\sin A - \sin B} = \dfrac{\tan \tfrac{1}{2}(A+B)}{\tan \tfrac{1}{2}(A-B)}.$ 10. $\dfrac{\sin A + \sin B}{\cos A + \cos B} = \tan \tfrac{1}{2}(A+B).$

11. $\sin A + \sin 3A + \sin 5A + \sin 7A = 4 \cos A \cos 2A \sin 4A.$

12. $\sin 2x + \sin 4x + \sin 6x = 4 \cos x \cos 2x \sin 3x.$

13. $\sin x - \sin 2x + \sin 3x = 4 \sin \tfrac{1}{2} x \cos x \cos \tfrac{3}{2} x.$

14. $\sin x + \sin y + \sin z - \sin(x+y+z) = 4 \sin \dfrac{x+y}{2} \sin \dfrac{y+z}{2} \sin \dfrac{z+x}{2}.$

15. Given $a/b = s/t$ we see on adding or subtracting unity from each fraction that
$$\dfrac{a+b}{b} = \dfrac{s+t}{t}, \quad \dfrac{a-b}{b} = \dfrac{s-t}{t}, \quad \dfrac{a+b}{a-b} = \dfrac{s+t}{s-t},$$

the third equation following by division. Applying this principle of "composition and division" to the law of sines

$$\frac{a}{b} = \frac{\sin A}{\sin B},$$

we get

$$\frac{a+b}{a-b} = \frac{\sin A + \sin B}{\sin A - \sin B}.$$

Replacing the second member by its value in Ex. 9, we have the law of tangents (Art. 88).

If A, B, C are angles of a triangle, prove that

16.* $\sin A + \sin B + \sin C = 4 \cos \frac{1}{2} A \cos \frac{1}{2} B \cos \frac{1}{2} C$.
17.* $\sin A + \sin B - \sin C = 4 \sin \frac{1}{2} A \sin \frac{1}{2} B \cos \frac{1}{2} C$.
18.* $\cos A + \cos B + \cos C = 1 + 4 \sin \frac{1}{2} A \sin \frac{1}{2} B \sin \frac{1}{2} C$.
19.* $\cos A - \cos B + \cos C + 1 = 4 \cos \frac{1}{2} A \sin \frac{1}{2} B \cos \frac{1}{2} C$.
20.* $\sin 2A + \sin 2B + \sin 2C = 4 \sin A \sin B \sin C$.
21.* $\sin 4A + \sin 4B + \sin 4C = -4 \sin 2A \sin 2B \sin 2C$.

105. Trigonometric equations. Unlike an identity, an equation is true only for special values. The exercises below include only equations which can be solved by methods wholly similar to those employed in the following four illustrative examples. More difficult equations are solved graphically in Arts. 109, 112.

EXAMPLE 1. Find the positive angles $<360°$ for which

$$2 \sin^2 x + 3 \cos x = 2.$$

Solution. Replacing $\sin^2 x$ by $1 - \cos^2 x$, we get $3 \cos x - 2 \cos^2 x = 0$. Hence $\cos x = 0$ or $3/2$. The second value must be discarded since $\cos x$ cannot exceed 1 numerically. Thus $\cos x = 0$, $x = 90°$ or $270°$.

EXAMPLE 2. Find the positive angles $<360°$ for which

$$\cos x + \cos 2x + \cos 3x = 0.$$

Solution. By formula (24),

$$\cos 3x + \cos x = 2 \cos 2x \cos x.$$

Hence the proposed equation becomes

$$\cos 2x (2 \cos x + 1) = 0.$$

Hence either $\cos 2x = 0$ or $2 \cos x = -1$. The positive solutions $<360°$ of the latter are $x = 120°, 240°$. Next, $\cos 2x = 0$ only when $2x$ is $90°$ or $270°$ or one of these angles increased by a multiple of 360°, whence x is 45° or 135° or one of these angles increased by a multiple of 180°. But if we add 180° more than once, we obtain an angle $> 360°$. Hence the answers are 45°, 135°, 225°, 315°, together with the former angles 120°, 240°.

EXAMPLE 3. Find the positive angles $<360°$ for which $\tan 2x = 2 \sin x$.

Solution. By formula (16),
$$\tan 2x = \frac{2 \tan x}{1-\tan^2 x} = \frac{2 \sin x}{\cos x\,(1-\tan^2 x)}.$$

Thus the last fraction shall be equal to $2 \sin x$. This is evidently true if $\sin x = 0$, whence $x = 0°$ or $180°$. Next, if the common factor $2 \sin x$ is not zero, it may be cancelled, and we obtain
$$\frac{1}{\cos x\,(1-\tan^2 x)} = 1, \quad \sec x = 1 - \tan^2 x.$$

We recall the identity $\sec^2 x = 1 + \tan^2 x$. Adding, we get
$$\sec^2 x + \sec x = 2.$$

Solving this as a quadratic equation for $\sec x$, we obtain $\sec x = 1$ or -2. Hence $\cos x = 1$ or $-1/2$, and the positive angles $<360°$ are 0°, 120°, 240°. These with the former angle 180° give the four answers.

EXAMPLE 4. Find the positive angles $<360°$ for which
$$20 \cos y - 15 \sin y = 12.$$

Solution. The most obvious method of solution is to transpose $15 \sin y$, square each of the new members, replace $\cos^2 y$ by $1 - \sin^2 y$, and solve the resulting quadratic equation for $\sin y$. But only part of the angles found in this manner will satisfy the given equation. For, when we square each member of an equation $x = a$, we obtain an equation $x^2 = a^2$ having a solution $x = -a$ which does not satisfy the former equation $x = a$.

To give a solution which shall not introduce extraneous values, divide each member by $\sqrt{20^2 + 15^2} = 25$. We get
$$\frac{4}{5} \cos y - \frac{3}{5} \sin y = \frac{12}{25}.$$

We can find an angle x such that $\sin x = 4/5$, $\cos x = 3/5$. By Table I, $x = 53°8'$, nearly. Hence our equation becomes
$$\sin (x - y) = 0.48.$$

By the same table, $53°8' - y$ is equal to $28°41'$ or $180° - 28°41'$, or one of these angles increased by a multiple of 360°. Hence the positive values $<360°$ of y are $24°27'$ and $261°49'$.

Exercises on Trigonometric Equations

Find all the positive angles $<360°$ which satisfy the following equations, excluding angles for which any of the functions are undefined:

1. $2 \sin^2 x + 3 \cos x = 0$.
2. $16 \sin^2 x + 24 \cos x = 9$.
3. $2 \cos^2 x + 5 \sin x = 4$.
4. $2 \tan x \sin x = 3$.
5. $\cos x + \cos 2x = -1$.
6. $\cos x + \sec x = \frac{5}{2}$.
7. $\tan A + \cot A = 2$.
8. $\sin 3A = \cos 2A \ [= \sin(90° - 2A)]$.
9. $\tan^2 y + \cot^2 y = 2$.
10. $\sec^2 y + \csc^2 y = 4$.
11. $\sin 2x = 2 \sin x$.
12. $\tan(45° - x) + \tan(45° + x) = 4$.
13. $\sin^4 x + \cos^4 x = 1$.
14. $\tan x + \tan 2x = \tan 3x \ [= \tan(x + 2x)]$.
15. $\tan x \sec x = -\sqrt{2}$.
16. $\sin 2x \cos x = \sin x$.
17. $4 \tan B - \cot B = 3$.
18. $\tan B - \cot B = \cot 2B$.
19. $\tan 2\theta = \tan \theta$.
20. $\csc \theta - \cot \theta = \sin \frac{1}{2} \theta$.
21. $6 \tan^2 \theta - 4 \sin^2 \theta = 1$.
22. $\csc \theta = 1 + \cot \theta$.

By converting one or both members into a product (Art. 104), solve

23. $\sin 3x + \sin x = -\sin 2x$.
24. $\sin 2x - \sin x = \cos 2x - \cos x$.
25. $\cos x - \cos 3x = \sin 2x$.
26. $\sin x + \sin 3x = \cos x - \cos 3x$.
27. $\sin 5A + \sin 3A = \cos A$.
28. $\cos 7A + \cos A = -\cos 5A - \cos 3A$.
29. $\sin 4A - \sin 2A = \cos 3A$.
30. $\sin(A + 120°) + \sin(A + 60°) = 1.5$.

By the second method of Example 4, solve

31. $\sin x + \cos x = \sqrt{2}$.
32. $5 \sin x + 12 \cos x = 6.5$.
33. $2 \cos x - \sin x = 1$.
34. $5 \sin x + 2 \cos x = 5$.

CHAPTER XI

GRAPHS OF THE TRIGONOMETRIC FUNCTIONS AND THEIR INVERSES, RADIANS

106. Line representations of the trigonometric functions.
Consider any angle A in its trigonometric position and recall the definitions (Art. 83) that $\sin A = y/r$, $\cos A = x/r$, etc., where x and y are the coördinates of any point P of the terminal side of angle A, while r is the distance from P to the origin O. Since r is the denominator of the fractions defining $\sin A$ and $\cos A$, take $r = 1$ for convenience, i.e., take OP as the unit of length of our drawings. Then $\sin A$ is represented to scale by the ordinate y (PF in Figs. 81, 82; $-PF$ in Figs. 83, 84) and $\cos A$ is repre-

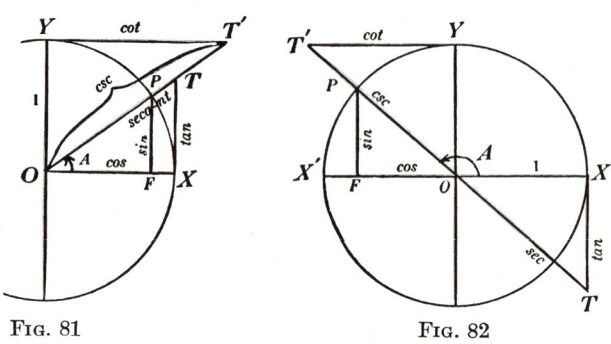

FIG. 81   FIG. 82

sented by the abscissa x (OF in Figs. 81, 84; $-OF$ in Figs. 82, 83). Hence *the sine of an angle in its trigonometric position is equal, in magnitude and sign, to the ordinate of the point P in which the terminal side of the angle intersects the unit circle. The cosine is equal to the abscissa of P.*

Next, consider $\tan A = y/x$, where $x \neq 0$. First, let A be in the first or fourth quadrant, so that the abscissa x is positive.

Since it is convenient to have our present denominator x equal to unity, we choose the point $T = (x, y)$ on the terminal side of angle A such that its abscissa x shall be OX, the unit of length in our figures. Then the corresponding ordinate y (TX in Fig. 81, $-TX$ in Fig. 84) represents to scale $\tan A = y/1$. Second, let A be in the second or third quadrant, so that the abscissa is negative. We write $\tan A = y/x$ in the form $\tan A = (-y)/(-x)$ and choose the point $T = (-x, -y)$ on the prolongation of the terminal side of A such that its positive abscissa $-x$ shall be OX, the unit of length. Then the corresponding ordinate $-y$ ($-TX$ in Fig. 82, TX in Fig. 83) represents $\tan A = (-y)/1$. Hence, *the tangent of an angle in its trigonometric position is equal, in magnitude and sign, to the ordinate of the point T in which the terminal side of the angle, prolonged if necessary,*

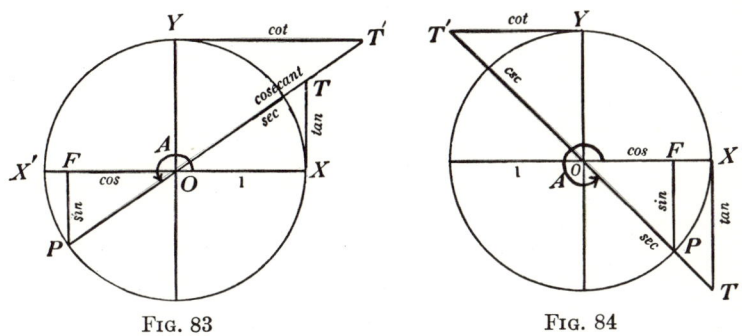

Fig. 83   Fig. 84

intersects the line tangent to the unit circle at the point X on the initial side of the angle.

Similarly, *the cotangent of an angle in its trigonometric position is equal, in magnitude and sign, to the abscissa of the point T' in which the terminal side of the angle, prolonged if necessary, intersects the line tangent to the unit circle at the point Y on the positive y-axis.*

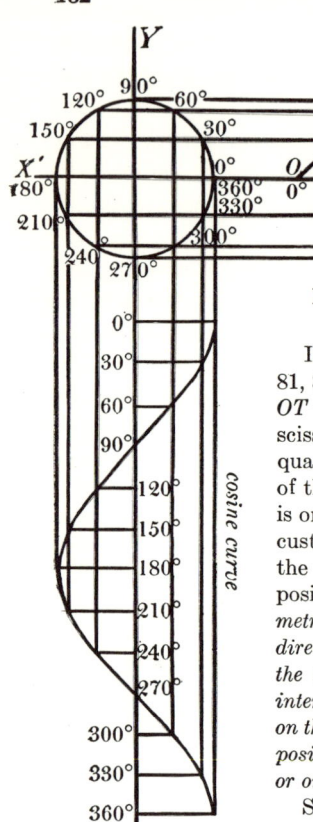

Fig. 85. Sine and Cosine Curves (Art. 107)

If angle A is in the first or fourth quadrant (Figs. 81, 84), sec $A = r/x$ is represented by the radius vector OT to the point in the terminal side of A whose abscissa x is $OX = 1$. If A is in the second or third quadrant (Figs. 82, 83), sec A is equal to the negative of the ratio of the length of OT to $OX = 1$; since T is on the prolongation of the terminal side of A, it is customary to regard OT as negative, while lines in the direction OP along the terminal side of A are positive. Hence *the secant of an angle in its trigonometric position is equal, in magnitude and sign, to the directed line OT from the origin to the point T in which the terminal side of the angle, prolonged if necessary, intersects the line tangent to the unit circle at the point X on the initial side of the angle, provided OT is counted positive or negative according as T is on the terminal side or on its prolongation.*

Similarly, *the cosecant of an angle in its trigonometric position is equal, in magnitude and sign, to the directed line OT' from the origin to the point T' in which the terminal side, prolonged if necessary (and then OT' is counted negative), intersects the line tangent to the unit circle at the point Y on the positive y-axis.*

107. The sine and cosine curves. These curves may be drawn rapidly by means of the line representations just discussed. Draw a circle whose radius is any convenient length representing unity.

Divide the circumference of the circle into 12 equal parts and label the points of division 0°, 30°, 60°, ..., 330° (Fig. 85). Through them draw lines parallel to the horizontal diameter $X'X$. Choose any convenient segment OA of $X'X$ to represent 360°, subdivide it into 12 equal parts, label the points of division 30°, 60°, .., 330°, and draw vertical lines through each to intersect the horizontal line through the point on the circumference with the same label. The points of intersection are points on the sine curve.

The abscissas of the points of the circumference marked 0°, 30°, .., 360° are the line representations of cos 0°, cos 30°, .., cos 360°. In the lower part of Fig. 85, they have been transferred (by means of parallels to YZ) into the positions of the horizontal segments extending from equally spaced points on YZ, labeled 0°, 30°, .., 360°. If we now rotate the page of the book until YZ becomes horizontal, with Z to the right of Y, we have a part of the cosine curve in its conventional position (Fig. 86).

Fig. 86. The Cosine Curve $y = \cos x$

Since $\sin(360° + x) = \sin x$, the part of the sine curve $y = \sin x$ from 360° to 720° is an exact copy of the part from 0° to 360° which is shown at the right of Fig. 85. Similarly for the part from $-360°$ to 0° (Fig. 87, which is drawn on different scales from those used in Fig. 85).

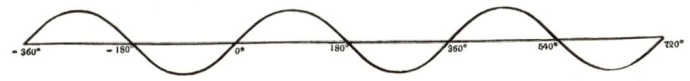

Fig. 87. The Sine Curve $y = \sin x$

108. The tangent curve. Using the line representation of the tangent function (Art. 106), we obtain the following construction of part of the tangent curve (Fig. 88):

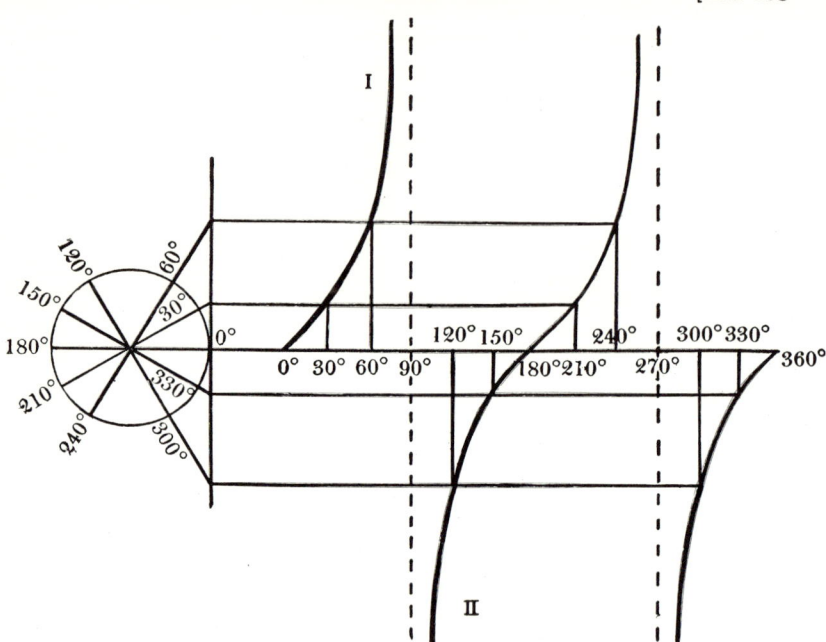

FIG. 88. THE TANGENT CURVE $y = \tan x$

When the arc of the circumference increases from 0° toward 90°, the representation of the tangent function by the intercept on the line tangent to the circle increases without limit. The corresponding part I of the tangent curve extends upward indefinitely, approaching nearer and nearer the vertical line through the point marked 90°, but always remaining to the left of it. When the angle decreases from 180° toward 90°, its tangent decreases from zero, through negative values, without limit. The corresponding part II of the tangent curve extends downward indefinitely, approaching nearer and nearer the vertical line through the point marked 90°, but always remaining to the right of it. We now see graphically why the tangent function is undefined at 90°, 270°, or any odd multiple of 90°.

Ch. XI] GRAPHS, RADIANS, INVERSE FUNCTIONS 155

If we elsewhere meet the statement that tan 90° is positive or negative infinity, written symbolically tan 90° = ± ∞, we should not understand this to define or give a value to tan 90°, but merely to mean that the tangent function increases or decreases without limit when the angle increases or decreases toward 90°, respectively. It is simpler in the case of the square of the tangent, for which we may appropriately write $\tan^2 90° = +\infty$.

EXERCISES ON GRAPHS OF TRIGONOMETRIC FUNCTIONS

1. By means of a circle and a line tangent to it at its highest point, construct the graphs of $y = \cot x$ and $y = \csc x$. For the latter, transfer by means of a pair of compasses the lines OT'' of Figs. 81–84, into vertical lines starting at equally spaced points marked 0°, 30°, ..., 360° on a horizontal line. While we may proceed similarly for $y = \cot x$, we may also

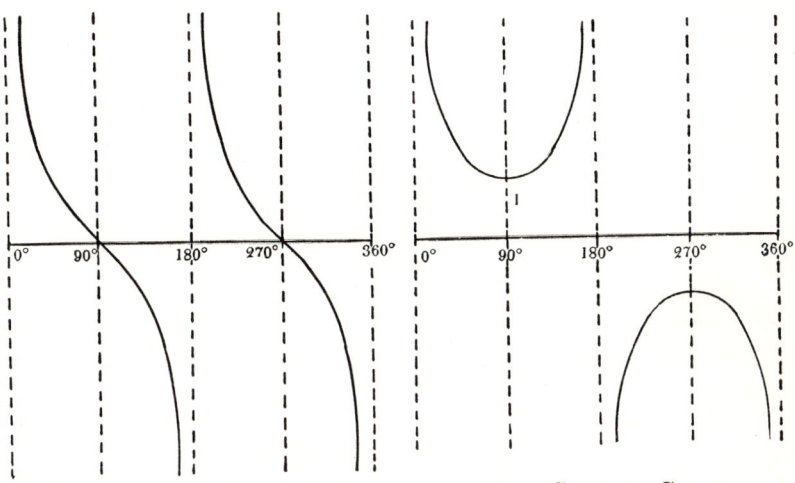

FIG. 89. COTANGENT CURVE   FIG. 90. COSECANT CURVE

draw it rapidly in a rotated position, by the method used for $y = \cos x$ in Art. 107.

2. Draw the secant curve and note that it may be derived from Fig. 90 by taking 90° from each angle, i.e., replacing the labels 90°, 180°, ..., by 0°, 90°, ...

3. In view of the preceding graphs, state the angles for which (a) cotangent is undefined, (b) cosecant, (c) secant.

4. Explain by means of the identity $\sin(A + 90°) = \cos A$ why the cosine curve may be obtained from the sine curve by replacing the labels $0°, 90°, 180°, \ldots$ on the latter by $-90°, 0°, 90°, \ldots$.

5. Since $\tan(A + 90°) = -\cot A$, how may we deduce the cotangent curve from the tangent curve?

6. State the identity which proves the second part of Ex. 2.

7. What property of the successive arches of the sine curve in Fig. 87 follows from the identity $\sin(180° + A) = -\sin A$?

109. Graphical solution of trigonometric equations; harmonic curves. If $a, b, c, \ldots$ are constants, the graph of
$$y = a \sin x + b \cos x + c \sin 2x + d \cos 2x + \cdots$$
is called a *harmonic curve*. Such curves occur frequently in physics. By means of the curve, we can solve the equation obtained by assigning to y any given value not too large numerically. This method of solving trigonometric equations is available when the special algebraic devices of Art. 105 fail.

EXAMPLE. Plot the harmonic curve whose equation is
(1) $\qquad y = \tfrac{1}{2} \sin x + \sin 2x,$
and find the positive angles $<360°$ for which
$$\tfrac{1}{2} \sin x + \sin 2x = 0.64.$$

Solution. First, we reproduce from Fig. 85 the graph of $y = \sin x$. Then, by bisecting the ordinates of several of its points, we obtain points on the graph of $y_1 = \tfrac{1}{2} \sin x$ (Fig. 91). To find points on $y_2 = \sin 2x$, take as the

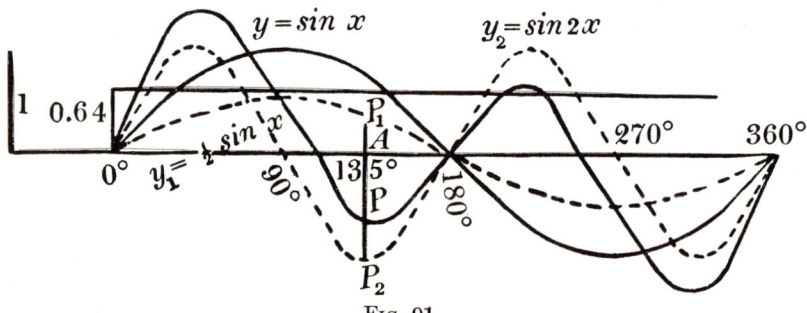

FIG. 91

ordinate of $x = 30°$ the ordinate sin 60° of $x = 60°$ in the graph of $y = \sin x$, etc. Corresponding to each value of x, the ordinate y of (1) is equal to $y_1 + y_2$, or the algebraic sum of the ordinates of the two dotted curves. For example, when $x = 135°$, $y_1 = AP_1$ is positive and $y_2 = -AP_2$ is negative and numerically larger than y_1; hence we lay off PP_2 equal to AP_1, upward from P_2, and obtain $y = y_1 + y_2 = -AP$, measured downward. The resulting graph of (1) is shown as a heavy curve in Fig. 91.

Next, we draw a line parallel to the x-axis at a distance 0.64 above it. This line is seen to cross the heavy curve at four points for which x is approximately 15°, 86°, 213°, 225°. More exact values will be found by interpolation, using Tables I and II.

For $x = 15°$ and $x = 15°30'$, the values of (1) are 0.6294 and 0.6486, whose difference is 0.0192. The desired value 0.64 exceeds the lesser by 0.0106. Then

$$\frac{106}{192} \times 30' = 16\tfrac{1}{2}', \quad x = 15°16\tfrac{1}{2}'.$$

When x is about 86°, set $x = 90° - A$. Then

$$y = \tfrac{1}{2} \cos A + \sin 2A.$$

For $A = 4°$, we get $y = 0.6380$. Since this is nearly the desired value 0.64, try $A = 4°5'$, which gives $y = 0.6409$. Since 20/29 of 5' is $3\tfrac{1}{2}'$, $A = 4°3\tfrac{1}{2}'$, whence $x = 85°56\tfrac{1}{2}'$.

For the large angles x, set $x = 180° + B$. Then

$$y = \sin 2B - \tfrac{1}{2} \sin B.$$

For $B = 45°$ and 46°, y equals 0.6464 and 0.6397. Since 64/67 of 60' is 57', $B = 45°57'$, $x = 225°57'$. Similarly, the fourth answer is $x = 212°49'$.

EXERCISES ON THE GRAPHICAL SOLUTION OF EQUATIONS

Solve graphically and by subsequent interpolations
1. $\tfrac{1}{2} \sin x + \sin 2x = 0.7$.   2. $\sin x + \sin 2x = 1.2$.
3. $2 \sin x + \sin 3x = 0.8$.   4. $2 \sin x - \sin \tfrac{1}{3} x = 0.4$.

110. The radian unit of angle. When we plotted the sine curve in Fig. 85, we were at liberty to choose any segment OA of the x-axis to represent the angle 360°, and any segment of the y-axis to represent sin 90° or the radius of the circle which we employed to secure the line representations of the sines of angles. A different choice of these two arbitrary units of measurements would have led to a different appearance of the graph. For the sake of simplicity and uniformity, it is desirable to have the same unit of length for the x's as for the y's. In particular, any two sine curves would then have the same shape, although one might be a magnification of the other (as in Figs. 85, 87), just as is true of any two circles. How shall we secure this desirable state of affairs?

We recall that the y's (or sines) were represented in Fig. 85 by vertical lines measured with respect to the radius of the circle as the unit of length. Since angles at the center are proportional to the arcs intercepted on the circumference, and since these arcs are measured naturally in terms of the radius as the unit of length, we shall obtain the desired goal of having the same unit of length for the x's (angles) as for the y's (sines), if we agree that an angle x has the same measure as its intercepted arc. *The resulting unit of angle, called a* **radian,** *is therefore an angle at the center of a circle which subtends an arc equal to the radius.*

Thus, in Fig. 92, if arc AB equals the radius r, angle AOB is a *radian*. Let DE be any second arc of the same circumference. Since angles at the center are proportional to their subtended arcs,

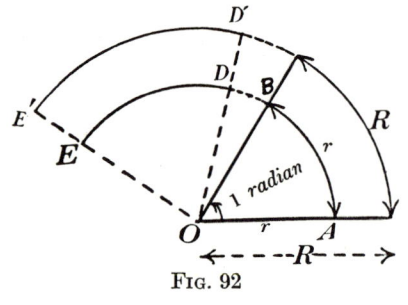

Fig. 92

$$\frac{\angle DOE}{\angle BOA} = \frac{\text{arc } DE}{\text{arc } AB} = \frac{\text{arc } DE}{r} = \frac{\text{arc } D'E'}{R},$$

or

$$\text{number of radians in angle at center} = \frac{\text{length of subtended arc}}{\text{length of radius}},$$

and this ratio is independent of the particular radius chosen. If $\angle DOE$ contains n radians, the first fraction is equal to n, so that arc DE is of length nr. *An angle of n radians at the center of a circle of radius r intercepts on the circumference an arc of length nr.*

Ch. XI] GRAPHS, RADIANS, INVERSE FUNCTIONS 159

Since the length of the semicircumference is πr, where $\pi = 3.1415926 +$, we have

(2) $\qquad \pi$ radians $= 180°$.

Thus one radian is equal to $180/\pi = 57.2958 -$ degrees, or approximately $57°17'45''$. The student should memorize formula (2).

REDUCTION OF DEGREES, MINUTES, AND SECONDS TO RADIANS

°	Radians	′	Radians	″	Radians
1	0.0174533	1	0.0002909	1	0.0000048
2	0.0349066	2	0.0005818	2	0.0000097
3	0.0523599	3	0.0008727	3	0.0000145
4	0.0698132	4	0.0011636	4	0.0000194
5	0.0872665	5	0.0014544	5	0.0000242
6	0.1047198	6	0.0017453	6	0.0000291
7	0.1221731	7	0.0020362	7	0.0000339
8	0.1396263	8	0.0023271	8	0.0000388
9	0.1570796	9	0.0026180	9	0.0000436

EXAMPLE. Find the number of radians in $73°36'40''$.

Solution. From the table we see that there are

```
1.221731 radians in 70°     (by shifting decimal point for 7°)
 .052360    "      "  3°
 .008727    "      " 30'    ( "      "      "      "      " 3' )
 .001745    "      "  6'
 .000194    "      " 40''   ( "      "      "      "      " 4'')
─────────
1.284757    "      " 73°36'40''.
```

Although not so stated at the time, the graphs (Figs. 85-90) of the trigonometric functions were actually drawn so that the units of lengths on the two axes are the same, since the length on the x-axis which represents $360°$ was chosen equal to 2π times the length of the radius of the auxiliary circle.

EXERCISES ON RADIANS

1. Find the number of radians in $45°$, $60°$, $-270°$.
2. Express in degrees $\pi/6$, $-\pi/4$, 1.570796 radians.

3. Copy Figs. 86 and 87, but label in terms of radians each angle which is a multiple of $90°$.

4. Using Fig. 89, sketch the cotangent curve for angles from -2π to $+3\pi$.

5. Find the number of radians in an angle at the center of a circle of radius 50 feet which intercepts an arc of 75 feet.

6. Find the length of an arc subtending an angle of 2.5 radians at the center of a circle of radius 50 feet.

7. Find the length of the radius of a circle at whose center an angle of 2.1 radians is subtended by an arc 42 feet long.

8. Find the length of an arc of $70°$ on a circle of 9 ft. radius, using $\pi = 22/7$.

9. If the angle of a sector of a circle of radius r contains n radians, the area of the sector is equal to the product $\frac{1}{2}nr^2$ of $n/(2\pi)$ by the area πr^2 of the circle. Subtracting the area $\frac{1}{2}r^2 \sin n$ of the triangle two of whose sides are radii and included angle is n (Art. 86), we obtain $\frac{1}{2}(n - \sin n) r^2$ as the area of the segment of the circle. Compute the area of a circular segment of radius 10 feet whose arc is $40°$.

10. Prove that $\cos \dfrac{3\pi}{11} + \cos \dfrac{5\pi}{11} + 2 \cos \dfrac{\pi}{11} \cos \dfrac{7\pi}{11} = 0$.

Express in terms of radians all solutions of the following equations:

11. $\cos x + \tan x = \sec x$. 12. $\cot x - \csc 2x = 1$.
13. $\tan 2x \tan 3x = 1$.

14. In field artillery, a *mil* is the angle subtended by an arc equal to $1/6400$ of the circumference. Show that a mil is approximately one-thousandth of a radian.

15.* An endless band passes around two wheels the diameter of one of which equals the circumference of the other. When the larger wheel makes one complete revolution, what is the number of radians in the angle described by the radius of the smaller wheel?

16.* Two straight railroad tracks intersect at P making an angle of $55°$. They are to be connected by a curved track, tangent to each, and forming a circular arc of radius 300 feet. Find the length of the curved track and the distance from P to the point of tangency.

17.* Three circles, whose radii are proportional to 1, 3, 5, are tangent externally. The points of tangency are the vertices of a curvilinear triangle whose area is 10 square inches. Find the radii.

Ch. XI] GRAPHS, RADIANS, INVERSE FUNCTIONS 161

18.* A railroad curve forms a circular arc of 19°13.4′, the radius to the center line of the track being 1680 feet. If the gauge is 5 feet, what is the difference in length of the two rails?

111. Approximate values of sines and tangents of small angles.

Let n be the number of radians in an acute angle ACT (Fig. 93). With C as a center and any radius $r = CA$, describe the arc AB. Let the tangent at A meet CB produced at T. The area of $\triangle TAC$ is

$\frac{1}{2} TA \cdot CA = \frac{1}{2} r^2 \tan n.$

The area of $\triangle CAB$ is $\frac{1}{2} r^2 \sin n$, and the area of sector CAB is $\frac{1}{2} r^2 n$ (Ex. 9, Art. 110). But

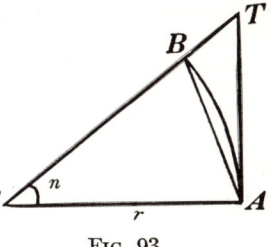

Fig. 93

$\triangle CAB <$ sector $CAB < \triangle TAC.$

Hence

$$\frac{1}{2} r^2 \sin n \ < \ \frac{1}{2} r^2 n \ < \ \frac{1}{2} r^2 \tan n,$$
$$\sin n \ < \ n \ < \ \tan n.$$

Dividing by the positive number $\sin n$ or $\tan n$, we get

$$1 < \frac{n}{\sin n} < \frac{1}{\cos n}, \quad \cos n < \frac{n}{\tan n} < 1.$$

But $\cos n$ approaches 1 when n approaches zero. Hence $n/\sin n$ and $n/\tan n$ each approaches 1 as n approaches zero, since each lies between 1 and a number which approaches 1. In other words, *the sine and the tangent of a very small angle are each approximately equal to the number of radians in the angle.*

For angles $<2°$, the approximation is sufficiently exact to 5 decimal places, as is clear from the following values:
$A = 1°30′ = 0.02618$ radians, $\sin A = 0.02618$, $\tan A = 0.02619,$
$B = 2° \ \ \ \ = 0.03491$ radians, $\sin B = 0.03490$, $\tan B = 0.03492.$

EXAMPLE 1. Find the inclination A of a railroad track to the horizontal if its grade is 1 per cent (i.e., rises 1 foot per 100 feet).

Solution. Since $\tan A = 0.01$, A contains approximately 0.01 radians. Since 1 radian is equal to 57.296 degrees, $A = 0.573° = 34.4′.$

EXAMPLE 2. A bolt 1 inch in diameter has 10 threads to the inch. Find the inclination A of the thread to a cross section of the bolt.

Solution. If a small part of the cylindrical surface of the bolt were flattened into a plane (as when a roll of paper is unrolled), a thread would appear as a straight line. The length of one thread is approximately π inches. The length of the 10 threads is 10π inches. Hence we have a plane right triangle with the hypotenuse 10π inches, a leg 1 inch (height of ten threads) and opposite angle A. Thus $\sin A = 1/(10\pi)$, which is the approximate number of radians in A. Its product $18/\pi^2$ by $180/\pi$ is the number N of degrees.

$$\log \pi = 0.49715 \qquad \begin{array}{l} \log 18 = 1.2553 \\ \log \pi^2 = 0.9943 \\ \hline \log N = 0.2610 \\ N = 1.824° = 1°49'. \end{array}$$

Exercises on Small Angles

1. How high is a tower which subtends 1° at a distance of 2 miles?

2. What is the per cent grade of a railroad track which is inclined 1° to the horizontal?

3. A bolt 2 inches in diameter has 6 threads to the inch. Find the inclination of the thread to a cross section of the bolt.

4. The diameter of the moon subtends the angle 31.5′ at the earth, and the moon is 239200 miles from the earth. Find the moon's diameter.

5. How high is a tower which subtends 40′ at a distance of 800 feet?

6. How far from the eye must a coin, one inch in diameter, be placed so as to just hide the moon, if its diameter subtends the angle 31′5″?

7. The sun is about 92 million miles from the earth and subtends the angle 32′ at the earth. Find the sun's diameter.

112. Equations involving both an angle and its trigonometric functions. In any such equation it is understood that the angle is measured in radians. Thus in Fig. 94, the unit of length is the same on the x-axis as on the y-axis.

EXAMPLE 1. Find the positive angles $<2\pi$ satisfying

$$x - \tfrac{1}{2} \sin x = \frac{\pi}{4},$$

which is a case of Kepler's equation in astronomy.

Ch. XI] GRAPHS, RADIANS, INVERSE FUNCTIONS   163

Solution. The required angles x are the abscissas of the points of intersection of $y = \sin x$ and $y = 2\left(x - \frac{\pi}{4}\right)$. The latter represents a straight line, two of whose points are $A = \left(\frac{\pi}{4}, 0\right)$ and $B = \left(\frac{\pi}{2}, \frac{\pi}{2}\right)$.

The abscissa x_1 of the point of intersection is just less than $5\pi/12$ or $75°$.

A more exact value of x_1 can be found by Table II and a table (Art. 110) of the radians in $1°, .., 9°$. We shall compute the values of

$$F = x - \tfrac{1}{2}\sin x - \frac{\pi}{4}$$

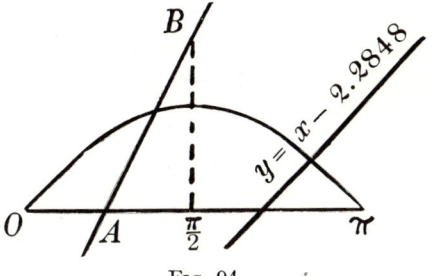

Fig. 94

for $x = 72°$ and $x = 73°$, and find that these values have opposite signs; hence F is zero for a value x_1 between $72°$ and $73°$.

$\sin 72° = 0.9511$	$\sin 73° = 0.9563$
$\tfrac{1}{2}\sin 72° = 0.4755$	$\tfrac{1}{2}\sin 73° = 0.4781$
$\frac{\pi}{4} = 0.7854$	$\frac{\pi}{4} = 0.7854$
1.2609	1.2635
$72° = 1.2566$ radians	$73° = 1.2741$ radians
$F = -0.0043$	$F = +0.0106$

The difference of the two F's is 0.0149. Hence x_1 exceeds $72°$ by

$$\frac{43}{149} \times 60' = 17'; \quad x_1 = 72°17', \text{ approximately.}$$

EXAMPLE 2. The area of a segment of a circle of radius 5 feet is 28.56 square feet. Find the length of the chord.

Solution. Let x be the number of radians in the angle at the center subtended by the chord. By Ex. 9, Art. 110,

$$\frac{25}{2}(x - \sin x) = 28.56, \quad x - \sin x = 2.2848.$$

Thus x is the abscissa of the point of intersection of $y = \sin x$ and $y = x - 2.2848$, whose graphs are shown in Fig. 94, the straight line being determined by the points having $x = 0$ and $x = \pi$. As in Ex. 1, we get $x = 155°4'$, nearly. The length of the chord is $10 \sin \tfrac{1}{2} x = 9.764$ ft.

Exercises on Trigonometric Equations

1. The area of a segment of a circle of radius 10 feet is 80 square feet. Find the length of the chord.

Find the angle at the center of a circle subtended by a chord which cuts off a segment the ratio of whose area to the circle is

    2. $1/8$.   3. $1/4$.   4. $3/8$.

Find the positive angles $<2\pi$ for which

    5. $x - \tfrac{1}{2}\sin x = \dfrac{\pi}{2}$.   6. $x - \tfrac{1}{4}\sin x = \dfrac{\pi}{3}$.   7. $x - \pi \sin x = 2$.

113. The inverse trigonometric functions. With most operations in mathematics there are associated inverse operations. For example, the direct operation may be the finding of the square $y = x^2$ of a given number x; the inverse operation then consists in finding a number x whose square is equal to a given number y, and there are two answers denoted by $x = \pm \sqrt{y}$. Again, we have often employed the direct operation of finding the cosine of a given angle; for example, finding the value $\tfrac{1}{2}$ of the cosine of 60°. Now the inverse operation consists in deducing an angle 60° (among the possible answers) when the value $\tfrac{1}{2}$ of its cosine is given, and we shall employ either of the symbols $\cos^{-1} \tfrac{1}{2}$ and arc $\cos \tfrac{1}{2}$ to denote any of the angles $n \cdot 360° \pm 60°$ whose cosine is $\tfrac{1}{2}$. The first symbol $\cos^{-1} \tfrac{1}{2}$ is read *inverse cosine of* $\tfrac{1}{2}$, and must be carefully distinguished from the reciprocal $1/(\cos \tfrac{1}{2})$ of $\cos \tfrac{1}{2}$, which is properly written $(\cos \tfrac{1}{2})^{-1}$. Thus the part -1 of our symbol is not an exponent. This possible, but only apparent, confusion is avoided by the use of our second symbol arc $\cos \tfrac{1}{2}$ which is read *arc whose cosine is* $\tfrac{1}{2}$. A simple illustration will make clear that we are not using the term inverse in the sense of reciprocal: let the direct operation be that of walking 4 miles north; then the inverse operation is that of walking 4 miles south, and not that of walking $\tfrac{1}{4}$ of a mile north.

Similarly, either of the symbols $\tan^{-1} 1$ and arc $\tan 1$ denotes any of the angles $n\pi + \pi/4$ (in radians) whose tangent is 1.

Ch. XI] GRAPHS, RADIANS, INVERSE FUNCTIONS 165

Again, $\sin^{-1} \frac{1}{2}$ or arc sin $\frac{1}{2}$ denotes any one of the angles $n \cdot 360° + 30°$ and $n \cdot 360° + 150°$ whose sine is $\frac{1}{2}$.

The nature of these inverse functions becomes clear from their graphs. To construct the graph of arc sin x, equate it to a variable y and plot the graph of the equation

(3) $\qquad\qquad y = \text{arc sin } x.$

Since this equation has the same meaning as $x = \sin y$, we may plot the graph of the latter instead of (3). To do this, start with the graph (Fig. 87) of $y = \sin x$, and rotate the plane of the paper 90° counter-clockwise; then the former positive x-axis becomes the new positive y-axis, while the former positive y-axis becomes the new negative x-axis. It remains therefore to reverse the direction of measuring the new abscissas, which amounts to revolving the graph in its new position through 180° about the vertical axis. We therefore obtain the graph (Fig. 95) of $x = \sin y$ and hence of (3). It lies between the vertical lines through the points with the abscissas -1 and $+1$, and consists of an infinite number of repetitions both upward and downward of the portion between $y = -\pi$ and $y = +\pi$. Hence for each value of x which is admissible (i.e., between -1 and $+1$), there is an infinite number of values of y, viz., the ordinates of the points (P, P', P'', etc.) of intersection of the curve with the line parallel to OY and at a distance x to the right of OY or $-x$ to the left of OY, according as x is positive or negative.

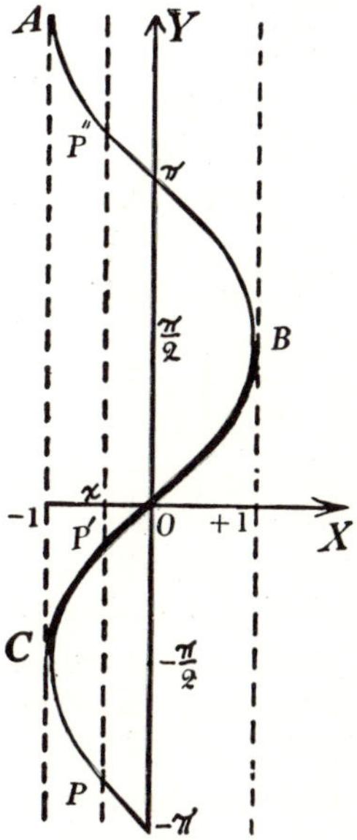

Fig. 95

Of the points, just mentioned, which have any given abscissa x (between -1 and $+1$), a single such point lies in the portion BOC (drawn heavier) of the curve and that point evidently has an ordinate which is numerically less than the ordinates of all of the remaining points of the curve having the same abscissa. This numerically least angle or arc whose sine is x is called the *principal value* of arc sin x or $\sin^{-1} x$ and designated by Arc sin x or $\text{Sin}^{-1} x$. By definition it lies between $-\pi/2$ and $+\pi/2$. For example,

$$\text{Arc sin } (-1/2) = -30° = -\pi/6.$$

Similarly, the principal value of an inverse tangent, cotangent, or cosecant is the value between $-\pi/2$ and $+\pi/2$, and the first letter in its name is written with a capital.

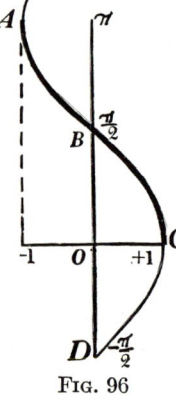

Fig. 96

But the principal value of an inverse cosine or secant is the positive value $\leq \pi$. For example,

$$\text{Arc cos } (-1/2) = 120° = 2\pi/3.$$

The reason for the latter definition becomes clear from the graph (Fig. 96) of $y = $ arc cos x. The portion BCD of the curve whose ordinates lie between $-\pi/2$ and $+\pi/2$ contains only points with positive abscissas. But any given number x, between -1 and $+1$, is the abscissa of a point of the portion ABC (drawn heavier), whose ordinate lies between 0 and π.

EXAMPLE 1. Prove that sec $(2 \cot^{-1} 2) = 5/3$.

Solution. Let A be any angle whose cotangent is 2. We are to find sec $2A$, given cot $A = 2$. Since $\csc^2 A = 1 + \cot^2 A = 5$, we get $\sin^2 A = 1/5$ and cos $2A = 1 - 2 \sin^2 A = 3/5$. Hence sec $2A = 5/3$.

EXAMPLE 2. If x and y are numerically <1, prove that

$$\sin (\text{Arc sin } x + \text{Arc sin } y) = x\sqrt{1-y^2} + y\sqrt{1-x^2}.$$

Solution. Write $A = $ Arc sin x, $B = $ Arc sin y, so that A and B are positive or negative acute angles. Since sin $A = x$, sin $B = y$, we have

$$\cos A = +\sqrt{1-x^2}, \cos B = +\sqrt{1-y^2},$$
$$\sin(A+B) = \sin A \cos B + \cos A \sin B = x\sqrt{1-y^2} + y\sqrt{1-x^2}.$$

Exercises on Inverse Functions

1. From the graphs (Figs. 88–90) of the tangent, cotangent, cosecant, and secant, derive the graphs of their inverse functions and justify the definition of their principal values.

Find the values of

2. $\sin(\text{Arc tan } 1)$.   3. $\sec(\text{Arc tan } 2)$.   4. $\cos(\text{Arc cos } \frac{1}{2})$.
5. $\tan(2 \cos^{-1} \frac{1}{2})$.   6. $\cos(2 \tan^{-1} \frac{1}{3}\sqrt{3})$.   7. $\tan(\sin^{-1} \frac{2}{3})$.

Prove the following formulas (with x and y numerically <1 in Exs. 8, 10, 12, 14 and 15):

8. $\cos(2 \cos^{-1} x) = 2x^2 - 1$.   9. $\tan(2 \tan^{-1} c) = \dfrac{2c}{1-c^2}$.
10. $\text{Arc cos } x = \frac{1}{2} \text{Arc cos}(2x^2 - 1)$ if $0 \lesseqgtr x \lesseqgtr 1$.
11. $\text{Arc sin } \frac{1}{2} + \text{Arc sin } 1 = \dfrac{2\pi}{3}$.
12. $\sin^{-1} x + \cos^{-1} x = \frac{1}{2}\pi$.
13. $\sin^{-1} 1 - \sin^{-1} \frac{1}{2} = \cos^{-1} \frac{1}{2}$.
14. $\cos(\sin^{-1} x - \sin^{-1} y) = xy + \sqrt{1-x^2} \cdot \sqrt{1-y^2}$.
15. $\sin(\sin^{-1} x - \sin^{-1} y) = x\sqrt{1-y^2} - y\sqrt{1-x^2}$.
16. $\text{Tan}^{-1} x - \text{Tan}^{-1} y = \text{Tan}^{-1} \dfrac{x-y}{1+xy}$, if $x>0, y>0$.
17. $2 \text{Tan}^{-1} \frac{2}{3} = \text{Tan}^{-1} \frac{12}{5}$.   18. $3 \sin^{-1} \frac{1}{4} = \sin^{-1} \frac{11}{16}$.
19. $\sin^{-1} \frac{3}{5} + \sin^{-1} \frac{8}{17} = \sin^{-1} \frac{77}{85}$.   20. $\cos^{-1} \frac{4}{5} + \cos^{-1} \frac{12}{13} = \cos^{-1} \frac{33}{65}$.
21. $\text{Arc tan } \frac{1}{2} + \text{Arc tan } \frac{1}{3} = \dfrac{\pi}{4}$.   22. $\text{Tan}^{-1} \frac{1}{6} + \text{Tan}^{-1} \frac{5}{7} = \dfrac{\pi}{4}$.
23. $2 \text{Tan}^{-1} \frac{1}{3} + \text{Tan}^{-1} \frac{1}{7} = \dfrac{\pi}{4}$.   24. $\text{Tan}^{-1} \frac{1}{2} + \text{Tan}^{-1} 2 = \dfrac{\pi}{2}$.

25.* $\text{Tan}^{-1} x + \text{Tan}^{-1} y = n\pi + \text{Tan}^{-1} \dfrac{x+y}{1-xy}$, where $n = 1$ if x and y are positive and $xy > 1$; $n = -1$ if x and y are negative and $xy > 1$; $n = 0$ in all remaining cases.

26.* $\text{Arc tan } 5 + \text{Arc tan}(-3) = \text{Arc tan } \frac{1}{8}$.

Solve and discuss the two equations:

27.* $\cos^{-1} x + \cos^{-1}(1-x) = \cos^{-1}(-x)$.
28.* $\tan^{-1}(x+1) + \tan^{-1}(x-1) = \tan^{-1} \frac{8}{31}$.

LIST AND INDEX OF FORMULAS

$$\csc A = \frac{1}{\sin A}, \qquad \sec A = \frac{1}{\cos A}, \qquad \cot A = \frac{1}{\tan A}.$$

$$\sin^2 A + \cos^2 A = 1, \qquad \tan A = \frac{\sin A}{\cos A}, \qquad \cot A = \frac{\cos A}{\sin A},$$

$$\sec^2 A = 1 + \tan^2 A, \qquad \csc^2 A = 1 + \cot^2 A \qquad \text{(pp. 13, 109)}.$$

$$\log MN = \log M + \log N, \qquad \log N^p = p \log N,$$

$$\log \frac{M}{N} = \log M - \log N, \qquad \log \sqrt[r]{N} = \frac{\log N}{r} \qquad \text{(pp. 36, 37)}.$$

In a right triangle with hypotenuse c and leg b adjacent to $\angle A$,

$$\tan \tfrac{1}{2} A = \sqrt{\frac{c-b}{c+b}} \qquad \text{(p. 51)};$$

$$\text{Area} = \tfrac{1}{2} ab = \tfrac{1}{2} a^2 \cot A = \tfrac{1}{2} c^2 \sin A \cos A \qquad \text{(p. 53)}.$$

Navigation (D = distance, C = course, pp. 62, 67, 69, 74):
    diff. lat. $= D \cos C$,   dep. $= D \sin C$,
    dep. $=$ (diff. longitude) $\times$ (cos lat.),
    diff. long. $=$ (merid. diff. lat.) $\times \tan C$.

Surveying (D = length of course, B = true bearing, p. 84):
    lat. $= D \cos B$,   dep. $= D \sin B$.

$\sin(90°-x) = \cos x, \quad \cos(90°-x) = \sin x, \quad \tan(90°-x) = \cot x,$
$\sin(90°+x) = \cos x, \quad \cos(90°+x) = -\sin x, \quad \tan(90°+x) = -\cot x,$
$\sin(180°-x) = \sin x, \quad \cos(180°-x) = -\cos x, \quad \tan(180°-x) = -\tan x,$
$\sin(180°+x) = -\sin x, \quad \cos(180°+x) = -\cos x, \quad \tan(180°+x) = \tan x,$
$\sin(360°-x) = \sin(-x) = -\sin x, \quad \sin(270° \pm x) = -\cos x,$
$\cos(360°-x) = \cos(-x) = \cos x, \quad \cos(270° \pm x) = \pm \sin x,$
$\tan(360°-x) = \tan(-x) = -\tan x, \quad \tan(270° \pm x) = \mp \cot x.$

Analogous formulas for secant, cosecant, cotangent, pp. 17, 111–4, 134–7.

Law of sines: $\dfrac{a}{\sin A} = \dfrac{b}{\sin B} = \dfrac{c}{\sin C}$ (p. 115).

Law of cosines: $a^2 = b^2 + c^2 - 2bc \cos A$ (p. 126).

Law of tangents: $\dfrac{a-b}{a+b} = \dfrac{\tan \tfrac{1}{2}(A-B)}{\tan \tfrac{1}{2}(A+B)} = \dfrac{\tan \tfrac{1}{2}(A-B)}{\cot \tfrac{1}{2} C}$ (p. 117).

Half-angle formulas (pp. 130–1, 145):

$$\tan \tfrac{1}{2}A = \frac{r}{s-a}, \quad \tan \tfrac{1}{2}B = \frac{r}{s-b}, \quad \tan \tfrac{1}{2}C = \frac{r}{s-c},$$

$$s = \tfrac{1}{2}(a+b+c), \quad r = \sqrt{\frac{(s-a)(s-b)(s-c)}{s}};$$

$$\sin \tfrac{1}{2}A = \sqrt{\frac{(s-b)(s-c)}{bc}}, \quad \cos \tfrac{1}{2}A = \sqrt{\frac{s(s-a)}{bc}}, \quad \tan \tfrac{1}{2}A = \sqrt{\frac{(s-b)(s-c)}{s(s-a)}}.$$

Area of triangle $= \tfrac{1}{2}bc \sin A = \sqrt{s(s-a)(s-b)(s-c)}$ (pp. 115, 129).

Addition and subtraction theorems (pp. 133, 136, 138–9):

$$\sin(A+B) = \sin A \cos B + \cos A \sin B,$$
$$\cos(A+B) = \cos A \cos B - \sin A \sin B,$$
$$\sin(A-B) = \sin A \cos B - \cos A \sin B,$$
$$\cos(A-B) = \cos A \cos B + \sin A \sin B,$$

$$\tan(A+B) = \frac{\tan A + \tan B}{1 - \tan A \tan B}, \quad \cot(A+B) = \frac{\cot A \cot B - 1}{\cot A + \cot B},$$

$$\tan(A-B) = \frac{\tan A - \tan B}{1 + \tan A \tan B}, \quad \cot(A-B) = \frac{\cot A \cot B + 1}{\cot B - \cot A}.$$

Functions of double angles (pp. 140–1):

$$\sin 2A = 2 \sin A \cos A, \qquad \cos 2A = \cos^2 A - \sin^2 A,$$
$$\cos 2A = 1 - 2 \sin^2 A, \qquad \cos 2A = 2 \cos^2 A - 1,$$
$$\tan 2A = \frac{2 \tan A}{1 - \tan^2 A}, \qquad \cot 2A = \frac{\cot^2 A - 1}{2 \cot A}.$$

Functions of half angles (p. 144):

$$\sin \frac{x}{2} = \pm \sqrt{\frac{1 - \cos x}{2}}, \qquad \cos \frac{x}{2} = \pm \sqrt{\frac{1 + \cos x}{2}},$$

$$\tan \frac{x}{2} = \pm \sqrt{\frac{1 - \cos x}{1 + \cos x}}, \qquad \cot \frac{x}{2} = \pm \sqrt{\frac{1 + \cos x}{1 - \cos x}}.$$

Sums or differences expressed as products (p. 146):

$$\sin x + \sin y = 2 \sin \tfrac{1}{2}(x+y) \cos \tfrac{1}{2}(x-y),$$
$$\sin x - \sin y = 2 \cos \tfrac{1}{2}(x+y) \sin \tfrac{1}{2}(x-y),$$
$$\cos x + \cos y = 2 \cos \tfrac{1}{2}(x+y) \cos \tfrac{1}{2}(x-y),$$
$$\cos x - \cos y = -2 \sin \tfrac{1}{2}(x+y) \sin \tfrac{1}{2}(x-y).$$

Miscellaneous formulas for heights and distances (pp. 55, 57, 120, 137–8), trajectories (p. 143), multiple angles (p. 141), length of arc of circle (p. 158), π radians $= 180°$ (p. 159).

INDEX
INCLUDING INDEX TO DEFINITIONS

Abscissa, 103.
Absolute error, **3.**
Acre, 82.
Addition theorem for cosine, 136.
  for sine, 133.
  for tangent, cotangent, 138.
Altitude, 115.
Angle, general, 105.
  in trigonometric position, 106.
  measurement of, 99.
  negative, 105.
  of depression, 5, 99.
  of elevation, 5, 99.
  of incidence, 31.
  of refraction, 32.
  positive, 105.
  quadrant of, 106.
Area of field, 83, 86.
  oblique triangle, 115, 128–9.
  right triangle, 53.
Axis, 104.
Azimuth, 100.

Balancing surveys, 84, 101.
Bearing, 83, 93, 94.
  reverse, 94.

Casting out nines, **51.**
Chain, 82.
Characteristic, **39.**
Co-function, 17.
Collimation, 99.
Compass, 61, 76.
  circle, 92.
  course, 77.
  surveyor's, 91.
Complementary angle, 16.
Component force, 30, 131.
Coördinates, 103.
Cosecant, 7, 107.
  curve, 155.
Cosine, 7, 107.
  arc, 164.
  curve, 152–3.
  inverse, 164.
  law of, 126.
Cotangent, 7, 107.
  curve, 155.
Course, 61, 77, 83.
  made good, 65.
Critical angle, 33.
Cross wires, 98.

Dead reckoning, 59, 79.
Decagon, 54.
Declination, 94.
Deflection angle, 100.
Departure, 62, 84.
  in mid lat., 69.

Deviation, 76.
Direct angle, 100.
Directed line, 152.
Double meridian dist., 86.

Equator, 60.
Error, 23, 51, 52.
  of closure, 86.
Extraction of roots, 37, **41.**

Force, 29, 131.
Function, 6.

Grade, 5.
Graphs, 150.
Gunter's chain, 82.

Half-angle formulas, 130.
Harmonic curve, 156.
Heights and distances, 9, 28, 55, 137.
Hexagon, 54.
Horizontal angle, 4, 99.
  line, 4.
  plane, 4.
  range, 143.

Identities, 16, 110.
Index laws, 34.
  of refraction, 32.
Interpolation, 19, 27, 63.
Inverse functions, 164.
Isosceles triangle, 53.

Kepler's equation, 162.
Knot, 80.

Latitude, 60, 84.
  in, 62.
Law of cosines, 126.
  sines, 115.
  tangents, 117.
Leeway, 76.
Level, 92, 98.
Limb of transit, 98.
Logarithm, 36.
Logarithmic scales, 43.
Longitude, 60, 66.

Made good, 65.
Magnetic, 94.
Mantissa, 39.
Maps, 71, 88.
Mercator chart, 71.
  sailing, 73.
Meridian, 59.
  distance, 86.
  magnetic, 76.
  prime, 60.

INDEX

Meridional parts, 72.
    difference of lat., 74.
Middle latitude sailing, 68.
Mil, 160.
Mollweide's equations, 117.

Natural functions, 19.
Nautical astronomy, 59.
    mile, 60.
Navigation, 59.

Oblique triangle, 115.
Octagon, 54.
Ordinate, 103.
Origin, 104.

Parallel of latitude, 60.
    sailing, 66.
Parallelogram of forces, 29.
Parts of triangle, 21.
Patent log, 61.
Pentagon, 53.
Perimeter, 129.
Piloting, 59.
Plane Sailing, 62.
Plotting, 88, 104.
Plumb line, 4.
Points of compass, 61.
Poles, 59, 94.
Polygon, 53.
Protractor, 1.

Quadrants, 106.

Radian, 158.
Radius vector, 104.
    of inscribed circle, 129.
Rational, 35.
Reciprocal, 7.
Refraction of light, 31.
Relative error, 3.
Resultant of forces, 29, 131.
Rhumb line, 68, 73.
Right triangle, 19, 48, 125.

Sailing, Mercator's, 73.
    middle latitude, 68.
    parallel, 66.
    plane, 62.
    traverse, 64.
Secant, 7, 107.
    curve, 155.
Sight vane, 91.
Significant, 38.

Sine, 6, 7, 107.
    arc, 165.
    curve, 152–3.
    inverse, 165.
    law of, 115.
    of small angle, 161.
Slide rule, 44.
Slope, 5.
Spirit level, 4.
Square-ruled paper, 2, 104.
Stadia wires, 99.
Statute mile, 60.
Subtraction theorems for sine and cosine, 136.
    for tangent and cotangent, 138.
Surveying, 82.
    instruments, 89.

Tangent, 5, 7, 107.
    curve, 154.
    law of, 117.
    of 90°, 155.
    of small angle, 161.
Tape, 82.
Telescope, 96.
Trajectory, 142.
Transit, 96.
Traverse, 99.
    sailing, 64.
    table, 26, 63.
Trigonometric equations, 147, 156, 162.
Trigonometric functions, 6, 107.
    inverse of, 164.
    line representation, 150.
    of double angle, 140.
    of half angle, 144.
    of multiple angle, 141.
    of several angles, 133.
    reduced to acute angles, 111.
    sum of, expressed as a product, 145.
True bearing, 83.
    course, 61, 77.

Undefined, 108, 154.
Unit's place, 38.

Variation, 76, 94.
    charts, 95.
Vernier, 89, 95.
    double, 90.
    plate, 96.
Vertical angle, 4.
    circle, 98.
    line, 4.
    plane, 4.

ANSWERS
TO CERTAIN OF THE FIRST FIVE EXERCISES OF EACH SET

Pages 8, 9

1. $\sin 45° = \cos 45° = \frac{1}{2}\sqrt{2}$, $\tan 45° = \cot 45° = 1$, $\sec 45° = \csc 45° = \sqrt{2}$.
2. $\sin 60° = \frac{1}{2}\sqrt{3}$, $\cos 60° = \frac{1}{2}$, $\tan 60° = \sqrt{3}$, $\csc 60° = \frac{2}{3}\sqrt{3}$, $\sec 60° = 2$, $\cot 60° = \frac{1}{3}\sqrt{3}$.
3. $\sin 30° = \frac{1}{2}$, $\cos 30° = \frac{1}{2}\sqrt{3}$, $\tan 30° = \frac{1}{3}\sqrt{3}$, $\csc 30° = 2$, $\sec 30° = \frac{2}{3}\sqrt{3}$, $\cot 30° = \sqrt{3}$.
5. $\sin = \frac{3}{5}$, $\cos = \frac{4}{5}$, $\tan = \frac{3}{4}$, $\cot = \frac{4}{3}$, $\sec = \frac{5}{4}$, $\csc = \frac{5}{3}$.

Pages 10, 11

1. $40(3+\sqrt{3})$.   2. $6+11\sqrt{3}$.   3. 250.

Page 12

1. 53°, see ans. 1, page 14.   3. $67\frac{1}{2}°$, $\frac{5}{12}$, $1\frac{3}{12}$.   5. 53°, 20 ft.

Page 14

1. $\sin A = \frac{4}{5}$, $\cos A = \frac{3}{5}$, $\tan A = \frac{4}{3}$, $\cot A = \frac{3}{4}$, $\sec A = \frac{5}{3}$, $\csc A = \frac{5}{4}$.
3. $\sin A = \frac{8}{17}$, $\cos A = \frac{15}{17}$, $\tan A = \frac{8}{15}$, $\cot A = \frac{15}{8}$, $\sec A = \frac{17}{15}$, $\csc A = \frac{17}{8}$.

Pages 17, 18

1. $\cos 25°$, $\sin 70°$, $\cot 34° 40'$, $\tan 7° 48'$, $\csc 23°$, $\sec 23°$.
2. $\sin 70° = \cos 20°$, $\cos 70° = \sin 20°$, $\tan 70° = \cot 20°$.   5. 45°.

Page 21

1. (a) 0.3156, 0.9488, 0.3327, 3.006   3. 2.0051.
4. $x = 27° 10'$, $y = 40° 3'$, $z = 64° 47'$, $w = 82° 58'$.

Pages 24, 25

1. $a = 281.9$, $b = 102.6$.   2. $a = 10.72$, $c = 41.41$.
5. $A = 19° 12'$, $B = 70° 48'$, $a = 5.916$.

Pages 28, 29

1. 60.   2. 901.1.   5. 888.4.

Page 31

1. 13 lbs., 22° 37'.   3. 85.02 lbs.   4. 6.12 miles.

Page 33

1. 4.49 ft.   3. 56.28 ft.

Pages 37, 38

1. $5, -1, -3, \frac{2}{3}$.   2. 2.   3. (b) 1.38021,   (c) 0.35218.

Pages 41, 42

1. 141.8, 0.01668, 0.0002154.   2. 464.7.   3. 4.152.

ANSWERS

Page 47
1. $9.7018-10$, $9.8645-10$, $9.9689-10$.
2. $x = 42° 57'$, $y = 24° 45'$, $z = 87° 5\frac{1}{2}'$, $w = 70° 27'$.

Page 52
1. $a = 536.6$, $b = 1006$.   2. $b = 130.1$, $c = 162.3$.
3. $A = 31° 24'$, $B = 58° 36'$, $b = 3666$.

Page 53
1. 297.4.   2. 857.7.
5. $a = 23.2$, $c = 30.63$, $A = 49° 14'$, $B = 40° 46'$.

Pages 54, 55
1. $A = 67° 22.9'$, $V = 45° 14.2'$, $h = 264.0$, $\triangle = 29040$.
2. $r = 41.11$, $h = 33.72$, $\triangle = 793.0$.

Pages 56–58
1. 69.95.   2. 0.298.   3. 1842 (approx.).

Pages 62, 63
1. 16.4 E, $43° 40.3'$ N.   3. 199.7, 58.4 W.

Page 64
1. $9° 21'$, 86.1 2. $15° 31'$, 93.4.

Pages 65, 66
1. S $24° 21'$ E, 69.6.   5. $33° 44'$ S, N $24° 46'$ W, 224.4.

Pages 67, 68
1. 125.0 E.   3. $166° 50'$ E.

Page 70
1. N $67° 29'$ E, 295.5.   3. $49° 10'$ S, $176°$ W.

Pages 75, 76
2. S $40° 47.2'$ E, 4754.   5. $47° 10'$ N, $32° 15'$ W.

Page 78, top
1. $12°$.   4. $23°$.

Page 78, bottom
1. $34° 49'$ N, 39.3 W.   2. 600, N $56° 20'$ W.

Pages 79–81
1. $45° 1.9'$ N, $13° 18.7'$ W.   3. $51° 19.5'$ N, $24° 9'$ W.

Page 88
1. 2.370.   3. 15.137.

Pages 95, 96
1. N $72°$ E.   2. S $86° 45'$ W.   5. $8° 50'$ W.

Pages 100, 101
1. S $18° 5'$ W, N $38°$ W.   2. S $57° 22'$ E, N $75° 26'$ E, S $56° 14'$ E.

ANSWERS

Page 102
1. 12.101 acres.
3. 226330 sq. ft. = 5.1958 acres.

Page 104
1. 5, center at origin and radius 5.
4. 100.

Page 106
1. Third, third, first, third, first.
5. 3819° 44′.

Pages 109, 110

2.

	135°	150°	210°	225°	240°	300°	315°	330°
sin	$\dfrac{1}{\sqrt{2}}$	$\dfrac{1}{2}$	$-\dfrac{1}{2}$	$\dfrac{-1}{\sqrt{2}}$	$\dfrac{-\sqrt{3}}{2}$	$\dfrac{-\sqrt{3}}{2}$	$\dfrac{-1}{\sqrt{2}}$	$-\dfrac{1}{2}$
cos	$\dfrac{-1}{\sqrt{2}}$	$\dfrac{-\sqrt{3}}{2}$	$\dfrac{-\sqrt{3}}{2}$	$\dfrac{-1}{\sqrt{2}}$	$-\dfrac{1}{2}$	$\dfrac{1}{2}$	$\dfrac{1}{\sqrt{2}}$	$\dfrac{\sqrt{3}}{2}$
tan	-1	$\dfrac{-1}{\sqrt{3}}$	$\dfrac{1}{\sqrt{3}}$	1	$\sqrt{3}$	$-\sqrt{3}$	-1	$\dfrac{-1}{\sqrt{3}}$

Page 114
1. -0.8660. 2. -0.2679. 3. -0.2588.

Pages 118–120
1. $C = 76°\ 48'$, $b = 74.17$, $c = 118.9$. 5. $A = 35°2.6'$, $B = 82°\ 25.4'$, $c = 228.7$.

Page 126
1. One. 2. Two. 4. None. 5. Two.

Page 128
1. $b^2 = a^2 + c^2 - 2ac \cos B$, $\cos B = (a^2 + c^2 - b^2)/(2ac)$.
2. $A = 28°\ 57'$, $B = 46°\ 34'$, $C = 104°\ 29'$.
5. $a = 6.456$, $B = 80°\ 46'$, $C = 63°\ 48'$.

Page 131, top
1. 2.905, see ans. 2, page 128. 5. 630.
2. 1499, $A = 46°\ 26.3'$, $B = 75°\ 13.5'$, $C = 58°\ 20.2'$.

Pages 131, bottom, 132
1. 56° 15′, 29° 55′. 2. 1114, 18° 23′. 4. 640, 364.

Page 136
1. $\tfrac{1}{4}\sqrt{2}(\sqrt{3} - 1)$, $\tfrac{1}{4}\sqrt{2}(\sqrt{3} + 1)$. 5. $\tfrac{63}{65}, \tfrac{56}{65}$.

Page 138
3. 2.467. 4. 457.8.

Pages 139, 140
2. $2 + \sqrt{3}$, $2 - \sqrt{3}$. 4. $\tfrac{6}{7}, \tfrac{2}{9}$. 5. 16° 6′.

ANSWERS

Pages 141, 142
2. $\frac{24}{25}, \frac{7}{25}, \frac{24}{7}$. **4.** $4\cos^3 A - 3\cos A$.

Pages 143, 144
2. 108250. **3.** $25°, 65°$. **5.** 36.95.

Page 145
1. $\frac{1}{2}\sqrt{2-\sqrt{3}}, \frac{1}{2}\sqrt{2+\sqrt{3}}, 2-\sqrt{3}$.

Page 146
2. $2\sin 2x \cos x$. **3.** $2\sin 2x \sin x$.

Page 149
1. $120°, 240°$. **4.** $60°, 300°$. **5.** $90°, 120°, 240°, 270°$

Page 156
3. $(a), (b)$ $0, 180°, 360°$; (c) $90°, 270°$.

Page 157
1. $16° 51', 84° 9'$ (maximum 0.6636 at $x = 219° 26'$).

Pages 159–161
1. $\pi/4 = 0.7854, \pi/3, -\frac{3}{2}\pi$. **5.** 1.5.

Page 162
1. 184.3 ft. **3.** $1° 31'$. **4.** 2192 miles.

Page 164
1. 18.36. **2.** $101° 12'$. **5.** $115° 47.6'$.

Page 167
2. $1/\sqrt{2}$. **3.** $\sqrt{5}$. **5.** $-\sqrt{3}$.

TABLES

	PAGE
EXAMPLES SHOWING HOW THE TABLES ARE USED	2
TABLES I, II. NATURAL SINES AND COSINES	3
TABLES III, IV, V. NATURAL TANGENTS AND COTANGENTS . . .	5
TABLE VI. TRAVERSE TABLE	8
TABLE VII. LOGARITHMS OF NUMBERS	26
TABLE VIII. LOGARITHMS OF THE TRIGONOMETRIC FUNCTIONS .	30
TABLE IX. MERIDIONAL PARTS	35

Examples Showing How the Tables Are Used

Examples. Find by Table I sin 25° 23′ and cos 64° 37′.

Angle < 45°
degrees at *left*
minutes at *top*

sin 25° 20′ = 0.4279
sin 25° 30′ = 0.4305
_____

$\frac{3}{10}$ × .0026 =
To the upper number *add*   .0008
∴ sin 25° 23′ = 0.4287

Angle > 45°
degrees at *right*
minutes at *bottom*

cos 64° 30′ = 0.4305
cos 64° 40′ = 0.4279
_____

$\frac{7}{10}$ × .0026 =
From the upper number *subtract*   .0018
∴ cos 64° 37′ = 0.4287

Or in P.P. tablette headed 26, read entry 18 opposite to 7.

Example. Given cot x = 2, find the acute ∠x by Table V.

cot 26° 30′ = 2.006
cot 26° 40′ = 1.991
_____
   .015

2.006 − 2 = .006
$\frac{6}{15}$ × 10′ = 4′, x = 26° 34′.

Traverse Table VI gives, for each ∠A and each hypotenuse, distance, or number D, the lengths of the adjacent and opposite legs of the right triangle, or the latitude and departure, or the products $D\cos A$ and $D\sin A$.

For A = 44° and D = $\begin{cases} 85, \text{ adj.} = 61.14, \text{ opp.} = 59.05 \\ 300, \quad\quad\quad 215.80 \quad\quad\quad 208.40 \\ 385, \quad\quad\quad \overline{276.94} \quad\quad\quad \overline{267.45} \end{cases}$

Or multiply by 5 the entires adj. = 55.39, opp. = 53.49 for D = 385/5 = 77.

When seeking, by Table VII, the logarithm of a positive number N, use pages 26, 27 if the first digit of N is 1. When finding the mantissa (decimal part) of log N, ignore the decimal point in N. To the mantissa, prefix + p if the first significant digit of N lies p places to the left of unit's place in N, but prefix $\bar{p}$ if it lies p places to the right. For example,

log 16.17 = 1.2087,   log 0.01617 = $\bar{2}$.2087.

In Table VIII employ the labels at the *top* (including 9. or 10.) when reading angles at the *left*, but the labels at the *bottom* when reading angles at the *right*. Always annex −10. For example,

log sin 10° 30′ = 9.2606 − 10,   log tan 75° 40′ = 10.5926 − 10.

TABLE I. NATURAL SINES

°	0'	10'	20'	30'	40'	50'	60'	
0	0.0000	0029	0058	0087	0116	0145	0175	89
1	0.0175	0204	0233	0262	0291	0320	0349	88
2	0.0349	0378	0407	0436	0465	0494	0523	87
3	0.0523	0552	0581	0610	0640	0669	0698	86
4	0.0698	0727	0756	0785	0814	0843	0872	85
5	0.0872	0901	0929	0958	0987	1016	1045	84
6	0.1045	1074	1103	1132	1161	1190	1219	83
7	0.1219	1248	1276	1305	1334	1363	1392	82
8	0.1392	1421	1449	1478	1507	1536	1564	81
9	0.1564	1593	1622	1650	1679	1708	1736	80
10	0.1736	1765	1794	1822	1851	1880	1908	79
11	0.1908	1937	1965	1994	2022	2051	2079	78
12	0.2079	2108	2136	2164	2193	2221	2250	77
13	0.2250	2278	2306	2334	2363	2391	2419	76
14	0.2419	2447	2476	2504	2532	2560	2588	75
15	0.2588	2616	2644	2672	2700	2728	2756	74
16	0.2756	2784	2812	2840	2868	2896	2924	73
17	0.2924	2952	2979	3007	3035	3062	3090	72
18	0.3090	3118	3145	3173	3201	3228	3256	71
19	0.3256	3283	3311	3338	3365	3393	3420	70
20	0.3420	3448	3475	3502	3529	3557	3584	69
21	0.3584	3611	3638	3665	3692	3719	3746	68
22	0.3746	3773	3800	3827	3854	3881	3907	67
23	0.3907	3934	3961	3987	4014	4041	4067	66
24	0.4067	4094	4120	4147	4173	4200	4226	65
25	0.4226	4253	4279	4305	4331	4358	4384	64
26	0.4384	4410	4436	4462	4488	4514	4540	63
27	0.4540	4566	4592	4617	4643	4669	4695	62
28	0.4695	4720	4746	4772	4797	4823	4848	61
29	0.4848	4874	4899	4924	4950	4975	5000	60
30	0.5000	5025	5050	5075	5100	5125	5150	59
31	0.5150	5175	5200	5225	5250	5275	5299	58
32	0.5299	5324	5348	5373	5398	5422	5446	57
33	0.5446	5471	5495	5519	5544	5568	5592	56
34	0.5592	5616	5640	5664	5688	5712	5736	55
35	0.5736	5760	5783	5807	5831	5854	5878	54
36	0.5878	5901	5925	5948	5972	5995	6018	53
37	0.6018	6041	6065	6088	6111	6134	6157	52
38	0.6157	6180	6202	6225	6248	6271	6293	51
39	0.6293	6316	6338	6361	6383	6406	6428	50
40	0.6428	6450	6472	6494	6517	6539	6561	49
41	0.6561	6583	6604	6626	6648	6670	6691	48
42	0.6691	6713	6734	6756	6777	6799	6820	47
43	0.6820	6841	6862	6884	6905	6926	6947	46
44	0.6947	6967	6988	7009	7030	7050	7071	45
	60'	50'	40'	30'	20'	10'	0'	°

NATURAL COSINES

P. P.

	29	28
1	3	3
2	6	6
3	9	8
4	12	11
5	15	14
6	17	17
7	20	20
8	23	22
9	26	25

	27	26
1	3	3
2	5	5
3	8	8
4	11	10
5	14	13
6	16	16
7	19	18
8	22	21
9	24	23

	25	24
1	3	2
2	5	5
3	8	7
4	10	10
5	13	12
6	15	14
7	18	17
8	20	19
9	23	22

	23	22
1	2	2
2	5	4
3	7	7
4	9	9
5	12	11
6	14	13
7	16	15
8	18	18
9	21	20

	21
1	2
2	4
3	6
4	8
5	11
6	13
7	15
8	17
9	19

TABLE II. NATURAL COSINES

°	0′	10′	20′	30′	40′	50′	60′	
0	1.0000	1.	1.	1.	9999	9999	9998	89
1	0.9998	9998	9997	9997	96	95	94	88
2	94	93	92	90	89	88	86	87
3	86	85	83	81	80	78	76	86
4	76	74	71	69	67	64	62	85
5	62	59	57	54	51	48	45	84
6	45	42	39	36	32	29	25	83
7	25	9922	9918	9914	9911	9907	9903	82
8	0.9903	9899	9894	9890	9886	9881	9877	81
9	0.9877	9872	9868	9863	9858	9853	9848	80
10	0.9848	9843	9838	9833	9827	9822	9816	79
11	0.9816	9811	9805	9799	9793	9787	9781	78
12	0.9781	9775	9769	9763	9757	9750	9744	77
13	0.9744	9737	9730	9724	9717	9710	9703	76
14	0.9703	9696	9689	9681	9674	9667	9659	75
15	0.9659	9652	9644	9636	9628	9621	9613	74
16	0.9613	9605	9596	9588	9580	9572	9563	73
17	0.9563	9555	9546	9537	9528	9520	9511	72
18	0.9511	9502	9492	9483	9474	9465	9455	71
19	0.9455	9446	9436	9426	9417	9407	9397	70
20	0.9397	9387	9377	9367	9356	9346	9336	69
21	0.9336	9325	9315	9304	9293	9283	9272	68
22	0.9272	9261	9250	9239	9228	9216	9205	67
23	0.9205	9194	9182	9171	9159	9147	9135	66
24	0.9135	9124	9112	9100	9088	9075	9063	65
25	0.9063	9051	9038	9026	9013	9001	8988	64
26	0.8988	8975	8962	8949	8936	8923	8910	63
27	0.8910	8897	8884	8870	8857	8843	8829	62
28	0.8829	8816	8802	8788	8774	8760	8746	61
29	0.8746	8732	8718	8704	8689	8675	8660	60
30	0.8660	8646	8631	8616	8601	8587	8572	59
31	0.8572	8557	8542	8526	8511	8496	8480	58
32	0.8480	8465	8450	8434	8418	8403	8387	57
33	0.8387	8371	8355	8339	8323	8307	8290	56
34	0.8290	8274	8258	8241	8225	8208	8192	55
35	0.8192	8175	8158	8141	8124	8107	8090	54
36	0.8090	8073	8056	8039	8021	8004	7986	53
37	0.7986	7969	7951	7934	7916	7898	7880	52
38	0.7880	7862	7844	7826	7808	7790	7771	51
39	0.7771	7753	7735	7716	7698	7679	7660	50
40	0.7660	7642	7623	7604	7585	7566	7547	49
41	0.7547	7528	7509	7490	7470	7451	7431	48
42	0.7431	7412	7392	7373	7353	7333	7314	47
43	0.7314	7294	7274	7254	7234	7214	7193	46
44	0.7193	7173	7153	7133	7112	7092	7071	45
	60′	50′	40′	30′	20′	10′	0′	°

Do not use to find angle: see Art. 15.

NATURAL SINES

P. P.

	11	12
1	1	1
2	2	2
3	3	4
4	4	5
5	6	6
6	7	7
7	8	8
8	9	10
9	11	10

	13	14
1	1	1
2	3	3
3	4	4
4	5	6
5	7	7
6	8	8
7	9	10
8	10	11
9	12	13

	15	16
1	2	2
2	3	3
3	5	5
4	6	6
5	8	8
6	9	10
7	11	11
8	12	13
9	14	14

	17	18
1	2	2
2	3	4
3	5	5
4	7	7
5	9	9
6	10	11
7	12	13
8	14	14
9	15	16

	19	21
1	2	2
2	4	4
3	6	6
4	8	8
5	10	11
6	11	13
7	13	15
8	15	17
9	17	19

TABLE III. NATURAL COTANGENTS

°	′	0′	1′	2′	3′	4′	5′	6′	7′	8′	9′		
0	0		3438	1719	1146	859.4	687.5	573.0	491.1	429.7	382.0		50
	10	343.8	312.5	286.5	264.4	245.6	229.2	214.9	202.2	191.0	180.9		40
	20	171.9	163.7	156.3	149.5	143.2	137.5	132.2	127.3	122.8	118.5		30
	30	114.6	110.9	107.4	104.2	101.1	98.22	95.49	92.91	90.46	88.14		20
	40	85.94	83.84	81.85	79.94	78.13	76.39	74.73	73.14	71.62	70.15		10
	50	68.75	67.40	66.11	64.86	63.66	62.50	61.38	60.31	59.27	58.26	**89**	0
1	0	57.29	56.35	55.44	54.56	53.71	52.88	52.08	51.30	50.55	49.82		50
	10	49.10	48.41	47.74	47.09	46.45	45.83	45.23	44.64	44.07	43.51		40
	20	42.96	42.43	41.92	41.41	40.92	40.44	39.97	39.51	39.06	38.62		30
	30	38.19	37.77	37.36	36.96	36.56	36.18	35.80	35.43	35.07	34.72		20
	40	34.37	34.03	33.69	33.37	33.05	32.73	32.42	32.12	31.82	31.53		10
	50	31.24	30.96	30.68	30.41	30.14	29.88	29.62	29.37	29.12	28.88	**88**	0
2	0	28.64	28.40	28.17	27.94	27.71	27.49	27.27	27.06	26.84	26.64		50
	10	26.43	26.23	26.03	25.83	25.64	25.45	25.26	25.08	24.90	24.72		40
	20	24.54	24.37	24.20	24.03	23.86	23.69	23.53	23.37	23.21	23.06		30
	30	22.90	22.75	22.60	22.45	22.31	22.16	22.02	21.88	21.74	21.61		20
	40	21.47	21.34	21.20	21.07	20.95	20.82	20.69	20.57	20.45	20.33		10
	50	20.21	20.09	19.97	19.85	19.74	19.63	19.52	19.41	19.30	19.19	**87**	0
3	0	19.08	18.98	18.87	18.77	18.67	18.56	18.46	18.37	18.27	18.17		50
	10	18.07	17.98	17.89	17.79	17.70	17.61	17.52	17.43	17.34	17.26		40
	20	17.17	17.08	17.00	16.92	16.83	16.75	16.67	16.59	16.51	16.43		30
	30	16.35	16.27	16.20	16.12	16.04	15.97	15.89	15.82	15.75	15.68	**86**	20
5	40	10.078	10.048	10.019	9.989	9.960	9.931	9.902	9.873	9.845	9.816		10
	50	9.788	9.760	9.732	9.704	9.677	9.649	9.622	9.595	9.568	9.541	**84**	0
6	0	9.514	9.488	9.461	9.435	9.409	9.383	9.357	9.332	9.306	9.281		50
	10	9.255	9.230	9.205	9.180	9.156	9.131	9.106	9.082	9.058	9.034		40
	20	9.010	8.986	8.962	8.939	8.915	8.892	8.869	8.846	8.823	8.800		30
	30	8.777	8.754	8.732	8.709	8.687	8.665	8.643	8.621	8.599	8.577		20
	40	8.556	8.534	8.513	8.491	8.470	8.449	8.428	8.407	8.386	8.366		10
	50	8.345	8.324	8.304	8.284	8.264	8.243	8.223	8.204	8.184	8.164	**83**	0
7	0	8.144	8.125	8.105	8.086	8.067	8.048	8.028	8.009	7.991	7.972		50
	10	7.953	7.934	7.916	7.897	7.879	7.861	7.842	7.824	7.806	7.788		40
	20	7.770	7.753	7.735	7.717	7.700	7.682	7.665	7.647	7.630	7.613		30
	30	7.596	7.579	7.562	7.545	7.528	7.511	7.495	7.478	7.462	7.445		20
	40	7.429	7.412	7.396	7.380	7.364	7.348	7.332	7.316	7.300	7.284		10
	50	7.269	7.253	7.238	7.222	7.207	7.191	7.176	7.161	7.146	7.130	**82**	0
8	0	7.115	7.100	7.085	7.071	7.056	7.041	7.026	7.012	6.997	6.983		50
	10	6.968	6.954	6.940	6.925	6.911	6.897	6.883	6.869	6.855	6.841		40
	20	6.827	6.813	6.799	6.786	6.772	6.758	6.745	6.731	6.718	6.704		30
	30	6.691	6.678	6.665	6.651	6.638	6.625	6.612	6.599	6.586	6.573		20
	40	6.561	6.548	6.535	6.522	6.510	6.497	6.485	6.472	6.460	6.447		10
	50	6.435	6.423	6.410	6.398	6.386	6.374	6.362	6.350	6.338	6.326	**81**	0
9	0	6.314	6.302	6.290	6.278	6.267	6.255	6.243	6.232	6.220	6.209		50
	10	6.197	6.186	6.174	6.163	6.152	6.140	6.129	6.118	6.107	6.096		40
	20	6.084	6.073	6.062	6.051	6.041	6.030	6.019	6.008	5.997	5.986		30
	30	5.976	5.965	5.954	5.944	5.933	5.923	5.912	5.902	5.892	5.881		20
	40	5.871	5.861	5.850	5.840	5.830	5.820	5.810	5.799	5.789	5.779		10
	50	5.769	5.759	5.749	5.740	5.730	5.720	5.710	5.700	5.691	5.681	**80**	0
10	0	5.671	5.662	5.652	5.642	5.633	5.623	5.614	5.605	5.595	5.586		50
	10	5.576	5.567	5.558	5.549	5.539	5.530	5.521	5.512	5.503	5.494		40
	20	5.485	5.475	5.466	5.458	5.449	5.440	5.431	5.422	5.413	5.404		30
	30	5.396	5.387	5.378	5.369	5.361	5.352	5.343	5.335	5.326	5.318		20
	40	5.309	5.301	5.292	5.284	5.276	5.267	5.259	5.250	5.242	5.234		10
	50	5.226	5.217	5.209	5.201	5.193	5.185	5.177	5.169	5.161	5.153	**79**	0
		10′	9′	8′	7′	6′	5′	4′	3′	2′	1′	°	′

NATURAL TANGENTS

TABLE IV. NATURAL TANGENTS

°	0′	10′	20′	30′	40′	50′	60′	
0	0.0000	0029	0058	0087	0116	0145	0175	89
1	0.0175	0204	0233	0262	0291	0320	0349	88
2	0.0349	0378	0407	0437	0466	0495	0524	87
3	0.0524	0553	0582	0612	0641	0670	0699	86
4	0.0699	0729	0758	0787	0816	0846	0875	85
5	0.0875	0904	0934	0963	0992	1022	1051	84
6	0.1051	1080	1110	1139	1169	1198	1228	83
7	0.1228	1257	1287	1317	1346	1376	1405	82
8	0.1405	1435	1465	1495	1524	1554	1584	81
9	0.1584	1614	1644	1673	1703	1733	1763	80
10	0.1763	1793	1823	1853	1883	1914	1944	79
11	0.1944	1974	2004	2035	2065	2095	2126	78
12	0.2126	2156	2186	2217	2247	2278	2309	77
13	0.2309	2339	2370	2401	2432	2462	2493	76
14	0.2493	2524	2555	2586	2617	2648	2679	75
15	0.2679	2711	2742	2773	2805	2836	2867	74
16	0.2867	2899	2931	2962	2994	3026	3057	73
17	0.3057	3089	3121	3153	3185	3217	3249	72
18	0.3249	3281	3314	3346	3378	3411	3443	71
19	0.3443	3476	3508	3541	3574	3607	3640	70
20	0.3640	3673	3706	3739	3772	3805	3839	69
21	0.3839	3872	3906	3939	3973	4006	4040	68
22	0.4040	4074	4108	4142	4176	4210	4245	67
23	0.4245	4279	4314	4348	4383	4417	4452	66
24	0.4452	4487	4522	4557	4592	4628	4663	65
25	0.4663	4699	4734	4770	4806	4841	4877	64
26	0.4877	4913	4950	4986	5022	5059	5095	63
27	0.5095	5132	5169	5206	5243	5280	5317	62
28	0.5317	5354	5392	5430	5467	5505	5543	61
29	0.5543	5581	5619	5658	5696	5735	5774	60
30	0.5774	5812	5851	5890	5930	5969	6009	59
31	0.6009	6048	6088	6128	6168	6208	6249	58
32	0.6249	6289	6330	6371	6412	6453	6494	57
33	0.6494	6536	6577	6619	6661	6703	6745	56
34	0.6745	6787	6830	6873	6916	6959	7002	55
35	0.7002	7046	7089	7133	7177	7221	7265	54
36	0.7265	7310	7355	7400	7445	7490	7536	53
37	0.7536	7581	7627	7673	7720	7766	7813	52
38	0.7813	7860	7907	7954	8002	8050	8098	51
39	0.8098	8146	8195	8243	8292	8342	8391	50
40	0.8391	8441	8491	8541	8591	8642	8693	49
41	0.8693	8744	8796	8847	8899	8952	9004	48
42	0.9004	9057	9110	9163	9217	9271	9325	47
43	0.9325	9380	9435	9490	9545	9601	9657	46
44	0.9657	9713	9770	9827	9884	9942	1.	45
°	60′	50′	40′	30′	20′	10′	0′	°

NATURAL COTANGENTS

P. P.

	29	31	32	33	34
1	3	3	3	3	3
2	6	6	6	7	7
3	9	9	10	10	10
4	12	12	13	13	14
5	15	16	16	17	17
6	17	19	19	20	20
7	20	22	22	23	24
8	23	25	26	26	27
9	26	28	29	30	31

	35	36	37	38	39
1	4	4	4	4	4
2	7	7	7	8	8
3	11	11	11	11	12
4	14	14	15	15	16
5	18	18	19	19	20
6	21	22	22	23	23
7	25	25	26	27	27
8	28	29	30	30	31
9	32	32	33	34	35

	41	42	43	44	45
1	4	4	4	4	5
2	8	8	9	9	9
3	12	13	13	13	14
4	16	17	17	18	18
5	21	21	22	22	23
6	25	25	26	26	27
7	29	29	30	31	32
8	33	34	34	35	36
9	37	38	39	40	41

	46	47	48	49	51	52
1	5	5	5	5	5	5
2	9	9	10	10	10	10
3	14	14	14	15	15	16
4	18	19	19	20	20	21
5	23	24	24	25	26	26
6	28	28	29	29	31	31
7	32	33	34	34	36	36
8	37	38	38	39	41	42
9	41	42	43	44	46	47

	53	54	55	56	57	58
1	5	5	6	6	6	6
2	11	11	11	11	11	12
3	16	16	17	17	17	17
4	21	22	22	22	23	23
5	27	27	28	28	29	29
6	32	32	33	34	34	35
7	37	38	39	39	40	41
8	42	43	44	45	46	46
9	48	49	50	50	51	52

TABLE V.   NATURAL COTANGENTS

P. P.

	79	77	74	72	68
1	8	8	7	7	7
2	16	16	15	14	14
3	24	23	22	22	20
4	32	31	30	29	27
5	40	39	37	36	34
6	48	46	44	43	41
7	56	54	52	51	48
8	64	61	59	58	54
9	71	69	67	65	61

	67	64	63	62	59
1	7	6	7	6	6
2	14	13	13	12	12
3	20	19	19	19	18
4	27	26	26	25	24
5	34	32	32	31	30
6	40	39	38	37	35
7	47	45	45	43	41
8	54	52	51	50	47
9	60	58	57	56	53

	28	27	26	25	24
1	3	3	3	3	2
2	6	5	5	5	5
3	8	8	8	8	7
4	11	11	10	10	10
5	14	14	13	13	12
6	17	16	16	15	14
7	20	19	18	18	17
8	22	22	21	20	19
9	25	24	23	23	22

	23	22	21	19	18	17
1	2	2	2	2	2	2
2	5	4	4	4	4	3
3	7	7	6	6	5	5
4	9	9	8	8	7	7
5	12	11	11	10	9	9
6	14	13	13	11	11	10
7	16	15	15	13	13	12
8	18	18	17	15	14	14
9	21	20	19	17	16	15

	16	15	14	13	12	11
1	2	2	1	1	1	1
2	3	3	3	3	2	2
3	5	5	4	4	4	3
4	6	6	6	5	5	4
5	8	8	7	7	6	6
6	10	9	8	8	7	7
7	11	11	10	9	8	8
8	13	12	11	10	10	9
9	14	14	13	12	11	10

°	0′	10′	20′	30′	40′	50′	60′	
	\multicolumn{7}{c}{Do not interpolate between two numbers in italics; use Table III}	
3	*19.08*	*18.07*	*17.17*	*16.35*	*15.60*	14.92	14.30	86
4	14.30	13.73	13.20	12.71	12.25	11.83	11.43	85
5	11.43	11.06	10.71	10.39	10.08	*9.788*	*9.514*	84
6	*9.514*	*9.255*	*9.010*	8.777	8.556	*8.345*	*8.144*	83
7	*8.144*	*7.953*	*7.770*	*7.596*	*7.429*	*7.269*	*7.115*	82
8	*7.115*	*6.968*	*6.827*	*6.691*	*6.561*	*6.435*	*6.314*	81
9	*6.314*	*6.197*	*6.084*	*5.976*	*5.871*	*5.769*	*5.671*	80
10	*5.671*	*5.576*	*5.485*	*5.396*	*5.309*	*5.226*	*5.145*	79
11	5.145	5.066	4.989	4.915	4.843	4.773	4.705	78
12	4.705	4.638	4.574	4.511	4.449	4.390	4.331	77
13	4.331	4.275	4.219	4.165	4.113	4.061	4.011	76
14	4.011	3.962	3.914	3.867	3.821	3.776	3.732	75
15	3.732	3.689	3.647	3.606	3.566	3.526	3.487	74
16	3.487	3.450	3.412	3.376	3.340	3.305	3.271	73
17	3.271	3.237	3.204	3.172	3.140	3.108	3.078	72
18	3.078	3.047	3.018	2.989	2.960	2.932	2.904	71
19	2.904	2.877	2.850	2.824	2.798	2.773	2.747	70
20	2.747	2.723	2.699	2.675	2.651	2.628	2.605	69
21	2.605	2.583	2.560	2.539	2.517	2.496	2.475	68
22	2.475	2.455	2.434	2.414	2.394	2.375	2.356	67
23	2.356	2.337	2.318	2.300	2.282	2.264	2.246	66
24	2.246	2.229	2.211	2.194	2.177	2.161	2.145	65
25	2.145	2.128	2.112	2.097	2.081	2.066	2.050	64
26	2.050	2.035	2.020	2.006	1.991	1.977	1.963	63
27	1.963	1.949	1.935	1.921	1.907	1.894	1.881	62
28	1.881	1.868	1.855	1.842	1.829	1.816	1.804	61
29	1.804	1.792	1.780	1.767	1.756	1.744	1.732	60
30	1.732	1.720	1.709	1.698	1.686	1.675	1.664	59
31	1.664	1.653	1.643	1.632	1.621	1.611	1.600	58
32	1.600	1.590	1.580	1.570	1.560	1.550	1.540	57
33	1.540	1.530	1.520	1.511	1.501	1.492	1.483	56
34	1.483	1.473	1.464	1.455	1.446	1.437	1.428	55
35	1.428	1.419	1.411	1.402	1.393	1.385	1.376	54
36	1.376	1.368	1.360	1.351	1.343	1.335	1.327	53
37	1.327	1.319	1.311	1.303	1.295	1.288	1.280	52
38	1.280	1.272	1.265	1.257	1.250	1.242	1.235	51
39	1.235	1.228	1.220	1.213	1.206	1.199	1.192	50
40	1.192	1.185	1.178	1.171	1.164	1.157	1.150	49
41	1.150	1.144	1.137	1.130	1.124	1.117	1.111	48
42	1.111	1.104	1.098	1.091	1.085	1.079	1.072	47
43	1.072	1.066	1.060	1.054	1.048	1.042	1.036	46
44	1.036	1.030	1.024	1.018	1.012	1.006	1.000	45
	60′	50′	40′	30′	20′	10′	0′	°

NATURAL TANGENTS

TABLE VI. TRAVERSE TABLE

	1°		2°		3°		4°		5°	
D	D cos	D sin	D cos	D sin	D cos	D sin	D cos	D sin	D cos	D sin	D
hyp.	adj.	opp.	adj.	opp.	adj.	opp.	adj.	opp.	adj.	opp.	hyp.
dis.	lat.	dep.	lat.	dep.	lat.	dep.	lat.	dep.	lat.	dep.	dis.
11	11.00	0.19	10.99	0.38	10.98	0.58	10.97	0.77	10.96	0.96	11
12	12.00	0.21	11.99	0.42	11.98	0.63	11.97	0.84	11.95	1.05	12
13	13.00	0.23	12.99	0.45	12.98	0.68	12.97	0.91	12.95	1.13	13
14	14.00	0.24	13.99	0.49	13.98	0.73	13.97	0.98	13.95	1.22	14
15	15.00	0.26	14.99	0.52	14.98	0.79	14.96	1.05	14.94	1.31	15
16	16.00	0.28	15.99	0.56	15.98	0.84	15.96	1.12	15.94	1.39	16
17	17.00	0.30	16.99	0.59	16.98	0.89	16.96	1.19	16.94	1.48	17
18	18.00	0.31	17.99	0.63	17.98	0.94	17.96	1.26	17.93	1.57	18
19	19.00	0.33	18.99	0.66	18.97	0.99	18.95	1.33	18.93	1.66	19
20	20.00	0.35	19.99	0.70	19.97	1.05	19.95	1.40	19.92	1.74	20
21	21.00	0.37	20.99	0.73	20.97	1.10	20.95	1.46	20.92	1.83	21
22	22.00	0.38	21.99	0.77	21.97	1.15	21.95	1.53	21.92	1.92	22
23	23.00	0.40	22.99	0.80	22.97	1.20	22.94	1.60	22.91	2.00	23
24	24.00	0.42	23.99	0.84	23.97	1.26	23.94	1.67	23.91	2.09	24
25	25.00	0.44	24.98	0.87	24.97	1.31	24.94	1.74	24.90	2.18	25
26	26.00	0.45	25.98	0.91	25.96	1.36	25.94	1.81	25.90	2.27	26
27	27.00	0.47	26.98	0.94	26.96	1.41	26.93	1.88	26.90	2.35	27
28	28.00	0.49	27.98	0.98	27.96	1.47	27.93	1.95	27.89	2.44	28
29	29.00	0.51	28.98	1.01	28.96	1.52	28.93	2.02	28.89	2.53	29
30	30.00	0.52	29.98	1.05	29.96	1.57	29.93	2.09	29.89	2.61	30
31	31.00	0.54	30.98	1.08	30.96	1.62	30.92	2.16	30.88	2.70	31
32	32.00	0.56	31.98	1.12	31.96	1.67	31.92	2.23	31.88	2.79	32
33	32.99	0.58	32.98	1.15	32.95	1.73	32.92	2.30	32.87	2.88	33
34	33.99	0.59	33.98	1.19	33.95	1.78	33.92	2.37	33.87	2.96	34
35	34.99	0.61	34.98	1.22	34.95	1.83	34.91	2.44	34.87	3.05	35
36	35.99	0.63	35.98	1.26	35.95	1.88	35.91	2.51	35.86	3.14	36
37	36.99	0.65	36.98	1.29	36.95	1.94	36.91	2.58	36.86	3.22	37
38	37.99	0.66	37.98	1.33	37.95	1.99	37.91	2.65	37.86	3.31	38
39	38.99	0.68	38.98	1.36	38.95	2.04	38.90	2.72	38.85	3.40	39
40	39.99	0.70	39.98	1.40	39.95	2.09	39.90	2.79	39.85	3.49	40
41	40.99	0.72	40.98	1.43	40.94	2.15	40.90	2.86	40.84	3.57	41
42	41.99	0.73	41.97	1.47	41.94	2.20	41.90	2.93	41.84	3.66	42
43	42.99	0.75	42.97	1.50	42.94	2.25	42.90	3.00	42.84	3.75	43
44	43.99	0.77	43.97	1.54	43.94	2.30	43.89	3.07	43.83	3.83	44
45	44.99	0.79	44.97	1.57	44.94	2.36	44.89	3.14	44.83	3.92	45
46	45.99	0.80	45.97	1.61	45.94	2.41	45.89	3.21	45.82	4.01	46
47	46.99	0.82	46.97	1.64	46.94	2.46	46.89	3.28	46.82	4.10	47
48	47.99	0.84	47.97	1.68	47.93	2.51	47.88	3.35	47.82	4.18	48
49	48.99	0.86	48.97	1.71	48.93	2.56	48.88	3.42	48.81	4.27	49
50	49.99	0.87	49.97	1.74	49.93	2.62	49.88	3.49	49.81	4.36	50
51	50.99	0.89	50.97	1.78	50.93	2.67	50.88	3.56	50.81	4.44	51
52	51.99	0.91	51.97	1.81	51.93	2.72	51.87	3.63	51.80	4.53	52
53	52.99	0.92	52.97	1.85	52.93	2.77	52.87	3.70	52.80	4.62	53
54	53.99	0.94	53.97	1.88	53.93	2.83	53.87	3.77	53.79	4.71	54
55	54.99	0.96	54.97	1.92	54.92	2.88	54.87	3.84	54.79	4.79	55
56	55.99	0.98	55.97	1.95	55.92	2.93	55.86	3.91	55.79	4.88	56
57	56.99	0.99	56.97	1.99	56.92	2.98	56.86	3.98	56.78	4.97	57
58	57.99	1.01	57.96	2.02	57.92	3.04	57.86	4.05	57.78	5.06	58
59	58.99	1.03	58.96	2.06	58.92	3.09	58.86	4.12	58.78	5.14	59
dis.	dep.	lat.	dep.	lat.	dep.	lat.	dep.	lat.	dep.	lat.	dis.
hyp.	opp.	adj.	opp.	adj.	opp.	adj.	opp.	adj.	opp.	adj.	hyp.
D	D sin	D cos	D sin	D cos	D sin	D cos	D sin	D cos	D sin	D cos	D
	89°		88°		87°		86°		85°		

8

TABLE VI. TRAVERSE TABLE

	1°		2°		3°		4°		5°		
D	D cos	D sin	D cos	D sin	D cos	D sin	D cos	D sin	D cos	D sin	D
hyp.	adj.	opp.	adj.	opp.	adj.	opp.	adj.	opp.	adj.	opp.	hyp.
dis.	lat.	dep.	lat.	dep.	lat.	dep.	lat.	dep.	lat.	dep.	dis.
60	59.99	1.05	59.96	2.09	59.92	3.14	59.85	4.19	59.77	5.23	60
61	60.99	1.06	60.96	2.13	60.92	3.19	60.85	4.26	60.77	5.32	61
62	61.99	1.08	61.96	2.16	61.92	3.24	61.85	4.32	61.76	5.40	62
63	62.99	1.10	62.96	2.20	62.91	3.30	62.85	4.39	62.76	5.49	63
64	63.99	1.12	63.96	2.23	63.91	3.35	63.84	4.46	63.76	5.58	64
65	64.99	1.13	64.96	2.27	64.91	3.40	64.84	4.53	64.75	5.67	65
66	65.99	1.15	65.96	2.30	65.91	3.45	65.84	4.60	65.75	5.75	66
67	66.99	1.17	66.96	2.34	66.91	3.51	66.84	4.67	66.75	5.84	67
68	67.99	1.19	67.96	2.37	67.91	3.56	67.83	4.74	67.74	5.93	68
69	68.99	1.20	68.96	2.41	68.91	3.61	68.83	4.81	68.74	6.01	69
70	69.99	1.22	69.96	2.44	69.90	3.66	69.83	4.88	69.73	6.10	70
71	70.99	1.24	70.96	2.48	70.90	3.72	70.83	4.95	70.73	6.19	71
72	71.99	1.26	71.96	2.51	71.90	3.77	71.82	5.02	71.73	6.28	72
73	72.99	1.27	72.96	2.55	72.90	3.82	72.82	5.09	72.72	6.36	73
74	73.99	1.29	73.95	2.58	73.90	3.87	73.82	5.16	73.72	6.45	74
75	74.99	1.31	74.95	2.62	74.90	3.93	74.82	5.23	74.71	6.54	75
76	75.99	1.33	75.95	2.65	75.90	3.98	75.81	5.30	75.71	6.62	76
77	76.99	1.34	76.95	2.69	76.89	4.03	76.81	5.37	76.71	6.71	77
78	77.99	1.36	77.95	2.72	77.89	4.08	77.81	5.44	77.70	6.80	78
79	78.99	1.38	78.95	2.76	78.89	4.13	78.81	5.51	78.70	6.89	79
80	79.99	1.40	79.95	2.79	79.89	4.19	79.81	5.58	79.70	6.97	80
81	80.99	1.41	80.95	2.83	80.89	4.24	80.80	5.65	80.69	7.06	81
82	81.99	1.43	81.95	2.86	81.89	4.29	81.80	5.72	81.69	7.15	82
83	82.99	1.45	82.95	2.90	82.89	4.34	82.80	5.79	82.68	7.23	83
84	83.99	1.47	83.95	2.93	83.88	4.40	83.80	5.86	83.68	7.32	84
85	84.99	1.48	84.95	2.97	84.88	4.45	84.79	5.93	84.68	7.41	85
86	85.99	1.50	85.95	3.00	85.88	4.50	85.79	6.00	85.67	7.50	86
87	86.99	1.52	86.95	3.04	86.88	4.55	86.79	6.07	86.67	7.58	87
88	87.99	1.54	87.95	3.07	87.88	4.61	87.79	6.14	87.67	7.67	88
89	88.99	1.55	88.95	3.11	88.88	4.66	88.78	6.21	88.66	7.76	89
90	89.99	1.57	89.95	3.14	89.88	4.71	89.78	6.28	89.66	7.84	90
91	90.99	1.59	90.94	3.18	90.88	4.76	90.78	6.35	90.65	7.93	91
92	91.99	1.61	91.94	3.21	91.87	4.81	91.78	6.42	91.65	8.02	92
93	92.99	1.62	92.94	3.25	92.87	4.87	92.77	6.49	92.65	8.11	93
94	93.99	1.64	93.94	3.28	93.87	4.92	93.77	6.56	93.64	8.19	94
95	94.99	1.66	94.94	3.32	94.87	4.97	94.77	6.63	94.64	8.28	95
96	95.99	1.68	95.94	3.35	95.87	5.02	95.77	6.70	95.63	8.37	96
97	96.99	1.69	96.94	3.39	96.87	5.08	96.76	6.77	96.63	8.45	97
98	97.99	1.71	97.94	3.42	97.87	5.13	97.76	6.84	97.63	8.54	98
99	98.98	1.73	98.94	3.46	98.86	5.18	98.76	6.91	98.62	8.63	99
100	99.98	1.75	99.94	3.49	99.86	5.23	99.76	6.98	99.62	8.72	100
200	199.97	3.49	199.88	6.98	199.73	10.47	199.51	13.95	199.24	17.43	200
300	299.95	5.24	299.82	10.47	299.59	15.70	299.27	20.93	298.86	26.15	300
400	399.94	6.98	399.76	13.96	399.45	20.93	399.03	27.90	398.48	34.86	400
500	499.92	8.73	499.70	17.45	499.31	26.17	498.78	34.88	498.10	43.58	500
600	599.91	10.47	599.63	20.94	599.18	31.40	598.54	41.85	597.72	52.29	600
700	699.89	12.22	699.57	24.43	699.04	36.64	698.29	48.83	697.34	61.01	700
800	799.88	13.96	799.51	27.92	798.90	41.87	798.05	55.80	796.96	69.72	800
900	899.86	15.71	899.45	31.41	898.77	47.10	897.81	62.78	896.58	78.44	900
dis.	dep.	lat.	dep.	lat.	dep.	lat.	dep.	lat.	dep.	lat.	dis.
hyp.	opp.	adj.	opp.	adj.	opp.	adj.	opp.	adj.	opp.	adj.	hyp.
D	D sin	D cos	D sin	D cos	D sin	D cos	D sin	D cos	D sin	D cos	D
	89°		88°		87°		86°		85°		

TABLE VI. TRAVERSE TABLE

	6°		7°		8°		9°		10°	
D	D cos	D sin	D cos	D sin	D cos	D sin	D cos	D sin	D cos	D sin	D
hyp.	adj.	opp.	adj.	opp.	adj.	opp.	adj.	opp.	adj.	opp.	hyp.
dis.	lat.	dep.	lat.	dep.	lat.	dep.	lat.	dep.	lat.	dep.	dis.
11	10.94	1.15	10.92	1.34	10.89	1.53	10.86	1.72	10.83	1.91	11
12	11.93	1.25	11.91	1.46	11.88	1.67	11.85	1.88	11.82	2.08	12
13	12.93	1.36	12.90	1.58	12.87	1.81	12.84	2.03	12.80	2.26	13
14	13.92	1.46	13.90	1.71	13.86	1.95	13.83	2.19	13.79	2.43	14
15	14.92	1.57	14.89	1.83	14.85	2.09	14.82	2.35	14.77	2.60	15
16	15.91	1.67	15.88	1.95	15.84	2.23	15.80	2.50	15.76	2.78	16
17	16.91	1.78	16.87	2.07	16.83	2.37	16.79	2.66	16.74	2.95	17
18	17.90	1.88	17.87	2.19	17.82	2.51	17.78	2.82	17.73	3.13	18
19	18.90	1.99	18.86	2.32	18.82	2.64	18.77	2.97	18.71	3.30	19
20	19.89	2.09	19.85	2.44	19.81	2.78	19.75	3.13	19.70	3.47	20
21	20.88	2.20	20.84	2.56	20.80	2.92	20.74	3.29	20.68	3.65	21
22	21.88	2.30	21.84	2.68	21.79	3.06	21.73	3.44	21.67	3.82	22
23	22.87	2.40	22.83	2.80	22.78	3.20	22.72	3.60	22.65	3.99	23
24	23.87	2.51	23.82	2.92	23.77	3.34	23.70	3.75	23.64	4.17	24
25	24.86	2.61	24.81	3.05	24.76	3.48	24.69	3.91	24.62	4.34	25
26	25.86	2.72	25.81	3.17	25.75	3.62	25.68	4.07	25.61	4.51	26
27	26.85	2.82	26.80	3.29	26.74	3.76	26.67	4.22	26.59	4.69	27
28	27.85	2.93	27.79	3.41	27.73	3.90	27.66	4.38	27.57	4.86	28
29	28.84	3.03	28.78	3.53	28.72	4.04	28.64	4.54	28.56	5.04	29
30	29.84	3.14	29.78	3.66	29.71	4.18	29.63	4.69	29.54	5.21	30
31	30.83	3.24	30.77	3.78	30.70	4.31	30.62	4.85	30.53	5.38	31
32	31.82	3.34	31.76	3.90	31.69	4.45	31.61	5.01	31.51	5.56	32
33	32.82	3.45	32.75	4.02	32.68	4.59	32.59	5.16	32.50	5.73	33
34	33.81	3.55	33.75	4.14	33.67	4.73	33.58	5.32	33.48	5.90	34
35	34.81	3.66	34.74	4.27	34.66	4.87	34.57	5.48	34.47	6.08	35
36	35.80	3.76	35.73	4.39	35.65	5.01	35.56	5.63	35.45	6.25	36
37	36.80	3.87	36.72	4.51	36.64	5.15	36.54	5.79	36.44	6.42	37
38	37.79	3.97	37.72	4.63	37.63	5.29	37.53	5.94	37.42	6.60	38
39	38.79	4.08	38.71	4.75	38.62	5.43	38.52	6.10	38.41	6.77	39
40	39.78	4.18	39.70	4.87	39.61	5.57	39.51	6.26	39.39	6.95	40
41	40.78	4.29	40.70	5.00	40.60	5.71	40.50	6.41	40.38	7.12	41
42	41.77	4.39	41.69	5.12	41.59	5.85	41.48	6.57	41.36	7.29	42
43	42.76	4.49	42.68	5.24	42.58	5.98	42.47	6.73	42.35	7.47	43
44	43.76	4.60	43.67	5.36	43.57	6.12	43.46	6.88	43.33	7.64	44
45	44.75	4.70	44.67	5.48	44.56	6.26	44.45	7.04	44.32	7.81	45
46	45.75	4.81	45.66	5.61	45.55	6.40	45.43	7.20	45.30	7.99	46
47	46.74	4.91	46.65	5.73	46.54	6.54	46.42	7.35	46.29	8.16	47
48	47.74	5.02	47.64	5.85	47.53	6.68	47.41	7.51	47.27	8.34	48
49	48.73	5.12	48.63	5.97	48.52	6.82	48.40	7.67	48.26	8.51	49
50	49.73	5.23	49.63	6.09	49.51	6.96	49.38	7.82	49.24	8.68	50
51	50.72	5.33	50.62	6.22	50.50	7.10	50.37	7.98	50.23	8.86	51
52	51.72	5.44	51.61	6.34	51.49	7.24	51.36	8.13	51.21	9.03	52
53	52.71	5.54	52.60	6.46	52.48	7.38	52.35	8.29	52.19	9.20	53
54	53.70	5.64	53.60	6.58	53.47	7.52	53.34	8.45	53.18	9.38	54
55	54.70	5.75	54.59	6.70	54.46	7.65	54.32	8.60	54.16	9.55	55
56	55.69	5.85	55.58	6.82	55.46	7.79	55.31	8.76	55.15	9.72	56
57	56.69	5.96	56.58	6.95	56.45	7.93	56.30	8.92	56.13	9.90	57
58	57.68	6.06	57.57	7.07	57.44	8.07	57.29	9.07	57.12	10.07	58
59	58.68	6.17	58.56	7.19	58.43	8.21	58.27	9.23	58.10	10.25	59
dis.	dep.	lat.	dep.	lat.	dep.	lat.	dep.	lat.	dep.	lat.	dis.
hyp.	opp.	adj.	opp.	adj.	opp.	adj.	opp.	adj.	opp.	adj.	hyp.
D	D sin	D cos	D sin	D cos	D sin	D cos	D sin	D cos	D sin	D cos	D
	84°		83°		82°		81°		80°		

TABLE VI. TRAVERSE TABLE

	6°		7°		8°		9°		10°		
D	D cos	D sin	D cos	D sin	D cos	D sin	D cos	D sin	D cos	D sin	D
hyp.	adj.	opp.	adj.	opp.	adj.	opp.	adj.	opp.	adj.	opp.	hyp.
dis.	lat.	dep.	lat.	dep.	lat.	dep.	lat.	dep.	lat.	dep.	dis.
60	59.67	6.27	59.55	7.31	59.42	8.35	59.26	9.39	59.09	10.42	60
61	60.67	6.38	60.55	7.43	60.41	8.49	60.25	9.54	60.07	10.59	61
62	61.66	6.48	61.54	7.56	61.40	8.63	61.24	9.70	61.06	10.77	62
63	62.65	6.59	62.53	7.68	62.39	8.77	62.22	9.86	62.04	10.94	63
64	63.65	6.69	63.52	7.80	63.38	8.91	63.21	10.01	63.03	11.11	64
65	64.64	6.79	64.52	7.92	64.37	9.05	64.20	10.17	64.01	11.29	65
66	65.64	6.90	65.51	8.04	65.36	9.19	65.19	10.32	65.00	11.46	66
67	66.63	7.00	66.50	8.17	66.35	9.32	66.18	10.48	65.98	11.63	67
68	67.63	7.11	67.49	8.29	67.34	9.46	67.16	10.64	66.97	11.81	68
69	68.62	7.21	68.49	8.41	68.33	9.60	68.15	10.79	67.95	11.98	69
70	69.62	7.32	69.48	8.53	69.32	9.74	69.14	10.95	68.94	12.16	70
71	70.61	7.42	70.47	8.65	70.31	9.88	70.13	11.11	69.92	12.33	71
72	71.61	7.53	71.46	8.77	71.30	10.02	71.11	11.26	70.91	12.50	72
73	72.60	7.63	72.46	8.90	72.29	10.16	72.10	11.42	71.89	12.68	73
74	73.59	7.74	73.45	9.02	73.28	10.30	73.09	11.58	72.88	12.85	74
75	74.59	7.84	74.44	9.14	74.27	10.44	74.08	11.73	73.86	13.02	75
76	75.58	7.94	75.43	9.26	75.26	10.58	75.06	11.89	74.85	13.20	76
77	76.58	8.05	76.43	9.38	76.25	10.72	76.05	12.05	75.83	13.37	77
78	77.57	8.15	77.42	9.51	77.24	10.86	77.04	12.20	76.82	13.54	78
79	78.57	8.26	78.41	9.63	78.23	10.99	78.03	12.36	77.80	13.72	79
80	79.56	8.36	79.40	9.75	79.22	11.13	79.02	12.51	78.78	13.89	80
81	80.56	8.47	80.40	9.87	80.21	11.27	80.00	12.67	79.77	14.07	81
82	81.55	8.57	81.39	9.99	81.20	11.41	80.99	12.83	80.75	14.24	82
83	82.55	8.68	82.38	10.12	82.19	11.55	81.98	12.98	81.74	14.41	83
84	83.54	8.78	83.37	10.24	83.18	11.69	82.97	13.14	82.72	14.59	84
85	84.53	8.88	84.37	10.36	84.17	11.83	83.95	13.30	83.71	14.76	85
86	85.53	8.99	85.36	10.48	85.16	11.97	84.94	13.45	84.69	14.93	86
87	86.52	9.09	86.35	10.60	86.15	12.11	85.93	13.61	85.68	15.11	87
88	87.52	9.20	87.34	10.72	87.14	12.25	86.92	13.77	86.66	15.28	88
89	88.51	9.30	88.34	10.85	88.13	12.39	87.90	13.92	87.65	15.45	89
90	89.51	9.41	89.33	10.97	89.12	12.53	88.89	14.08	88.63	15.63	90
91	90.50	9.51	90.32	11.09	90.11	12.66	89.88	14.24	89.62	15.80	91
92	91.50	9.62	91.31	11.21	91.10	12.80	90.87	14.39	90.60	15.98	92
93	92.49	9.72	92.31	11.33	92.09	12.94	91.86	14.55	91.59	16.15	93
94	93.49	9.83	93.30	11.46	93.09	13.08	92.84	14.70	92.57	16.32	94
95	94.48	9.93	94.29	11.58	94.08	13.22	93.83	14.86	93.56	16.50	95
96	95.47	10.03	95.28	11.70	95.07	13.36	94.82	15.02	94.54	16.67	96
97	96.47	10.14	96.28	11.82	96.06	13.50	95.81	15.17	95.53	16.84	97
98	97.46	10.24	97.27	11.94	97.05	13.64	96.79	15.33	96.51	17.02	98
99	98.46	10.35	98.26	12.07	98.04	13.78	97.78	15.49	97.50	17.19	99
100	99.45	10.45	99.25	12.19	99.03	13.92	98.77	15.64	98.48	17.36	100
200	198.90	20.91	198.51	24.37	198.05	27.83	197.54	31.29	196.96	34.73	200
300	298.36	31.36	297.76	36.56	297.08	41.75	296.31	46.93	295.44	52.09	300
400	397.81	41.81	397.02	48.75	396.11	55.67	395.08	62.57	393.92	69.46	400
500	497.26	52.26	496.27	60.93	495.13	69.59	493.84	78.22	492.40	86.82	500
600	596.71	62.72	595.53	73.12	594.16	83.50	592.61	93.86	590.88	104.19	600
700	696.17	73.17	694.78	85.31	693.19	97.42	691.38	109.50	689.37	121.55	700
800	795.62	83.62	794.04	97.50	792.21	111.34	790.15	125.15	787.85	138.92	800
900	895.07	94.08	893.29	109.68	891.24	125.26	888.92	140.79	886.33	156.28	900
dis.	dep.	lat.	dep.	lat.	dep.	lat.	dep.	lat.	dep.	lat.	dis.
hyp.	opp.	adj.	opp.	adj.	opp.	adj.	opp.	adj.	opp.	adj.	hyp.
D	D sin	D cos	D sin	D cos	D sin	D cos	D sin	D cos	D sin	D cos	D

| | 84° | 83° | 82° | 81° | 80° | |

TABLE VI. TRAVERSE TABLE

	11°		12°		13°		14°		15°	
D	D cos	D sin	D cos	D sin	D cos	D sin	D cos	D sin	D cos	D sin	D
hyp.	adj.	opp.	adj.	opp.	adj.	opp.	adj.	opp.	adj.	opp.	hyp.
dis.	lat.	dep.	lat.	dep.	lat.	dep.	lat.	dep.	lat.	dep.	dis.
11	10.80	2.10	10.76	2.29	10.72	2.47	10.67	2.66	10.63	2.85	11
12	11.78	2.29	11.74	2.49	11.69	2.70	11.64	2.90	11.59	3.11	12
13	12.76	2.48	12.72	2.70	12.67	2.92	12.61	3.15	12.56	3.36	13
14	13.74	2.67	13.69	2.91	13.64	3.15	13.58	3.39	13.52	3.62	14
15	14.72	2.86	14.67	3.12	14.62	3.37	14.55	3.63	14.49	3.88	15
16	15.71	3.05	15.65	3.33	15.59	3.60	15.52	3.87	15.45	4.14	16
17	16.69	3.24	16.63	3.53	16.57	3.82	16.50	4.11	16.42	4.40	17
18	17.67	3.43	17.61	3.74	17.54	4.05	17.47	4.35	17.39	4.66	18
19	18.65	3.63	18.58	3.95	18.51	4.27	18.44	4.60	18.35	4.92	19
20	19.63	3.82	19.56	4.16	19.49	4.50	19.41	4.84	19.32	5.18	20
21	20.61	4.01	20.54	4.37	20.46	4.72	20.38	5.08	20.28	5.44	21
22	21.60	4.20	21.52	4.57	21.44	4.95	21.35	5.32	21.25	5.69	22
23	22.58	4.39	22.50	4.78	22.41	5.17	22.32	5.56	22.22	5.95	23
24	23.56	4.58	23.48	4.99	23.38	5.40	23.29	5.81	23.18	6.21	24
25	24.54	4.77	24.45	5.20	24.36	5.62	24.26	6.05	24.15	6.47	25
26	25.52	4.96	25.43	5.41	25.33	5.85	25.23	6.29	25.11	6.73	26
27	26.50	5.15	26.41	5.61	26.31	6.07	26.20	6.53	26.08	6.99	27
28	27.49	5.34	27.39	5.82	27.28	6.30	27.17	6.77	27.05	7.25	28
29	28.47	5.53	28.37	6.03	28.26	6.52	28.14	7.02	28.01	7.51	29
30	29.45	5.72	29.34	6.24	29.23	6.75	29.11	7.26	28.98	7.76	30
31	30.43	5.92	30.32	6.45	30.21	6.97	30.08	7.50	29.94	8.02	31
32	31.41	6.11	31.30	6.65	31.18	7.20	31.05	7.74	30.91	8.28	32
33	32.39	6.30	32.28	6.86	32.15	7.42	32.02	7.98	31.88	8.54	33
34	33.38	6.49	33.26	7.07	33.13	7.65	32.99	8.23	32.84	8.80	34
35	34.36	6.68	34.24	7.28	34.10	7.87	33.96	8.47	33.81	9.06	35
36	35.34	6.87	35.21	7.48	35.08	8.10	34.93	8.71	34.77	9.32	36
37	36.32	7.06	36.19	7.69	36.05	8.32	35.90	8.95	35.74	9.58	37
38	37.30	7.25	37.17	7.90	37.03	8.55	36.87	9.19	36.71	9.84	38
39	38.28	7.44	38.15	8.11	38.00	8.77	37.84	9.44	37.67	10.09	39
40	39.27	7.63	39.13	8.32	38.97	9.00	38.81	9.68	38.64	10.35	40
41	40.25	7.82	40.10	8.52	39.95	9.22	39.78	9.92	39.60	10.61	41
42	41.23	8.01	41.08	8.73	40.92	9.45	40.75	10.16	40.57	10.87	42
43	42.21	8.20	42.06	8.94	41.90	9.67	41.72	10.40	41.53	11.13	43
44	43.19	8.40	43.04	9.15	42.87	9.90	42.69	10.64	42.50	11.39	44
45	44.17	8.59	44.02	9.36	43.85	10.12	43.66	10.89	43.47	11.65	45
46	45.15	8.78	44.99	9.56	44.82	10.35	44.63	11.13	44.43	11.91	46
47	46.14	8.97	45.97	9.77	45.80	10.57	45.60	11.37	45.40	12.16	47
48	47.12	9.16	46.95	9.98	46.77	10.80	46.57	11.61	46.36	12.42	48
49	48.10	9.35	47.93	10.19	47.74	11.02	47.54	11.85	47.33	12.68	49
50	49.08	9.54	48.91	10.40	48.72	11.25	48.51	12.10	48.30	12.94	50
51	50.06	9.73	49.89	10.60	49.69	11.47	49.49	12.34	49.26	13.20	51
52	51.04	9.92	50.86	10.81	50.67	11.70	50.46	12.58	50.23	13.46	52
53	52.03	10.11	51.84	11.02	51.64	11.92	51.43	12.82	51.19	13.72	53
54	53.01	10.30	52.82	11.23	52.62	12.15	52.40	13.06	52.16	13.98	54
55	53.99	10.49	53.80	11.44	53.59	12.37	53.37	13.31	53.13	14.24	55
56	54.97	10.69	54.78	11.64	54.56	12.60	54.34	13.55	54.09	14.49	56
57	55.95	10.88	55.75	11.85	55.54	12.82	55.31	13.79	55.06	14.75	57
58	56.93	11.07	56.73	12.06	56.51	13.05	56.28	14.03	56.02	15.01	58
59	57.92	11.26	57.71	12.27	57.49	13.27	57.25	14.27	56.99	15.27	59
dis.	dep.	lat.	dep.	lat.	dep.	lat.	dep.	lat.	dep.	lat.	dis.
hyp.	opp.	adj.	opp.	adj.	opp.	adj.	opp.	adj.	opp.	adj.	hyp.
D	D sin	D cos	D sin	D cos	D sin	D cos	D sin	D cos	D sin	D cos	D
	79°		78°		77°		76°		75°		

TABLE VI. TRAVERSE TABLE

	11°		12°		13°		14°		15°	
D	D cos	D sin	D cos	D sin	D cos	D sin	D cos	D sin	D cos	D sin	D
hyp.	adj.	opp.	adj.	opp.	adj.	opp.	adj.	opp.	adj.	opp.	hyp.
dis.	lat.	dep.	lat.	dep.	lat.	dep.	lat.	dep.	lat.	dep.	dis.
60	58.90	11.45	58.69	12.47	58.46	13.50	58.22	14.52	57.96	15.53	60
61	59.88	11.64	59.67	12.68	59.44	13.72	59.19	14.76	58.92	15.79	61
62	60.86	11.83	60.65	12.89	60.41	13.95	60.16	15.00	59.89	16.05	62
63	61.84	12.02	61.62	13.10	61.39	14.17	61.13	15.24	60.85	16.31	63
64	62.82	12.21	62.60	13.31	62.36	14.40	62.10	15.48	61.82	16.56	64
65	63.81	12.40	63.58	13.51	63.33	14.62	63.07	15.72	62.79	16.82	65
66	64.79	12.59	64.56	13.72	64.31	14.85	64.04	15.97	63.75	17.08	66
67	65.77	12.78	65.54	13.93	65.28	15.07	65.01	16.21	64.72	17.34	67
68	66.75	12.98	66.51	14.14	66.26	15.30	65.98	16.45	65.68	17.60	68
69	67.73	13.17	67.49	14.35	67.23	15.52	66.95	16.69	66.65	17.86	69
70	68.71	13.36	68.47	14.55	68.21	15.75	67.92	16.93	67.61	18.12	70
71	69.70	13.55	69.45	14.76	69.18	15.97	68.89	17.18	68.58	18.38	71
72	70.68	13.74	70.43	14.97	70.15	16.20	69.86	17.42	69.55	18.63	72
73	71.66	13.93	71.40	15.18	71.13	16.42	70.83	17.66	70.51	18.89	73
74	72.64	14.12	72.38	15.39	72.10	16.65	71.80	17.90	71.48	19.15	74
75	73.62	14.31	73.36	15.59	73.08	16.87	72.77	18.14	72.44	19.41	75
76	74.60	14.50	74.34	15.80	74.05	17.10	73.74	18.39	73.41	19.67	76
77	75.59	14.69	75.32	16.01	75.03	17.32	74.71	18.63	74.38	19.93	77
78	76.57	14.88	76.30	16.22	76.00	17.55	75.68	18.87	75.34	20.19	78
79	77.55	15.07	77.27	16.43	76.98	17.77	76.65	19.11	76.31	20.45	79
80	78.53	15.26	78.25	16.63	77.95	18.00	77.62	19.35	77.27	20.71	80
81	79.51	15.46	79.23	16.84	78.92	18.22	78.59	19.60	78.24	20.96	81
82	80.49	15.65	80.21	17.05	79.90	18.45	79.56	19.84	79.21	21.22	82
83	81.48	15.84	81.19	17.26	80.87	18.67	80.53	20.08	80.17	21.48	83
84	82.46	16.03	82.16	17.46	81.85	18.90	81.50	20.32	81.14	21.74	84
85	83.44	16.22	83.14	17.67	82.82	19.12	82.48	20.56	82.10	22.00	85
86	84.42	16.41	84.12	17.88	83.80	19.35	83.45	20.81	83.07	22.26	86
87	85.40	16.60	85.10	18.09	84.77	19.57	84.42	21.05	84.04	22.52	87
88	86.38	16.79	86.08	18.30	85.74	19.80	85.39	21.29	85.00	22.78	88
89	87.36	16.98	87.06	18.50	86.72	20.02	86.36	21.53	85.97	23.03	89
90	88.35	17.17	88.03	18.71	87.69	20.25	87.33	21.77	86.93	23.29	90
91	89.33	17.36	89.01	18.92	88.67	20.47	88.30	22.01	87.90	23.55	91
92	90.31	17.55	89.99	19.13	89.64	20.70	89.27	22.26	88.87	23.81	92
93	91.29	17.75	90.97	19.34	90.62	20.92	90.24	22.50	89.83	24.07	93
94	92.27	17.94	91.95	19.54	91.59	21.15	91.21	22.74	90.80	24.33	94
95	93.25	18.13	92.92	19.75	92.57	21.37	92.18	22.98	91.76	24.59	95
96	94.24	18.32	93.90	19.96	93.54	21.60	93.15	23.22	92.73	24.85	96
97	95.22	18.51	94.88	20.17	94.51	21.82	94.12	23.47	93.69	25.11	97
98	96.20	18.70	95.86	20.38	95.49	22.05	95.09	23.71	94.66	25.36	98
99	97.18	18.89	96.84	20.58	96.46	22.27	96.06	23.95	95.63	25.62	99
100	98.16	19.08	97.81	20.79	97.44	22.50	97.03	24.19	96.59	25.88	100
200	196.33	38.16	195.63	41.58	194.87	44.99	194.06	48.38	193.19	51.76	200
300	294.49	57.24	293.44	62.37	292.31	67.49	291.09	72.58	289.78	77.65	300
400	392.65	76.32	391.26	83.16	389.75	89.98	388.12	96.77	386.37	103.53	400
500	490.81	95.40	489.07	103.96	487.19	112.48	485.15	120.96	482.96	129.41	500
600	588.98	114.49	586.89	124.75	584.62	134.97	582.18	145.15	579.56	155.29	600
700	687.14	133.57	684.70	145.54	682.06	157.47	679.21	169.35	676.15	181.17	700
800	785.30	152.65	782.52	166.33	779.50	179.96	776.24	193.54	772.74	207.06	800
900	883.46	171.73	880.33	187.12	876.93	202.46	873.27	217.73	869.33	232.94	900
dis.	dep.	lat.	dep.	lat.	dep.	lat.	dep.	lat.	dep.	lat.	dis.
hyp.	opp.	adj.	opp.	adj.	opp.	adj.	opp.	adj.	opp.	adj.	hyp.
D	D sin	D cos	D sin	D cos	D sin	D cos	D sin	D cos	D sin	D cos	D
	79°		78°		77°		76°		75°		

TABLE VI. TRAVERSE TABLE

	16°		17°		18°		19°		20°	
D	D cos	D sin	D cos	D sin	D cos	D sin	D cos	D sin	D cos	D sin	D
hyp.	adj.	opp.	adj.	opp.	adj.	opp.	adj.	opp.	adj.	opp.	hyp.
dis.	lat.	dep.	lat.	dep.	lat.	dep.	lat.	dep.	lat.	dep.	dis.
11	10.57	3.03	10.52	3.22	10.46	3.40	10.40	3.58	10.34	3.76	11
12	11.54	3.31	11.48	3.51	11.41	3.71	11.35	3.91	11.28	4.10	12
13	12.50	3.58	12.43	3.80	12.36	4.02	12.29	4.23	12.22	4.45	13
14	13.46	3.86	13.39	4.09	13.31	4.33	13.24	4.56	13.16	4.79	14
15	14.42	4.13	14.34	4.39	14.27	4.64	14.18	4.88	14.10	5.13	15
16	15.38	4.41	15.30	4.68	15.22	4.94	15.13	5.21	15.04	5.47	16
17	16.34	4.69	16.26	4.97	16.17	5.25	16.07	5.53	15.97	5.81	17
18	17.30	4.96	17.21	5.26	17.12	5.56	17.02	5.86	16.91	6.16	18
19	18.26	5.24	18.17	5.56	18.07	5.87	17.96	6.19	17.85	6.50	19
20	19.23	5.51	19.13	5.85	19.02	6.18	18.91	6.51	18.79	6.84	20
21	20.19	5.79	20.08	6.14	19.97	6.49	19.86	6.84	19.73	7.18	21
22	21.15	6.06	21.04	6.43	20.92	6.80	20.80	7.16	20.67	7.52	22
23	22.11	6.34	21.99	6.72	21.87	7.11	21.75	7.49	21.61	7.87	23
24	23.07	6.62	22.95	7.02	22.83	7.42	22.69	7.81	22.55	8.21	24
25	24.03	6.89	23.91	7.31	23.78	7.73	23.64	8.14	23.49	8.55	25
26	24.99	7.17	24.86	7.60	24.73	8.03	24.58	8.46	24.43	8.89	26
27	25.95	7.44	25.82	7.89	25.68	8.34	25.53	8.79	25.37	9.23	27
28	26.92	7.72	26.78	8.19	26.63	8.65	26.47	9.12	26.31	9.58	28
29	27.88	7.99	27.73	8.48	27.58	8.96	27.42	9.44	27.25	9.92	29
30	28.84	8.27	28.69	8.77	28.53	9.27	28.37	9.77	28.19	10.26	30
31	29.80	8.54	29.65	9.06	29.48	9.58	29.31	10.09	29.13	10.60	31
32	30.76	8.82	30.60	9.36	30.43	9.89	30.26	10.42	30.07	10.94	32
33	31.72	9.10	31.56	9.65	31.38	10.20	31.20	10.74	31.01	11.29	33
34	32.68	9.37	32.51	9.94	32.34	10.51	32.15	11.07	31.95	11.63	34
35	33.64	9.65	33.47	10.23	33.29	10.82	33.09	11.39	32.89	11.97	35
36	34.61	9.92	34.43	10.53	34.24	11.12	34.04	11.72	33.83	12.31	36
37	35.57	10.20	35.38	10.82	35.19	11.43	34.98	12.05	34.77	12.65	37
38	36.53	10.47	36.34	11.11	36.14	11.74	35.93	12.37	35.71	13.00	38
39	37.49	10.75	37.30	11.40	37.09	12.05	36.88	12.70	36.65	13.34	39
40	38.45	11.03	38.25	11.69	38.04	12.36	37.82	13.02	37.59	13.68	40
41	39.41	11.30	39.21	11.99	38.99	12.67	38.77	13.35	38.53	14.02	41
42	40.37	11.58	40.16	12.28	39.94	12.98	39.71	13.67	39.47	14.36	42
43	41.33	11.85	41.12	12.57	40.90	13.29	40.66	14.00	40.41	14.71	43
44	42.30	12.13	42.08	12.86	41.85	13.60	41.60	14.32	41.35	15.05	44
45	43.26	12.40	43.03	13.16	42.80	13.91	42.55	14.65	42.29	15.39	45
46	44.22	12.68	43.99	13.45	43.75	14.21	43.49	14.98	43.23	15.73	46
47	45.18	12.95	44.95	13.74	44.70	14.52	44.44	15.30	44.17	16.07	47
48	46.14	13.23	45.90	14.03	45.65	14.83	45.38	15.63	45.11	16.42	48
49	47.10	13.51	46.86	14.33	46.60	15.14	46.33	15.95	46.04	16.76	49
50	48.06	13.78	47.82	14.62	47.55	15.45	47.28	16.28	46.98	17.10	50
51	49.02	14.06	48.77	14.91	48.50	15.76	48.22	16.60	47.92	17.44	51
52	49.99	14.33	49.73	15.20	49.45	16.07	49.17	16.93	48.86	17.79	52
53	50.95	14.61	50.68	15.50	50.41	16.38	50.11	17.26	49.80	18.13	53
54	51.91	14.88	51.64	15.79	51.36	16.69	51.06	17.58	50.74	18.47	54
55	52.87	15.16	52.60	16.08	52.31	17.00	52.00	17.91	51.68	18.81	55
56	53.83	15.44	53.55	16.37	53.26	17.30	52.95	18.23	52.62	19.15	56
57	54.79	15.71	54.51	16.67	54.21	17.61	53.89	18.56	53.56	19.50	57
58	55.75	15.99	55.47	16.96	55.16	17.92	54.84	18.88	54.50	19.84	58
59	56.71	16.26	56.42	17.25	56.11	18.23	55.79	19.21	55.44	20.18	59
dis.	dep.	lat.	dep.	lat.	dep.	lat.	dep.	lat.	dep.	lat.	dis.
hyp.	opp.	adj.	opp.	adj.	opp.	adj.	opp.	adj.	opp.	adj.	hyp.
D	D sin	D cos	D sin	D cos	D sin	D cos	D sin	D cos	D sin	D cos	D
	74°		73°		72°		71°		70°		

TABLE VI. TRAVERSE TABLE 15

	16°			17°		18°		19°		20°		
D	D cos	D sin	D cos	D sin	D cos	D sin	D cos	D sin	D cos	D sin	D
hyp.	adj.	opp.	adj.	opp.	adj.	opp.	adj.	opp.	adj.	opp.	hyp.
dis.	lat.	dep.	lat.	dep.	lat.	dep.	lat.	dep.	lat.	dep.	dis.
60	57.68	16.54	57.38	17.54	57.06	18.54	56.73	19.53	56.38	20.52	60
61	58.64	16.81	58.33	17.83	58.01	18.85	57.68	19.86	57.32	20.86	61
62	59.60	17.09	59.29	18.13	58.97	19.16	58.62	20.19	58.26	21.21	62
63	60.56	17.37	60.25	18.42	59.92	19.47	59.57	20.51	59.20	21.55	63
64	61.52	17.64	61.20	18.71	60.87	19.78	60.51	20.84	60.14	21.89	64
65	62.48	17.92	62.16	19.00	61.82	20.09	61.46	21.16	61.08	22.23	65
66	63.44	18.19	63.12	19.30	62.77	20.40	62.40	21.49	62.02	22.57	66
67	64.40	18.47	64.07	19.59	63.72	20.70	63.35	21.81	62.96	22.92	67
68	65.37	18.74	65.03	19.88	64.67	21.01	64.30	22.14	63.90	23.26	68
69	66.33	19.02	65.99	20.17	65.62	21.32	65.24	22.46	64.84	23.60	69
70	67.29	19.29	66.94	20.47	66.57	21.63	66.19	22.79	65.78	23.94	70
71	68.25	19.57	67.90	20.76	67.53	21.94	67.13	23.12	66.72	24.28	71
72	69.21	19.85	68.80	21.05	68.48	22.25	68.08	23.44	67.66	24.63	72
73	70.17	20.12	69.81	21.34	69.43	22.56	69.02	23.77	68.60	24.97	73
74	71.13	20.40	70.77	21.64	70.38	22.87	69.97	24.09	69.54	25.31	74
75	72.09	20.67	71.72	21.93	71.33	23.18	70.91	24.42	70.48	25.65	75
76	73.06	20.95	72.68	22.22	72.28	23.49	71.86	24.74	71.42	25.99	76
77	74.02	21.22	73.64	22.51	73.23	23.79	72.80	25.07	72.36	26.34	77
78	74.98	21.50	74.59	22.80	74.18	24.10	73.75	25.39	73.30	26.68	78
79	75.94	21.78	75.55	23.10	75.13	24.41	74.70	25.72	74.24	27.02	79
80	76.90	22.05	76.50	23.39	76.08	24.72	75.64	26.05	75.18	27.36	80
81	77.86	22.33	77.46	23.68	77.04	25.03	76.59	26.37	76.12	27.70	81
82	78.82	22.60	78.42	23.97	77.99	25.34	77.53	26.70	77.05	28.05	82
83	79.78	22.88	79.37	24.27	78.94	25.65	78.48	27.02	77.99	28.39	83
84	80.75	23.15	80.33	24.56	79.89	25.96	79.42	27.35	78.93	28.73	84
85	81.71	23.43	81.29	24.85	80.84	26.27	80.37	27.67	79.87	29.07	85
86	82.67	23.70	82.24	25.14	81.79	26.58	81.31	28.00	80.81	29.41	86
87	83.63	23.98	83.20	25.44	82.74	26.88	82.26	28.32	81.75	29.76	87
88	84.59	24.26	84.15	25.73	83.69	27.19	83.21	28.65	82.69	30.10	88
89	85.55	24.53	85.11	26.02	84.64	27.50	84.15	28.98	83.63	30.44	89
90	86.51	24.81	86.07	26.31	85.60	27.81	85.10	29.30	84.57	30.78	90
91	87.47	25.08	87.02	26.61	86.55	28.12	86.04	29.63	85.51	31.12	91
92	88.44	25.36	87.98	26.90	87.50	28.43	86.99	29.95	86.45	31.47	92
93	89.40	25.63	88.94	27.19	88.45	28.74	87.93	30.28	87.39	31.81	93
94	90.36	25.91	89.89	27.48	89.40	29.05	88.88	30.60	88.33	32.15	94
95	91.32	26.19	90.85	27.78	90.35	29.36	89.82	30.93	89.27	32.49	95
96	92.28	26.46	91.81	28.07	91.30	29.67	90.77	31.25	90.21	32.83	96
97	93.24	26.74	92.76	28.36	92.25	29.97	91.72	31.58	91.15	33.18	97
98	94.20	27.01	93.72	28.65	93.20	30.28	92.66	31.91	92.09	33.52	98
99	95.16	27.29	94.67	28.94	94.15	30.59	93.61	32.23	93.03	33.86	99
100	96.13	27.56	95.63	29.24	95.11	30.90	94.55	32.56	93.97	34.20	100
200	192.25	55.13	191.26	58.47	190.21	61.80	189.10	65.11	187.94	68.40	200
300	288.38	82.69	286.89	87.71	285.32	92.71	283.66	97.67	281.91	102.61	300
400	384.50	110.25	382.52	116.95	380.42	123.61	378.21	130.23	375.88	136.81	400
500	480.63	137.82	478.15	146.19	475.53	154.51	472.76	162.78	469.85	171.01	500
600	576.76	165.38	573.78	175.42	570.63	185.41	567.31	195.34	563.82	205.21	600
700	672.88	192.95	669.41	204.66	665.74	216.31	661.86	227.90	657.79	239.41	700
800	769.01	220.51	765.04	233.90	760.85	247.21	756.42	260.45	751.75	273.62	800
900	865.14	248.07	860.67	263.13	855.95	278.12	850.97	293.01	845.72	307.82	900
dis.	dep.	lat.	dep.	lat.	dep.	lat.	dep.	lat.	dep.	lat.	dis.
hyp.	opp.	adj.	opp.	adj.	opp.	adj.	opp.	adj.	opp.	adj.	hyp.
D	D sin	D cos	D sin	D cos	D sin	D cos	D sin	D cos	D sin	D cos	D
	74°		73°		72°		71°		70°		

TABLE VI. TRAVERSE TABLE

	21°		22°		23°		24°		25°	
D	D cos	D sin	D cos	D sin	D cos	D sin	D cos	D sin	D cos	D sin	D
hyp.	adj.	opp.	adj.	opp.	adj.	opp.	adj.	opp.	adj.	opp.	hyp.
dis.	lat.	dep.	lat.	dep.	lat.	dep.	lat.	dep.	lat.	dep.	dis.
11	10.27	3.94	10.20	4.12	10.13	4.30	10.05	4.47	9.97	4.65	11
12	11.20	4.30	11.13	4.50	11.05	4.69	10.96	4.88	10.88	5.07	12
13	12.14	4.66	12.05	4.87	11.97	5.08	11.88	5.29	11.78	5.49	13
14	13.07	5.02	12.98	5.24	12.89	5.47	12.79	5.69	12.69	5.92	14
15	14.00	5.38	13.91	5.62	13.81	5.86	13.70	6.10	13.59	6.34	15
16	14.94	5.73	14.83	5.99	14.73	6.25	14.62	6.51	14.50	6.76	16
17	15.87	6.09	15.76	6.37	15.65	6.64	15.53	6.91	15.41	7.18	17
18	16.80	6.45	16.69	6.74	16.57	7.03	16.44	7.32	16.31	7.61	18
19	17.74	6.81	17.62	7.12	17.49	7.42	17.36	7.73	17.22	8.03	19
20	18.67	7.17	18.54	7.49	18.41	7.81	18.27	8.13	18.13	8.45	20
21	19.61	7.53	19.47	7.87	19.33	8.21	19.18	8.54	19.03	8.87	21
22	20.54	7.88	20.40	8.24	20.25	8.60	20.10	8.95	19.94	9.30	22
23	21.47	8.24	21.33	8.62	21.17	8.99	21.01	9.35	20.85	9.72	23
24	22.41	8.60	22.25	8.99	22.09	9.38	21.93	9.76	21.75	10.14	24
25	23.34	8.96	23.18	9.37	23.01	9.77	22.84	10.17	22.66	10.57	25
26	24.27	9.32	24.11	9.74	23.93	10.16	23.75	10.58	23.56	10.99	26
27	25.21	9.68	25.03	10.11	24.85	10.55	24.67	10.98	24.47	11.41	27
28	26.14	10.03	25.96	10.49	25.77	10.94	25.58	11.39	25.38	11.83	28
29	27.07	10.39	26.89	10.86	26.69	11.33	26.49	11.80	26.28	12.26	29
30	28.01	10.75	27.82	11.24	27.62	11.72	27.41	12.20	27.19	12.68	30
31	28.94	11.11	28.74	11.61	28.54	12.11	28.32	12.61	28.10	13.10	31
32	29.87	11.47	29.67	11.99	29.46	12.50	29.23	13.02	29.00	13.52	32
33	30.81	11.83	30.60	12.36	30.38	12.89	30.15	13.42	29.91	13.95	33
34	31.74	12.18	31.52	12.74	31.30	13.28	31.06	13.83	30.81	14.37	34
35	32.68	12.54	32.45	13.11	32.22	13.68	31.97	14.24	31.72	14.79	35
36	33.61	12.90	33.38	13.49	33.14	14.07	32.89	14.64	32.63	15.21	36
37	34.54	13.26	34.31	13.86	34.06	14.46	33.80	15.05	33.53	15.64	37
38	35.48	13.62	35.23	14.24	34.98	14.85	34.71	15.46	34.44	16.06	38
39	36.41	13.98	36.16	14.61	35.90	15.24	35.63	15.86	35.35	16.48	39
40	37.34	14.33	37.09	14.98	36.82	15.63	36.54	16.27	36.25	16.90	40
41	38.28	14.69	38.01	15.36	37.74	16.02	37.46	16.68	37.16	17.33	41
42	39.21	15.05	38.94	15.73	38.66	16.41	38.37	17.08	38.06	17.75	42
43	40.14	15.41	39.87	16.11	39.58	16.80	39.28	17.49	38.97	18.17	43
44	41.08	15.77	40.80	16.48	40.50	17.19	40.20	17.90	39.88	18.60	44
45	42.01	16.13	41.72	16.86	41.42	17.58	41.11	18.30	40.78	19.02	45
46	42.94	16.48	42.65	17.23	42.34	17.97	42.02	18.71	41.69	19.44	46
47	43.88	16.84	43.58	17.61	43.26	18.36	42.94	19.12	42.60	19.86	47
48	44.81	17.20	44.50	17.98	44.18	18.76	43.85	19.52	43.50	20.29	48
49	45.75	17.56	45.43	18.36	45.10	19.15	44.76	19.93	44.41	20.71	49
50	46.68	17.92	46.36	18.73	46.03	19.54	45.68	20.34	45.32	21.13	50
51	47.61	18.28	47.29	19.10	46.95	19.93	46.59	20.74	46.22	21.55	51
52	48.55	18.64	48.21	19.48	47.87	20.32	47.50	21.15	47.13	21.98	52
53	49.48	18.99	49.14	19.85	48.79	20.71	48.42	21.56	48.03	22.40	53
54	50.41	19.35	50.07	20.23	49.71	21.10	49.33	21.96	48.94	22.82	54
55	51.35	19.71	51.00	20.60	50.63	21.49	50.24	22.37	49.85	23.24	55
56	52.28	20.07	51.92	20.98	51.55	21.88	51.16	22.78	50.75	23.67	56
57	53.21	20.43	52.85	21.35	52.47	22.27	52.07	23.18	51.66	24.09	57
58	54.15	20.79	53.78	21.73	53.39	22.66	52.99	23.59	52.57	24.51	58
59	55.08	21.14	54.70	22.10	54.31	23.05	53.90	24.00	53.47	24.93	59
dis.	dep.	lat.	dep.	lat.	dep.	lat.	dep.	lat.	dep.	lat.	dis.
hyp.	opp.	adj.	opp.	adj.	opp.	adj.	opp.	adj.	opp.	adj.	hyp.
D	D sin	D cos	D sin	D cos	D sin	D cos	D sin	D cos	D sin	D cos	D
	69°		68°		67°		66°		65°	

TABLE VI. TRAVERSE TABLE

	21°		22°		23°		24°		25°	
D	D cos	D sin	D cos	D sin	D cos	D sin	D cos	D sin	D cos	D sin	D
hyp.	adj.	opp.	adj.	opp.	adj.	opp.	adj.	opp.	adj.	opp.	hyp.
dis.	lat.	dep.	lat.	dep.	lat.	dep.	lat.	dep.	lat.	dep.	dis.
60	56.01	21.50	55.63	22.48	55.23	23.44	54.81	24.40	54.38	25.36	60
61	56.95	21.86	56.56	22.85	56.15	23.83	55.73	24.81	55.28	25.78	61
62	57.88	22.22	57.49	23.23	57.07	24.23	56.64	25.22	56.19	26.20	62
63	58.82	22.58	58.41	23.60	57.99	24.62	57.55	25.62	57.10	26.62	63
64	59.75	22.94	59.34	23.97	58.91	25.01	58.47	26.03	58.00	27.05	64
65	60.68	23.29	60.27	24.35	59.83	25.40	59.38	26.44	58.91	27.47	65
66	61.62	23.65	61.19	24.72	60.75	25.79	60.29	26.84	59.82	27.89	66
67	62.55	24.01	62.12	25.10	61.67	26.18	61.21	27.25	60.72	28.32	67
68	63.48	24.37	63.05	25.47	62.59	26.57	62.12	27.66	61.63	28.74	68
69	64.42	24.73	63.98	25.85	63.51	26.96	63.03	28.06	62.54	29.16	69
70	65.35	25.09	64.90	26.22	64.44	27.35	63.95	28.47	63.44	29.58	70
71	66.28	25.44	65.83	26.60	65.36	27.74	64.86	28.88	64.35	30.01	71
72	67.22	25.80	66.76	26.97	66.28	28.13	65.78	29.28	65.25	30.43	72
73	68.15	26.16	67.68	27.35	67.20	28.52	66.69	29.69	66.16	30.85	73
74	69.08	26.52	68.61	27.72	68.12	28.91	67.60	30.10	67.07	31.27	74
75	70.02	26.88	69.54	28.10	69.04	29.30	68.52	30.51	67.97	31.70	75
76	70.95	27.24	70.47	28.47	69.96	29.70	69.43	30.91	68.88	32.12	76
77	71.89	27.59	71.39	28.84	70.88	30.09	70.34	31.32	69.79	32.54	77
78	72.82	27.95	72.32	29.22	71.80	30.48	71.26	31.73	70.69	32.96	78
79	73.75	28.31	73.25	29.59	72.72	30.87	72.17	32.13	71.60	33.39	79
80	74.69	28.67	74.17	29.97	73.64	31.26	73.08	32.54	72.50	33.81	80
81	75.62	29.03	75.10	30.34	74.56	31.65	74.00	32.95	73.41	34.23	81
82	76.55	29.39	76.03	30.72	75.48	32.04	74.91	33.35	74.32	34.65	82
83	77.49	29.74	76.96	31.09	76.40	32.43	75.82	33.76	75.22	35.08	83
84	78.42	30.10	77.88	31.47	77.32	32.82	76.74	34.17	76.13	35.50	84
85	79.35	30.46	78.81	31.84	78.24	33.21	77.65	34.57	77.04	35.92	85
86	80.29	30.82	79.74	32.22	79.16	33.60	78.56	34.98	77.94	36.35	86
87	81.22	31.18	80.66	32.59	80.08	33.99	79.48	35.39	78.85	36.77	87
88	82.16	31.54	81.59	32.97	81.00	34.38	80.39	35.79	79.76	37.19	88
89	83.09	31.89	82.52	33.34	81.92	34.78	81.31	36.20	80.66	37.61	89
90	84.02	32.25	83.45	33.71	82.85	35.17	82.22	36.61	81.57	38.04	90
91	84.96	32.61	84.37	34.09	83.77	35.56	83.13	37.01	82.47	38.46	91
92	85.89	32.97	85.30	34.46	84.69	35.95	84.05	37.42	83.38	38.88	92
93	86.82	33.33	86.23	34.84	85.61	36.34	84.96	37.83	84.29	39.30	93
94	87.76	33.69	87.16	35.21	86.53	36.73	85.87	38.23	85.19	39.73	94
95	88.69	34.04	88.08	35.59	87.45	37.12	86.79	38.64	86.10	40.15	95
96	89.62	34.40	89.01	35.96	88.37	37.51	87.70	39.05	87.01	40.57	96
97	90.56	34.76	89.94	36.34	89.29	37.90	88.61	39.45	87.91	40.99	97
98	91.49	35.12	90.86	36.71	90.21	38.29	89.53	39.86	88.82	41.42	98
99	92.42	35.48	91.79	37.09	91.13	38.68	90.44	40.27	89.72	41.84	99
100	93.36	35.84	92.72	37.46	92.05	39.07	91.35	40.67	90.63	42.26	100
200	186.72	71.67	185.44	74.92	184.10	78.15	182.71	81.35	181.26	84.52	200
300	280.07	107.51	278.16	112.38	276.15	117.22	274.06	122.02	271.89	126.79	300
400	373.43	143.35	370.87	149.84	368.20	156.29	365.42	162.69	362.52	169.05	400
500	466.79	179.18	463.59	187.30	460.25	195.37	456.77	203.37	453.15	211.31	500
600	560.15	215.02	556.31	224.76	552.30	234.44	548.13	244.04	543.78	253.57	600
700	653.51	250.86	649.03	262.22	644.35	273.51	639.48	284.72	634.42	295.83	700
800	746.86	286.69	741.75	299.69	736.40	312.58	730.84	325.39	725.05	338.09	800
900	840.22	322.53	834.47	337.15	828.45	351.66	822.19	366.06	815.68	380.36	900
dis.	dep.	lat.	dep.	lat.	dep.	lat.	dep.	lat.	dep.	lat.	dis.
hyp.	opp.	adj.	opp.	adj.	opp.	adj.	opp.	adj.	opp.	adj.	hyp.
D	D sin	D cos	D sin	D cos	D sin	D cos	D sin	D cos	D sin	D cos	D
	69°		68°		67°		66°		65°	

TABLE VI. TRAVERSE TABLE

	26°		27°		28°		29°		30°	
D	D cos	D sin	D cos	D sin	D cos	D sin	D cos	D sin	D cos	D sin	D
hyp.	adj.	opp.	adj.	opp.	adj.	opp.	adj.	opp.	adj.	opp.	hyp.
dis.	lat.	dep.	lat.	dep.	lat.	dep.	lat.	dep.	lat.	dep.	dis.
11	9.89	4.82	9.80	4.99	9.71	5.16	9.62	5.33	9.53	5.50	11
12	10.79	5.26	10.69	5.45	10.60	5.63	10.50	5.82	10.39	6.00	12
13	11.68	5.70	11.58	5.90	11.48	6.10	11.37	6.30	11.26	6.50	13
14	12.58	6.14	12.47	6.36	12.36	6.57	12.24	6.79	12.12	7.00	14
15	13.48	6.58	13.37	6.81	13.24	7.04	13.12	7.27	12.99	7.50	15
16	14.38	7.01	14.26	7.26	14.13	7.51	13.99	7.76	13.86	8.00	16
17	15.28	7.45	15.15	7.72	15.01	7.98	14.87	8.24	14.72	8.50	17
18	16.18	7.89	16.04	8.17	15.89	8.45	15.74	8.73	15.59	9.00	18
19	17.08	8.33	16.93	8.63	16.78	8.92	16.62	9.21	16.45	9.50	19
20	17.98	8.77	17.82	9.08	17.66	9.39	17.49	9.70	17.32	10.00	20
21	18.87	9.21	18.71	9.53	18.54	9.86	18.37	10.18	18.19	10.50	21
22	19.77	9.64	19.60	9.99	19.42	10.33	19.24	10.67	19.05	11.00	22
23	20.67	10.08	20.49	10.44	20.31	10.80	20.12	11.15	19.92	11.50	23
24	21.57	10.52	21.38	10.90	21.19	11.27	20.99	11.64	20.78	12.00	24
25	22.47	10.96	22.28	11.35	22.07	11.74	21.87	12.12	21.65	12.50	25
26	23.37	11.40	23.17	11.80	22.96	12.21	22.74	12.61	22.52	13.00	26
27	24.27	11.84	24.06	12.26	23.84	12.68	23.61	13.09	23.38	13.50	27
28	25.17	12.27	24.95	12.71	24.72	13.15	24.49	13.57	24.25	14.00	28
29	26.07	12.71	25.84	13.17	25.61	13.61	25.36	14.06	25.11	14.50	29
30	26.96	13.15	26.73	13.62	26.49	14.08	26.24	14.54	25.98	15.00	30
31	27.86	13.59	27.62	14.07	27.37	14.55	27.11	15.03	26.85	15.50	31
32	28.76	14.03	28.51	14.53	28.25	15.02	27.99	15.51	27.71	16.00	32
33	29.66	14.47	29.40	14.98	29.14	15.49	28.86	16.00	28.58	16.50	33
34	30.56	14.90	30.29	15.44	30.02	15.96	29.74	16.48	29.44	17.00	34
35	31.46	15.34	31.19	15.89	30.90	16.43	30.61	16.97	30.31	17.50	35
36	32.36	15.78	32.08	16.34	31.79	16.90	31.49	17.45	31.18	18.00	36
37	33.26	16.22	32.97	16.80	32.67	17.37	32.36	17.94	32.04	18.50	37
38	34.15	16.66	33.86	17.25	33.55	17.84	33.24	18.42	32.91	19.00	38
39	35.05	17.10	34.75	17.71	34.43	18.31	34.11	18.91	33.77	19.50	39
40	35.95	17.53	35.64	18.16	35.32	18.78	34.98	19.39	34.64	20.00	40
41	36.85	17.97	36.53	18.61	36.20	19.25	35.86	19.88	35.51	20.50	41
42	37.75	18.41	37.42	19.07	37.08	19.72	36.73	20.36	36.37	21.00	42
43	38.65	18.85	38.31	19.52	37.97	20.19	37.61	20.85	37.24	21.50	43
44	39.55	19.29	39.20	19.98	38.85	20.66	38.48	21.33	38.11	22.00	44
45	40.45	19.73	40.10	20.43	39.73	21.13	39.36	21.82	38.97	22.50	45
46	41.34	20.17	40.99	20.88	40.62	21.60	40.23	22.30	39.84	23.00	46
47	42.24	20.60	41.88	21.34	41.50	22.07	41.11	22.79	40.70	23.50	47
48	43.14	21.04	42.77	21.79	42.38	22.53	41.98	23.27	41.57	24.00	48
49	44.04	21.48	43.66	22.25	43.26	23.00	42.86	23.76	42.44	24.50	49
50	44.94	21.92	44.55	22.70	44.15	23.47	43.73	24.24	43.30	25.00	50
51	45.84	22.36	45.44	23.15	45.03	23.94	44.61	24.73	44.17	25.50	51
52	46.74	22.80	46.33	23.61	45.91	24.41	45.48	25.21	45.03	26.00	52
53	47.64	23.23	47.22	24.06	46.80	24.88	46.35	25.69	45.90	26.50	53
54	48.53	23.67	48.11	24.52	47.68	25.35	47.23	26.18	46.77	27.00	54
55	49.43	24.11	49.01	24.97	48.56	25.82	48.10	26.66	47.63	27.50	55
56	50.33	24.55	49.90	25.42	49.45	26.29	48.98	27.15	48.50	28.00	56
57	51.23	24.99	50.79	25.88	50.33	26.76	49.85	27.63	49.36	28.50	57
58	52.13	25.43	51.68	26.33	51.21	27.23	50.73	28.12	50.23	29.00	58
59	53.03	25.86	52.57	26.79	52.09	27.70	51.60	28.60	51.10	29.50	59
dis.	dep.	lat.	dep.	lat.	dep.	lat.	dep.	lat.	dep.	lat.	dis.
hyp.	opp.	adj.	opp.	adj.	opp.	adj.	opp.	adj.	opp.	adj.	hyp.
D	D sin	D cos	D sin	D cos	D sin	D cos	D sin	D cos	D sin	D cos	D
	64°		63°		62°		61°		60°	

TABLE VI. TRAVERSE TABLE 19

	26°		27°		28°		29°		30°	
D	D cos	D sin	D cos	D sin	D cos	D sin	D cos	D sin	D cos	D sin	D
hyp.	adj.	opp.	adj.	opp.	adj.	opp.	adj.	opp.	adj.	opp.	hyp.
dis.	lat.	dep.	lat.	dep.	lat.	dep.	lat.	dep.	lat.	dep.	dis.
60	53.93	26.30	53.46	27.24	52.98	28.17	52.48	29.09	51.96	30.00	60
61	54.83	26.74	54.35	27.69	53.86	28.64	53.35	29.57	52.83	30.50	61
62	55.73	27.18	55.24	28.15	54.74	29.11	54.23	30.06	53.69	31.00	62
63	56.62	27.62	56.13	28.60	55.63	29.58	55.10	30.54	54.56	31.50	63
64	57.52	28.06	57.02	29.06	56.51	30.05	55.98	31.03	55.43	32.00	64
65	58.42	28.49	57.92	29.51	57.39	30.52	56.85	31.51	56.29	32.50	65
66	59.32	28.93	58.81	29.96	58.27	30.99	57.72	32.00	57.16	33.00	66
67	60.22	29.37	59.70	30.42	59.16	31.45	58.60	32.48	58.02	33.50	67
68	61.12	29.81	60.59	30.87	60.04	31.92	59.47	32.97	58.89	34.00	68
69	62.02	30.25	61.48	31.33	60.92	32.39	60.35	33.45	59.76	34.50	69
70	62.92	30.69	62.37	31.78	61.81	32.86	61.22	33.94	60.62	35.00	70
71	63.81	31.12	63.26	32.23	62.69	33.33	62.10	34.42	61.49	35.50	71
72	64.71	31.56	64.15	32.69	63.57	33.80	62.97	34.91	62.35	36.00	72
73	65.61	32.00	65.04	33.14	64.46	34.27	63.85	35.39	63.22	36.50	73
74	66.51	32.44	65.93	33.60	65.34	34.74	64.72	35.88	64.09	37.00	74
75	67.41	32.88	66.83	34.05	66.22	35.21	65.60	36.36	64.95	37.50	75
76	68.31	33.32	67.72	34.50	67.10	35.68	66.47	36.85	65.82	38.00	76
77	69.21	33.75	68.61	34.96	67.99	36.15	67.35	37.33	66.68	38.50	77
78	70.11	34.19	69.50	35.41	68.87	36.62	68.22	37.82	67.55	39.00	78
79	71.00	34.63	70.39	35.87	69.75	37.09	69.09	38.30	68.42	39.50	79
80	71.90	35.07	71.28	36.32	70.64	37.56	69.97	38.78	69.28	40.00	80
81	72.80	35.51	72.17	36.77	71.52	38.03	70.84	39.27	70.15	40.50	81
82	73.70	35.95	73.06	37.23	72.40	38.50	71.72	39.75	71.01	41.00	82
83	74.60	36.38	73.95	37.68	73.28	38.97	72.59	40.24	71.88	41.50	83
84	75.50	36.82	74.84	38.14	74.17	39.44	73.47	40.72	72.75	42.00	84
85	76.40	37.26	75.74	38.59	75.05	39.91	74.34	41.21	73.61	42.50	85
86	77.30	37.70	76.63	39.04	75.93	40.37	75.22	41.69	74.48	43.00	86
87	78.20	38.14	77.52	39.50	76.82	40.84	76.09	42.18	75.34	43.50	87
88	79.09	38.58	78.41	39.95	77.70	41.31	76.97	42.66	76.21	44.00	88
89	79.99	39.01	79.30	40.41	78.58	41.78	77.84	43.15	77.08	44.50	89
90	80.89	39.45	80.19	40.86	79.47	42.25	78.72	43.63	77.94	45.00	90
91	81.79	39.89	81.08	41.31	80.35	42.72	79.59	44.12	78.81	45.50	91
92	82.69	40.33	81.97	41.77	81.23	43.19	80.46	44.60	79.67	46.00	92
93	83.59	40.77	82.86	42.22	82.11	43.66	81.34	45.09	80.54	46.50	93
94	84.49	41.21	83.75	42.68	83.00	44.13	82.21	45.57	81.41	47.00	94
95	85.39	41.65	84.65	43.13	83.88	44.60	83.09	46.06	82.27	47.50	95
96	86.28	42.08	85.54	43.58	84.76	45.07	83.96	46.54	83.14	48.00	96
97	87.18	42.52	86.43	44.04	85.65	45.54	84.84	47.03	84.00	48.50	97
98	88.08	42.96	87.32	44.49	86.53	46.01	85.71	47.51	84.87	49.00	98
99	88.98	43.40	88.21	44.95	87.41	46.48	86.59	48.00	85.74	49.50	99
100	89.88	43.84	89.10	45.40	88.29	46.95	87.46	48.48	86.60	50.00	100
200	179.76	87.67	178.20	90.80	176.59	93.89	174.92	96.96	173.21	100.00	200
300	269.64	131.51	267.30	136.20	264.88	140.84	262.39	145.44	259.81	150.00	300
400	359.52	175.35	356.40	181.60	353.18	187.79	349.85	193.92	346.41	200.00	400
500	449.40	219.19	445.50	227.00	441.47	234.74	437.31	242.40	433.01	250.00	500
600	539.28	263.02	534.60	272.39	529.77	281.68	524.77	290.89	519.62	300.00	600
700	629.16	306.86	623.70	317.79	618.06	328.63	612.23	339.37	606.22	350.00	700
800	719.04	350.70	712.81	363.19	706.36	375.58	699.70	387.85	692.82	400.00	800
900	808.91	394.53	801.91	408.59	794.65	422.52	787.16	436.33	779.42	450.00	900
dis.	dep.	lat.	dep.	lat.	dep.	lat.	dep.	lat.	dep.	lat.	dis.
hyp.	opp.	adj.	opp.	adj.	opp.	adj.	opp.	adj.	opp.	adj.	hyp.
D	D sin	D cos	D sin	D cos	D sin	D cos	D sin	D cos	D sin	D cos	D
	64°		63°		62°		61°		60°		

TABLE VI. TRAVERSE TABLE

D	31°		32°		33°		34°		35°	D
	D cos	D sin	D cos	D sin	D cos	D sin	D cos	D sin	D cos	D sin	
hyp.	adj.	opp.	adj.	opp.	adj.	opp.	adj.	opp.	adj.	opp.	hyp.
dis.	lat.	dep.	lat.	dep.	lat.	dep.	lat.	dep.	lat.	dep.	dis.
11	9.43	5.67	9.33	5.83	9.23	5.99	9.12	6.15	9.01	6.31	11
12	10.29	6.18	10.18	6.36	10.06	6.54	9.95	6.71	9.83	6.88	12
13	11.14	6.70	11.02	6.89	10.90	7.08	10.78	7.27	10.65	7.46	13
14	12.00	7.21	11.87	7.42	11.74	7.62	11.61	7.83	11.47	8.03	14
15	12.86	7.73	12.72	7.95	12.58	8.17	12.44	8.39	12.29	8.60	15
16	13.71	8.24	13.57	8.48	13.42	8.71	13.26	8.95	13.11	9.18	16
17	14.57	8.76	14.42	9.01	14.26	9.26	14.09	9.51	13.93	9.75	17
18	15.43	9.27	15.26	9.54	15.10	9.80	14.92	10.07	14.74	10.32	18
19	16.29	9.79	16.11	10.07	15.93	10.35	15.75	10.62	15.56	10.90	19
20	17.14	10.30	16.96	10.60	16.77	10.89	16.58	11.18	16.38	11.47	20
21	18.00	10.82	17.81	11.13	17.61	11.44	17.41	11.74	17.20	12.05	21
22	18.86	11.33	18.66	11.66	18.45	11.98	18.24	12.30	18.02	12.62	22
23	19.71	11.85	19.51	12.19	19.29	12.53	19.07	12.86	18.84	13.19	23
24	20.57	12.36	20.35	12.72	20.13	13.07	19.90	13.42	19.66	13.77	24
25	21.43	12.88	21.20	13.25	20.97	13.62	20.73	13.98	20.48	14.34	25
26	22.29	13.39	22.05	13.78	21.81	14.16	21.55	14.54	21.30	14.91	26
27	23.14	13.91	22.90	14.31	22.64	14.71	22.38	15.10	22.12	15.49	27
28	24.00	14.42	23.75	14.84	23.48	15.25	23.21	15.66	22.94	16.06	28
29	24.86	14.94	24.59	15.37	24.32	15.79	24.04	16.22	23.76	16.63	29
30	25.71	15.45	25.44	15.90	25.16	16.34	24.87	16.78	24.57	17.21	30
31	26.57	15.97	26.29	16.43	26.00	16.88	25.70	17.33	25.39	17.78	31
32	27.43	16.48	27.14	16.96	26.84	17.43	26.53	17.89	26.21	18.35	32
33	28.29	17.00	27.99	17.49	27.68	17.97	27.36	18.45	27.03	18.93	33
34	29.14	17.51	28.83	18.02	28.51	18.52	28.19	19.01	27.85	19.50	34
35	30.00	18.03	29.68	18.55	29.35	19.06	29.02	19.57	28.67	20.08	35
36	30.86	18.54	30.53	19.08	30.19	19.61	29.85	20.13	29.49	20.65	36
37	31.72	19.06	31.38	19.61	31.03	20.15	30.67	20.69	30.31	21.22	37
38	32.57	19.57	32.23	20.14	31.87	20.70	31.50	21.25	31.13	21.80	38
39	33.43	20.09	33.07	20.67	32.71	21.24	32.33	21.81	31.95	22.37	39
40	34.29	20.60	33.92	21.20	33.55	21.79	33.16	22.37	32.77	22.94	40
41	35.14	21.12	34.77	21.73	34.39	22.33	33.99	22.93	33.59	23.52	41
42	36.00	21.63	35.62	22.26	35.22	22.87	34.82	23.49	34.40	24.09	42
43	36.86	22.15	36.47	22.79	36.06	23.42	35.65	24.05	35.22	24.66	43
44	37.72	22.66	37.31	23.32	36.90	23.96	36.48	24.60	36.04	25.24	44
45	38.57	23.18	38.16	23.85	37.74	24.51	37.31	25.16	36.86	25.81	45
46	39.43	23.69	39.01	24.38	38.58	25.05	38.14	25.72	37.68	26.38	46
47	40.29	24.21	39.86	24.91	39.42	25.60	38.96	26.28	38.50	26.96	47
48	41.14	24.72	40.71	25.44	40.26	26.14	39.79	26.84	39.32	27.53	48
49	42.00	25.24	41.55	25.97	41.09	26.69	40.62	27.40	40.14	28.11	49
50	42.86	25.75	42.40	26.50	41.93	27.23	41.45	27.96	40.96	28.68	50
51	43.72	26.27	43.25	27.03	42.77	27.78	42.28	28.52	41.78	29.25	51
52	44.57	26.78	44.10	27.56	43.61	28.32	43.11	29.08	42.60	29.83	52
53	45.43	27.30	44.95	28.09	44.45	28.87	43.94	29.64	43.42	30.40	53
54	46.29	27.81	45.79	28.62	45.29	29.41	44.77	30.20	44.23	30.97	54
55	47.14	28.33	46.64	29.15	46.13	29.96	45.60	30.76	45.05	31.55	55
56	48.00	28.84	47.49	29.68	46.97	30.50	46.43	31.31	45.87	32.12	56
57	48.86	29.36	48.34	30.21	47.80	31.04	47.26	31.87	46.69	32.69	57
58	49.72	29.87	49.19	30.74	48.64	31.59	48.08	32.43	47.51	33.27	58
59	50.57	30.39	50.03	31.27	49.48	32.13	48.91	32.99	48.33	33.84	59
dis.	dep.	lat.	dep.	lat.	dep.	lat.	dep.	lat.	dep.	lat.	dis.
hyp.	opp.	adj.	opp.	adj.	opp.	adj.	opp.	adj.	opp.	adj.	hyp.
D	D sin	D cos	D sin	D cos	D sin	D cos	D sin	D cos	D sin	D cos	D
	59°		58°		57°		56°		55°	

TABLE VI. TRAVERSE TABLE 21

D	31°		32°		33°		34°		35°		D
	D cos	D sin	D cos	D sin	D cos	D sin	D cos	D sin	D cos	D sin	
hyp.	adj.	opp.	adj.	opp.	adj.	opp.	adj.	opp.	adj.	opp.	hyp.
dis.	lat.	dep.	lat.	dep.	lat.	dep.	lat.	dep.	lat.	dep.	dis.
60	51.43	30.90	50.88	31.80	50.32	32.68	49.74	33.55	49.15	34.41	60
61	52.29	31.42	51.73	32.33	51.16	33.22	50.57	34.11	49.97	34.99	61
62	53.14	31.93	52.58	32.85	52.00	33.77	51.40	34.67	50.79	35.56	62
63	54.00	32.45	53.43	33.38	52.84	34.31	52.23	35.23	51.61	36.14	63
64	54.86	32.96	54.28	33.91	53.67	34.86	53.06	35.79	52.43	36.71	64
65	55.72	33.48	55.12	34.44	54.51	35.40	53.89	36.35	53.24	37.28	65
66	56.57	33.99	55.97	34.97	55.35	35.95	54.72	36.91	54.06	37.86	66
67	57.43	34.51	56.82	35.50	56.19	36.49	55.55	37.46	54.88	38.43	67
68	58.29	35.02	57.67	36.03	57.03	37.04	56.37	38.03	55.70	39.00	68
69	59.14	35.54	58.52	36.56	57.87	37.58	57.20	38.58	56.52	39.58	69
70	60.00	36.05	59.36	37.09	58.71	38.12	58.03	39.14	57.34	40.15	70
71	60.86	36.57	60.21	37.62	59.55	38.67	58.86	39.70	58.16	40.72	71
72	61.72	37.08	61.06	38.15	60.38	39.21	59.69	40.26	58.98	41.30	72
73	62.57	37.60	61.91	38.68	61.22	39.76	60.52	40.82	59.80	41.87	73
74	63.43	38.11	62.76	39.21	62.06	40.30	61.35	41.38	60.62	42.44	74
75	64.29	38.63	63.60	39.74	62.90	40.85	62.18	41.94	61.44	43.02	75
76	65.14	39.14	64.45	40.27	63.74	41.39	63.01	42.50	62.26	43.59	76
77	66.00	39.66	65.30	40.80	64.58	41.94	63.84	43.06	63.07	44.17	77
78	66.86	40.17	66.15	41.33	65.42	42.48	64.66	43.62	63.89	44.74	78
79	67.72	40.69	67.00	41.86	66.25	43.03	65.49	44.18	64.71	45.31	79
80	68.57	41.20	67.84	42.39	67.09	43.57	66.32	44.74	65.53	45.89	80
81	69.43	41.72	68.69	42.92	67.93	44.12	67.15	45.29	66.35	46.46	81
82	70.29	42.23	69.54	43.45	68.77	44.66	67.98	45.85	67.17	47.03	82
83	71.14	42.75	70.39	43.98	69.61	45.20	68.81	46.41	67.99	47.61	83
84	72.00	43.26	71.24	44.51	70.45	45.75	69.64	46.97	68.81	48.18	84
85	72.86	43.78	72.08	45.04	71.29	46.29	70.47	47.53	69.63	48.75	85
86	73.72	44.29	72.93	45.57	72.13	46.84	71.30	48.09	70.45	49.33	86
87	74.57	44.81	73.78	46.10	72.96	47.38	72.13	48.65	71.27	49.90	87
88	75.43	45.32	74.63	46.63	73.80	47.93	72.96	49.21	72.09	50.47	88
89	76.29	45.84	75.48	47.16	74.64	48.47	73.78	49.77	72.90	51.05	89
90	77.15	46.35	76.32	47.69	75.48	49.02	74.61	50.33	73.72	51.62	90
91	78.00	46.87	77.17	48.22	76.32	49.56	75.44	50.89	74.54	52.20	91
92	78.86	47.38	78.02	48.75	77.16	50.11	76.27	51.45	75.36	52.77	92
93	79.72	47.90	78.87	49.28	78.00	50.65	77.10	52.00	76.18	53.34	93
94	80.57	48.41	79.72	49.81	78.83	51.20	77.93	52.56	77.00	53.92	94
95	81.43	48.93	80.56	50.34	79.67	51.74	78.76	53.12	77.82	54.49	95
96	82.29	49.44	81.41	50.87	80.51	52.29	79.59	53.68	78.64	55.06	96
97	83.15	49.96	82.26	51.40	81.35	52.83	80.42	54.24	79.46	55.64	97
98	84.00	50.47	83.11	51.93	82.19	53.37	81.25	54.80	80.28	56.21	98
99	84.86	50.99	83.96	52.46	83.03	53.92	82.07	55.36	81.10	56.78	99
100	85.72	51.50	84.80	52.99	83.87	54.46	82.90	55.92	81.92	57.36	100
200	171.43	103.01	169.61	105.98	167.73	108.93	165.81	111.84	163.83	114.72	200
300	257.15	154.51	254.41	158.98	251.60	163.39	248.71	167.76	245.75	172.07	300
400	342.87	206.02	339.22	211.97	335.47	217.86	331.62	223.68	327.66	229.43	400
500	428.58	257.52	424.02	264.96	419.34	272.32	414.52	279.60	409.58	286.79	500
600	514.30	309.02	508.83	317.95	503.20	326.78	497.42	335.52	491.49	344.15	600
700	600.02	360.53	593.63	370.94	587.07	381.25	580.33	391.44	573.41	401.50	700
800	685.73	412.03	678.44	423.94	670.94	435.71	663.23	447.35	655.32	458.86	800
900	771.45	463.53	763.24	476.93	754.80	490.18	746.13	503.27	737.24	516.22	900
dis.	dep.	lat.	dep.	lat.	dep.	lat.	dep.	lat.	dep.	lat.	dis.
hyp.	opp.	adj.	opp.	adj.	opp.	adj.	opp.	adj.	opp.	adj.	hyp.
D	D sin	D cos	D sin	D cos	D sin	D cos	D sin	D cos	D sin	D cos	D
	59°		58°		57°		56°		55°		

TABLE VI. TRAVERSE TABLE

	36°		37°		38°		39°		40°	
D	D cos	D sin	D cos	D sin	D cos	D sin	D cos	D sin	D cos	D sin	D
hyp.	adj.	opp.	adj.	opp.	adj.	opp.	adj.	opp.	adj.	opp.	hyp.
dis.	lat.	dep.	lat.	dep.	lat.	dep.	lat.	dep.	lat.	dep.	dis.
11	8.90	6.47	8.78	6.62	8.67	6.77	8.55	6.92	8.43	7.07	11
12	9.71	7.05	9.58	7.22	9.46	7.39	9.33	7.55	9.19	7.71	12
13	10.52	7.64	10.38	7.82	10.24	8.00	10.10	8.18	9.96	8.36	13
14	11.33	8.23	11.18	8.43	11.03	8.62	10.88	8.81	10.72	9.00	14
15	12.14	8.82	11.98	9.03	11.82	9.23	11.66	9.44	11.49	9.64	15
16	12.94	9.40	12.78	9.63	12.61	9.85	12.43	10.07	12.26	10.28	16
17	13.75	9.99	13.58	10.23	13.40	10.47	13.21	10.70	13.02	10.93	17
18	14.56	10.58	14.38	10.83	14.18	11.08	13.99	11.33	13.79	11.57	18
19	15.37	11.17	15.17	11.43	14.97	11.70	14.77	11.96	14.55	12.21	19
20	16.18	11.76	15.97	12.04	15.76	12.31	15.54	12.59	15.32	12.86	20
21	16.99	12.34	16.77	12.64	16.55	12.93	16.32	13.22	16.09	13.50	21
22	17.80	12.93	17.57	13.24	17.34	13.54	17.10	13.85	16.85	14.14	22
23	18.61	13.52	18.37	13.84	18.12	14.16	17.87	14.47	17.62	14.78	23
24	19.42	14.11	19.17	14.44	18.91	14.78	18.65	15.10	18.39	15.43	24
25	20.23	14.69	19.97	15.05	19.70	15.39	19.43	15.73	19.15	16.07	25
26	21.03	15.28	20.76	15.65	20.49	16.01	20.21	16.36	19.92	16.71	26
27	21.84	15.87	21.56	16.25	21.28	16.62	20.98	16.99	20.68	17.36	27
28	22.65	16.46	22.36	16.85	22.06	17.24	21.76	17.62	21.45	18.00	28
29	23.46	17.05	23.16	17.45	22.85	17.85	22.54	18.25	22.22	18.64	29
30	24.27	17.63	23.96	18.05	23.64	18.47	23.31	18.88	22.98	19.28	30
31	25.08	18.22	24.76	18.66	24.43	19.09	24.09	19.51	23.75	19.93	31
32	25.89	18.81	25.56	19.26	25.22	19.70	24.87	20.14	24.51	20.57	32
33	26.70	19.40	26.35	19.86	26.00	20.32	25.65	20.77	25.28	21.21	33
34	27.51	19.98	27.15	20.46	26.79	20.93	26.42	21.40	26.05	21.85	34
35	28.32	20.57	27.95	21.06	27.58	21.55	27.20	22.03	26.81	22.50	35
36	29.12	21.16	28.75	21.67	28.37	22.16	27.98	22.66	27.58	23.14	36
37	29.93	21.75	29.55	22.27	29.16	22.78	28.75	23.28	28.34	23.78	37
38	30.74	22.34	30.35	22.87	29.94	23.40	29.53	23.91	29.11	24.43	38
39	31.55	22.92	31.15	23.47	30.73	24.01	30.31	24.54	29.88	25.07	39
40	32.36	23.51	31.95	24.07	31.52	24.63	31.09	25.17	30.64	25.71	40
41	33.17	24.10	32.74	24.67	32.31	25.24	31.86	25.80	31.41	26.35	41
42	33.98	24.69	33.54	25.28	33.10	25.86	32.64	26.43	32.17	27.00	42
43	34.79	25.27	34.34	25.88	33.88	26.47	33.42	27.06	32.94	27.64	43
44	35.60	25.86	35.14	26.48	34.67	27.09	34.19	27.69	33.71	28.28	44
45	36.41	26.45	35.94	27.08	35.46	27.70	34.97	28.32	34.47	28.93	45
46	37.21	27.04	36.74	27.68	36.25	28.32	35.75	28.95	35.24	29.57	46
47	38.02	27.63	37.54	28.29	37.04	28.94	36.53	29.58	36.00	30.21	47
48	38.83	28.21	38.33	28.89	37.82	29.55	37.30	30.21	36.77	30.85	48
49	39.64	28.80	39.13	29.49	38.61	30.17	38.08	30.84	37.54	31.50	49
50	40.45	29.39	39.93	30.09	39.40	30.78	38.86	31.47	38.30	32.14	50
51	41.26	29.98	40.73	30.69	40.19	31.40	39.63	32.10	39.07	32.78	51
52	42.07	30.56	41.53	31.29	40.98	32.01	40.41	32.72	39.83	33.42	52
53	42.88	31.15	42.33	31.90	41.76	32.63	41.19	33.35	40.60	34.07	53
54	43.69	31.74	43.13	32.50	42.55	33.25	41.97	33.98	41.37	34.71	54
55	44.50	32.33	43.92	33.10	43.34	33.86	42.74	34.61	42.13	35.35	55
56	45.30	32.92	44.72	33.70	44.13	34.48	43.52	35.24	42.90	36.00	56
57	46.11	33.50	45.52	34.30	44.92	35.09	44.30	35.87	43.66	36.64	57
58	46.92	34.09	46.32	34.91	45.70	35.71	45.07	36.50	44.43	37.28	58
59	47.73	34.68	47.12	35.51	46.49	36.32	45.85	37.13	45.20	37.92	59
dis.	dep.	lat.	dep.	lat.	dep.	lat.	dep.	lat.	dep.	lat.	dis.
hyp.	opp.	adj.	opp.	adj.	opp.	adj.	opp.	adj.	opp.	adj.	hyp.
D	D sin	D cos	D sin	D cos	D sin	D cos	D sin	D cos	D sin	D cos	D
	54°		53°		52°		51°		50°		

TABLE VI. TRAVERSE TABLE

	36°		37°		38°		39°		40°		
D	D cos	D sin	D cos	D sin	D cos	D sin	D cos	D sin	D cos	D sin	D
hyp.	adj.	opp.	adj.	opp.	adj.	opp.	adj.	opp.	adj.	opp.	hyp.
dis.	lat.	dep.	lat.	dep.	lat.	dep.	lat.	dep.	lat.	dep.	dis.
60	48.54	35.27	47.92	36.11	47.28	36.94	46.63	37.76	45.96	38.57	60
61	49.35	35.85	48.72	36.71	48.07	37.56	47.41	38.39	46.73	39.21	61
62	50.16	36.44	49.52	37.31	48.86	38.17	48.18	39.02	47.49	39.85	62
63	50.97	37.03	50.31	37.91	49.64	38.79	48.96	39.65	48.26	40.50	63
64	51.78	37.62	51.11	38.52	50.43	39.40	49.74	40.28	49.03	41.14	64
65	52.59	38.21	51.91	39.12	51.22	40.02	50.51	40.91	49.79	41.78	65
66	53.40	38.79	52.71	39.72	52.01	40.63	51.29	41.54	50.56	42.42	66
67	54.20	39.38	53.51	40.32	52.80	41.25	52.07	42.16	51.32	43.07	67
68	55.01	39.97	54.31	40.92	53.58	41.86	52.85	42.79	52.09	43.71	68
69	55.82	40.56	55.11	41.53	54.37	42.48	53.52	43.42	52.86	44.35	69
70	56.63	41.14	55.90	42.13	55.16	43.10	54.40	44.05	53.62	45.00	70
71	57.44	41.73	56.70	42.73	55.95	43.71	55.18	44.68	54.39	45.64	71
72	58.25	42.32	57.50	43.33	56.74	44.33	55.95	45.31	55.16	46.28	72
73	59.06	42.91	58.30	43.93	57.52	44.94	56.73	45.94	55.92	46.92	73
74	59.87	43.50	59.10	44.53	58.31	45.56	57.51	46.57	56.69	47.57	74
75	60.68	44.08	59.90	45.14	59.10	46.17	58.29	47.20	57.45	48.21	75
76	61.49	44.67	60.70	45.74	59.89	46.79	59.06	47.83	58.22	48.85	76
77	62.29	45.26	61.49	46.34	60.68	47.41	59.84	48.46	58.99	49.49	77
78	63.10	45.85	62.29	46.94	61.46	48.02	60.62	49.09	59.75	50.14	78
79	63.91	46.43	63.09	47.54	62.25	48.64	61.39	49.72	60.52	50.78	79
80	64.72	47.02	63.89	48.15	63.04	49.25	62.17	50.35	61.28	51.42	80
81	65.53	47.61	64.69	48.75	63.83	49.87	62.95	50.97	62.05	52.07	81
82	66.34	48.20	65.49	49.35	64.62	50.48	63.73	51.60	62.82	52.71	82
83	67.15	48.79	66.29	49.95	65.40	51.10	64.50	52.23	63.58	53.35	83
84	67.96	49.37	67.09	50.55	66.19	51.72	65.28	52.86	64.35	53.99	84
85	68.77	49.96	67.88	51.15	66.98	52.33	66.06	53.49	65.11	54.64	85
86	69.58	50.55	68.68	51.76	67.77	52.95	66.83	54.12	65.88	55.28	86
87	70.38	51.14	69.48	52.36	68.56	53.56	67.61	54.75	66.65	55.92	87
88	71.19	51.73	70.28	52.96	69.34	54.18	68.39	55.38	67.41	56.57	88
89	72.00	52.31	71.08	53.56	70.13	54.79	69.17	56.01	68.18	57.21	89
90	72.81	52.90	71.88	54.16	70.92	55.41	69.94	56.64	68.94	57.85	90
91	73.62	53.49	72.68	54.77	71.71	56.03	70.72	57.27	69.71	58.49	91
92	74.43	54.08	73.47	55.37	72.50	56.64	71.50	57.90	70.48	59.14	92
93	75.24	54.66	74.27	55.97	73.28	57.26	72.27	58.53	71.24	59.78	93
94	76.05	55.25	75.07	56.57	74.07	57.87	73.05	59.16	72.01	60.42	94
95	76.86	55.84	75.87	57.17	74.86	58.49	73.83	59.79	72.77	61.06	95
96	77.67	56.43	76.67	57.77	75.65	59.10	74.61	60.41	73.54	61.71	96
97	78.47	57.02	77.47	58.38	76.44	59.72	75.38	61.04	74.31	62.35	97
98	79.28	57.60	78.27	58.98	77.22	60.33	76.16	61.67	75.07	62.99	98
99	80.09	58.19	79.06	59.58	78.01	60.95	76.94	62.30	75.84	63.64	99
100	80.90	58.78	79.86	60.18	78.80	61.57	77.71	62.93	76.60	64.28	100
200	161.80	117.56	159.73	120.36	157.60	123.13	155.43	125.86	153.21	128.56	200
300	242.71	176.34	239.59	180.54	236.40	184.70	233.14	188.80	229.81	192.84	300
400	323.61	235.11	319.45	240.73	315.20	246.26	310.86	251.73	306.42	257.12	400
500	404.51	293.89	399.32	300.91	394.01	307.83	388.57	314.66	383.02	321.39	500
600	485.41	352.67	479.18	361.09	472.81	369.40	466.29	377.59	459.63	385.67	600
700	566.31	411.45	559.04	421.27	551.61	430.96	544.00	440.52	536.23	449.95	700
800	647.21	470.23	638.91	481.45	630.41	492.53	621.72	503.46	612.84	514.23	800
900	728.12	529.01	718.77	541.63	709.21	554.09	699.43	566.39	689.44	578.51	900
dis.	dep.	lat.	dep.	lat.	dep.	lat.	dep.	lat.	dep.	lat.	dis.
hyp.	opp.	adj.	opp.	adj.	opp.	adj.	opp.	adj.	opp.	adj.	hyp.
D	D sin	D cos	D sin	D cos	D sin	D cos	D sin	D cos	D sin	D cos	D
	54°		53°		52°		51°		50°		

TABLE VI. TRAVERSE TABLE

	41°		42°		43°		44°		45°	
D	D cos	D sin	D cos	D sin	D cos	D sin	D cos	D sin	D cos	D sin	D
hyp.	adj.	opp.	adj.	opp.	adj.	opp.	adj.	opp.	adj.	opp.	hyp.
dis.	lat.	dep.	lat.	dep.	lat.	dep.	lat.	dep.	lat.	dep.	dis.
11	8.30	7.22	8.17	7.36	8.04	7.50	7.91	7.64	7.78	7.78	11
12	9.06	7.87	8.92	8.03	8.78	8.18	8.63	8.34	8.49	8.49	12
13	9.81	8.53	9.66	8.70	9.51	8.87	9.35	9.03	9.19	9.19	13
14	10.57	9.18	10.40	9.37	10.24	9.55	10.07	9.73	9.90	9.90	14
15	11.32	9.84	11.15	10.04	10.97	10.23	10.79	10.42	10.61	10.61	15
16	12.08	10.50	11.89	10.71	11.70	10.91	11.51	11.11	11.31	11.31	16
17	12.83	11.15	12.63	11.38	12.43	11.59	12.23	11.81	12.02	12.02	17
18	13.58	11.81	13.38	12.04	13.16	12.28	12.95	12.50	12.73	12.73	18
19	14.34	12.47	14.12	12.71	13.90	12.96	13.67	13.20	13.44	13.44	19
20	15.09	13.12	14.86	13.38	14.63	13.64	14.39	13.89	14.14	14.14	20
21	15.85	13.78	15.61	14.05	15.36	14.32	15.11	14.59	14.85	14.85	21
22	16.60	14.43	16.35	14.72	16.09	15.00	15.83	15.28	15.56	15.56	22
23	17.36	15.09	17.09	15.39	16.82	15.69	16.54	15.98	16.26	16.26	23
24	18.11	15.75	17.84	16.06	17.55	16.37	17.26	16.67	16.97	16.97	24
25	18.87	16.40	18.58	16.73	18.28	17.05	17.98	17.37	17.68	17.68	25
26	19.62	17.06	19.32	17.40	19.02	17.73	18.70	18.06	18.38	18.38	26
27	20.38	17.71	20.06	18.07	19.75	18.41	19.42	18.76	19.09	19.09	27
28	21.13	18.37	20.81	18.74	20.48	19.10	20.14	19.45	19.80	19.80	28
29	21.89	19.03	21.55	19.40	21.21	19.78	20.86	20.15	20.51	20.51	29
30	22.64	19.68	22.29	20.07	21.94	20.46	21.58	20.84	21.21	21.21	30
31	23.40	20.34	23.04	20.74	22.67	21.14	22.30	21.53	21.92	21.92	31
32	24.15	20.99	23.78	21.41	23.40	21.82	23.02	22.23	22.63	22.63	32
33	24.91	21.65	24.52	22.08	24.13	22.51	23.74	22.92	23.33	23.33	33
34	25.66	22.31	25.27	22.75	24.87	23.19	24.46	23.62	24.04	24.04	34
35	26.41	22.96	26.01	23.42	25.60	23.87	25.18	24.31	24.75	24.75	35
36	27.17	23.62	26.75	24.09	26.33	24.55	25.90	25.01	25.46	25.46	36
37	27.92	24.27	27.50	24.76	27.06	25.23	26.62	25.70	26.16	26.16	37
38	28.68	24.93	28.24	25.43	27.79	25.92	27.33	26.40	26.87	26.87	38
39	29.43	25.59	28.98	26.10	28.52	26.60	28.05	27.09	27.58	27.58	39
40	30.19	26.24	29.73	26.77	29.25	27.28	28.77	27.79	28.28	28.28	40
41	30.94	26.90	30.47	27.43	29.99	27.96	29.49	28.48	28.99	28.99	41
42	31.70	27.55	31.21	28.10	30.72	28.64	30.21	29.18	29.70	29.70	42
43	32.45	28.21	31.96	28.77	31.45	29.33	30.93	29.87	30.41	30.41	43
44	33.21	28.87	32.70	29.44	32.18	30.01	31.65	30.56	31.11	31.11	44
45	33.96	29.52	33.44	30.11	32.91	30.69	32.37	31.26	31.82	31.82	45
46	34.72	30.18	34.18	30.78	33.64	31.37	33.09	31.95	32.53	32.53	46
47	35.47	30.83	34.93	31.45	34.37	32.05	33.81	32.65	33.23	33.23	47
48	36.23	31.49	35.67	32.12	35.10	32.74	34.53	33.34	33.94	33.94	48
49	36.98	32.15	36.41	32.79	35.84	33.42	35.25	34.04	34.65	34.65	49
50	37.74	32.80	37.16	33.46	36.57	34.10	35.97	34.73	35.36	35.36	50
51	38.49	33.46	37.90	34.13	37.30	34.78	36.69	35.43	36.06	36.06	51
52	39.24	34.12	38.64	34.79	38.03	35.46	37.41	36.12	36.77	36.77	52
53	40.00	34.77	39.39	35.46	38.76	36.15	38.12	36.82	37.48	37.48	53
54	40.75	35.43	40.13	36.13	39.49	36.83	38.84	37.51	38.18	38.18	54
55	41.51	36.08	40.87	36.80	40.22	37.51	39.56	38.21	38.89	38.89	55
56	42.26	36.74	41.62	37.47	40.96	38.19	40.28	38.90	39.60	39.60	56
57	43.02	37.40	42.36	38.14	41.69	38.87	41.00	39.60	40.31	40.31	57
58	43.77	38.05	43.10	38.81	42.42	39.56	41.72	40.31	41.01	41.01	58
59	44.53	38.71	43.85	39.48	43.15	40.24	42.44	40.98	41.72	41.72	59
dis.	dep.	lat.	dep.	lat.	dep.	lat.	dep.	lat.	dep.	lat.	dis.
hyp.	opp.	adj.	opp.	adj.	opp.	adj.	opp.	adj.	opp.	adj.	hyp.
D	D sin	D cos	D sin	D cos	D sin	D cos	D sin	D cos	D sin	D cos	D
	49°		48°		47°		46°		45°	

TABLE VI. TRAVERSE TABLE

	41°		42°		43°		44°		45°		
D	D cos	D sin	D cos	D sin	D cos	D sin	D cos	D sin	D cos	D sin	D
hyp.	adj.	opp.	adj.	opp.	adj.	opp.	adj.	opp.	adj.	opp.	hyp.
dis.	lat.	dep.	lat.	dep.	lat.	dep.	lat.	dep.	lat.	dep.	dis.
60	45.28	39.36	44.59	40.15	43.88	40.92	43.16	41.68	42.43	42.43	60
61	46.04	40.02	45.33	40.82	44.61	41.60	43.88	42.37	43.13	43.13	61
62	46.79	40.68	46.07	41.49	45.34	42.28	44.60	43.07	43.84	43.84	62
63	47.55	41.33	46.82	42.16	46.08	42.97	45.32	43.76	44.55	44.55	63
64	48.30	41.99	47.56	42.82	46.81	43.65	46.04	44.46	45.25	45.25	64
65	49.06	42.64	48.30	43.49	47.54	44.33	46.76	45.15	45.96	45.96	65
66	49.81	43.30	49.05	44.16	48.27	45.01	47.48	45.85	46.67	46.67	66
67	50.57	43.96	49.79	44.83	49.00	45.69	48.20	46.54	47.38	47.38	67
68	51.32	44.61	50.53	45.50	49.73	46.38	48.92	47.24	48.08	48.08	68
69	52.07	45.27	51.28	46.17	50.46	47.06	49.63	47.93	48.79	48.79	69
70	52.83	45.92	52.02	46.84	51.19	47.74	50.35	48.63	49.50	49.50	70
71	53.58	46.58	52.76	47.51	51.93	48.42	51.07	49.32	50.20	50.20	71
72	54.34	47.24	53.51	48.18	52.66	49.10	51.79	50.02	50.91	50.91	72
73	55.09	47.89	54.25	48.85	53.39	49.79	52.51	50.71	51.62	51.62	73
74	55.85	48.55	54.99	49.52	54.12	50.47	53.23	51.40	52.33	52.33	74
75	56.60	49.20	55.74	50.18	54.85	51.15	53.95	52.10	53.03	53.03	75
76	57.36	49.86	56.48	50.85	55.58	51.83	54.67	52.79	53.74	53.74	76
77	58.11	50.52	57.22	51.52	56.31	52.51	55.39	53.49	54.45	54.45	77
78	58.87	51.17	57.97	52.19	57.05	53.20	56.11	54.18	55.15	55.15	78
79	59.62	51.83	58.71	52.86	57.78	53.88	56.83	54.88	55.86	55.86	79
80	60.38	52.48	59.45	53.53	58.51	54.56	57.55	55.57	56.57	56.57	80
81	61.13	53.14	60.19	54.20	59.24	55.24	58.27	56.27	57.28	57.28	81
82	61.89	53.80	60.94	54.87	59.97	55.92	58.99	56.96	57.98	57.98	82
83	62.64	54.45	61.68	55.54	60.70	56.61	59.71	57.66	58.69	58.69	83
84	63.40	55.11	62.42	56.21	61.43	57.29	60.42	58.35	59.40	59.40	84
85	64.15	55.76	63.17	56.88	62.17	57.97	61.14	59.05	60.10	60.10	85
86	64.90	56.42	63.91	57.55	62.90	58.65	61.86	59.74	60.81	60.81	86
87	65.66	57.08	64.65	58.21	63.63	59.33	62.58	60.44	61.52	61.52	87
88	66.41	57.73	65.40	58.88	64.36	60.02	63.30	61.13	62.23	62.23	88
89	67.17	58.39	66.14	59.55	65.09	60.70	64.02	61.82	62.93	62.93	89
90	67.92	59.05	66.88	60.22	65.82	61.38	64.74	62.52	63.64	63.64	90
91	68.68	59.70	67.63	60.89	66.55	62.06	65.46	63.21	64.35	64.35	91
92	69.43	60.36	68.37	61.56	67.28	62.74	66.18	63.91	65.05	65.05	92
93	70.19	61.01	69.11	62.23	68.02	63.43	66.90	64.60	65.76	65.76	93
94	70.94	61.67	69.86	62.90	68.75	64.11	67.62	65.30	66.47	66.47	94
95	71.70	62.33	70.60	63.57	69.48	64.79	68.34	65.99	67.18	67.18	95
96	72.45	62.98	71.34	64.24	70.21	65.47	69.06	66.69	67.88	67.88	96
97	73.21	63.64	72.08	64.91	70.94	66.15	69.78	67.38	68.59	68.59	97
98	73.96	64.29	72.83	65.57	71.67	66.84	70.50	68.08	69.30	69.30	98
99	74.72	64.95	73.57	66.24	72.40	67.52	71.21	68.77	70.00	70.00	99
100	75.47	65.61	74.31	66.91	73.14	68.20	71.93	69.47	70.71	70.71	100
200	150.94	131.21	148.63	133.83	146.27	136.40	143.87	138.93	141.42	141.42	200
300	226.41	196.82	222.94	200.74	219.41	204.60	215.80	208.40	212.13	212.13	300
400	301.88	262.42	297.26	267.65	292.54	272.80	287.74	277.86	282.84	282.84	400
500	377.35	328.03	371.57	334.57	365.68	341.00	359.67	347.33	353.55	353.55	500
600	452.83	393.64	445.89	401.48	438.81	409.20	431.60	416.80	424.26	424.26	600
700	528.30	459.24	520.20	468.39	511.95	477.40	503.54	486.26	494.97	494.97	700
800	603.77	524.85	594.52	535.30	585.08	545.60	575.47	555.73	565.69	565.69	800
900	679.24	590.45	668.83	602.22	658.22	613.80	647.41	625.19	636.40	636.40	900
dis.	dep.	lat.	dep.	lat.	dep.	lat.	dep.	lat.	dep.	lat.	dis.
hyp.	opp.	adj.	opp.	adj.	opp.	adj.	opp.	adj.	opp.	adj.	hyp.
D	D sin	D cos	D sin	D cos	D sin	D cos	D sin	D cos	D sin	D cos	D
	49°		48°		47°		46°		45°		

TABLE VII. LOGARITHMS OF NUMBERS

N	0	1	2	3	4	5	6	7	8	9
100	0000	0004	0009	0013	0017	0022	0026	0030	0035	0039
101	0043	0048	0052	0056	0060	0065	0069	0073	0077	0082
102	0086	0090	0095	0099	0103	0107	0111	0116	0120	0124
103	0128	0133	0137	0141	0145	0149	0154	0158	0162	0166
104	0170	0175	0179	0183	0187	0191	0195	0199	0204	0208
105	0212	0216	0220	0224	0228	0233	0237	0241	0245	0249
106	0253	0257	0261	0265	0269	0273	0278	0282	0286	0290
107	0294	0298	0302	0306	0310	0314	0318	0322	0326	0330
108	0334	0338	0342	0346	0350	0354	0358	0362	0366	0370
109	0374	0378	0382	0386	0390	0394	0398	0402	0406	0410
110	0414	0418	0422	0426	0430	0434	0438	0441	0445	0449
111	0453	0457	0461	0465	0469	0473	0477	0481	0484	0488
112	0492	0496	0500	0504	0508	0512	0515	0519	0523	0527
113	0531	0535	0538	0542	0546	0550	0554	0558	0561	0565
114	0569	0573	0577	0580	0584	0588	0592	0596	0599	0603
115	0607	0611	0615	0618	0622	0626	0630	0633	0637	0641
116	0645	0648	0652	0656	0660	0663	0667	0671	0674	0678
117	0682	0686	0689	0693	0697	0700	0704	0708	0711	0715
118	0719	0722	0726	0730	0734	0737	0741	0745	0748	0752
119	0755	0759	0763	0766	0770	0774	0777	0781	0785	0788
120	0792	0795	0799	0803	0806	0810	0813	0817	0821	0824
121	0828	0831	0835	0839	0842	0846	0849	0853	0856	0860
122	0864	0867	0871	0874	0878	0881	0885	0888	0892	0896
123	0899	0903	0906	0910	0913	0917	0920	0924	0927	0931
124	0934	0938	0941	0945	0948	0952	0955	0959	0962	0966
125	0969	0973	0976	0980	0983	0986	0990	0993	0997	1000
126	1004	1007	1011	1014	1017	1021	1024	1028	1031	1035
127	1038	1041	1045	1048	1052	1055	1059	1062	1065	1069
128	1072	1075	1079	1082	1086	1089	1092	1096	1099	1103
129	1106	1109	1113	1116	1119	1123	1126	1129	1133	1136
130	1139	1143	1146	1149	1153	1156	1159	1163	1166	1169
131	1173	1176	1179	1183	1186	1189	1193	1196	1199	1202
132	1206	1209	1212	1216	1219	1222	1225	1229	1232	1235
133	1239	1242	1245	1248	1252	1255	1258	1261	1265	1268
134	1271	1274	1278	1281	1284	1287	1290	1294	1297	1300
135	1303	1307	1310	1313	1316	1319	1323	1326	1329	1332
136	1335	1339	1342	1345	1348	1351	1355	1358	1361	1364
137	1367	1370	1374	1377	1380	1383	1386	1389	1392	1396
138	1399	1402	1405	1408	1411	1414	1418	1421	1424	1427
139	1430	1433	1436	1440	1443	1446	1449	1452	1455	1458
140	1461	1464	1467	1471	1474	1477	1480	1483	1486	1489
141	1492	1495	1498	1501	1504	1508	1511	1514	1517	1520
142	1523	1526	1529	1532	1535	1538	1541	1544	1547	1550
143	1553	1556	1559	1562	1565	1569	1572	1575	1578	1581
144	1584	1587	1590	1593	1596	1599	1602	1605	1608	1611
145	1614	1617	1620	1623	1626	1629	1632	1635	1638	1641
146	1644	1647	1649	1652	1655	1658	1661	1664	1667	1670
147	1673	1676	1679	1682	1685	1688	1691	1694	1697	1700
148	1703	1706	1708	1711	1714	1717	1720	1723	1726	1729
149	1732	1735	1738	1741	1744	1746	1749	1752	1755	1758
	0	1	2	3	4	5	6	7	8	9

TABLE VII. LOGARITHMS OF NUMBERS

N	0	1	2	3	4	5	6	7	8	9
150	1761	1764	1767	1770	1772	1775	1778	1781	1784	1787
151	1790	1793	1796	1798	1801	1804	1807	1810	1813	1816
152	1818	1821	1824	1827	1830	1833	1836	1838	1841	1844
153	1847	1850	1853	1855	1858	1861	1864	1867	1870	1872
154	1875	1878	1881	1884	1886	1889	1892	1895	1898	1901
155	1903	1906	1909	1912	1915	1917	1920	1923	1926	1928
156	1931	1934	1937	1940	1942	1945	1948	1951	1953	1956
157	1959	1962	1965	1967	1970	1973	1976	1978	1981	1984
158	1987	1989	1992	1995	1998	2000	2003	2006	2009	2011
159	2014	2017	2019	2022	2025	2028	2030	2033	2036	2038
160	2041	2044	2047	2049	2052	2055	2057	2060	2063	2066
161	2068	2071	2074	2076	2079	2082	2084	2087	2090	2092
162	2095	2098	2101	2103	2106	2109	2111	2114	2117	2119
163	2122	2125	2127	2130	2133	2135	2138	2140	2143	2146
164	2148	2151	2154	2156	2159	2162	2164	2167	2170	2172
165	2175	2177	2180	2183	2185	2188	2191	2193	2196	2198
166	2201	2204	2206	2209	2212	2214	2217	2219	2222	2225
167	2227	2230	2232	2235	2238	2240	2243	2245	2248	2251
168	2253	2256	2258	2261	2263	2266	2269	2271	2274	2276
169	2279	2281	2284	2287	2289	2292	2294	2297	2299	2302
170	2304	2307	2310	2312	2315	2317	2320	2322	2325	2327
171	2330	2333	2335	2338	2340	2343	2345	2348	2350	2353
172	2355	2358	2360	2363	2365	2368	2370	2373	2375	2378
173	2380	2383	2385	2388	2390	2393	2395	2398	2400	2403
174	2405	2408	2410	2413	2415	2418	2420	2423	2425	2428
175	2430	2433	2435	2438	2440	2443	2445	2448	2450	2453
176	2455	2458	2460	2463	2465	2467	2470	2472	2475	2477
177	2480	2482	2485	2487	2490	2492	2494	2497	2499	2502
178	2504	2507	2509	2512	2514	2516	2519	2521	2524	2526
179	2529	2531	2533	2536	2538	2541	2543	2545	2548	2550
180	2553	2555	2558	2560	2562	2565	2567	2570	2572	2574
181	2577	2579	2582	2584	2586	2589	2591	2594	2596	2598
182	2601	2603	2605	2608	2610	2613	2615	2617	2620	2622
183	2625	2627	2629	2632	2634	2636	2639	2641	2643	2646
184	2648	2651	2653	2655	2658	2660	2662	2665	2667	2669
185	2672	2674	2676	2679	2681	2683	2686	2688	2690	2693
186	2695	2697	2700	2702	2704	2707	2709	2711	2714	2716
187	2718	2721	2723	2725	2728	2730	2732	2735	2737	2739
188	2742	2744	2746	2749	2751	2753	2755	2758	2760	2762
189	2765	2767	2769	2772	2774	2776	2778	2781	2783	2785
190	2788	2790	2792	2794	2797	2799	2801	2804	2806	2808
191	2810	2813	2815	2817	2819	2822	2824	2826	2828	2831
192	2833	2835	2838	2840	2842	2844	2847	2849	2851	2853
193	2856	2858	2860	2862	2865	2867	2869	2871	2874	2876
194	2878	2880	2882	2885	2887	2889	2891	2894	2896	2898
195	2900	2903	2905	2907	2909	2911	2914	2916	2918	2920
196	2923	2925	2927	2929	2931	2934	2936	2938	2940	2942
197	2945	2947	2949	2951	2953	2956	2958	2960	2962	2964
198	2967	2969	2971	2973	2975	2978	2980	2982	2984	2986
199	2989	2991	2993	2995	2997	2999	3002	3004	3006	3008
	0	1	2	3	4	5	6	7	8	9

TABLE VII. LOGARITHMS OF NUMBERS

N	0	1	2	3	4	5	6	7	8	9
10	0000	0043	0086	0128	0170	0212	0253	0294	0334	0374
11	0414	0453	0492	0531	0569	0607	0645	0682	0719	0755
12	0792	0828	0864	0899	0934	0969	1004	1038	1072	1106
13	1139	1173	1206	1239	1271	1303	1335	1367	1399	1430
14	1461	1492	1523	1553	1584	1614	1644	1673	1703	1732
15	1761	1790	1818	1847	1875	1903	1931	1959	1987	2014
16	2041	2068	2095	2122	2148	2175	2201	2227	2253	2279
17	2304	2330	2355	2380	2405	2430	2455	2480	2504	2529
18	2553	2577	2601	2625	2648	2672	2695	2718	2742	2765
19	2788	2810	2833	2856	2878	2900	2923	2945	2967	2989
20	3010	3032	3054	3075	3096	3118	3139	3160	3181	3201
21	3222	3243	3263	3284	3304	3324	3345	3365	3385	3404
22	3424	3444	3464	3483	3502	3522	3541	3560	3579	3598
23	3617	3636	3655	3674	3692	3711	3729	3747	3766	3784
24	3802	3820	3838	3856	3874	3892	3909	3927	3945	3962
25	3979	3997	4014	4031	4048	4065	4082	4099	4116	4133
26	4150	4166	4183	4200	4216	4232	4249	4265	4281	4298
27	4314	4330	4346	4362	4378	4393	4409	4425	4440	4456
28	4472	4487	4502	4518	4533	4548	4564	4579	4594	4609
29	4624	4639	4654	4669	4683	4698	4713	4728	4742	4757
30	4771	4786	4800	4814	4829	4843	4857	4871	4886	4900
31	4914	4928	4942	4955	4969	4983	4997	5011	5024	5038
32	5051	5065	5079	5092	5105	5119	5132	5145	5159	5172
33	5185	5198	5211	5224	5237	5250	5263	5276	5289	5302
34	5315	5328	5340	5353	5366	5378	5391	5403	5416	5428
35	5441	5453	5465	5478	5490	5502	5514	5527	5539	5551
36	5563	5575	5587	5599	5611	5623	5635	5647	5658	5670
37	5682	5694	5705	5717	5729	5740	5752	5763	5775	5786
38	5798	5809	5821	5832	5843	5855	5866	5877	5888	5899
39	5911	5922	5933	5944	5955	5966	5977	5988	5999	6010
40	6021	6031	6042	6053	6064	6075	6085	6096	6107	6117
41	6128	6138	6149	6160	6170	6180	6191	6201	6212	6222
42	6232	6243	6253	6263	6274	6284	6294	6304	6314	6325
43	6335	6345	6355	6365	6375	6385	6395	6405	6415	6425
44	6435	6444	6454	6464	6474	6484	6493	6503	6513	6522
45	6532	6542	6551	6561	6571	6580	6590	6599	6609	6618
46	6628	6637	6646	6656	6665	6675	6684	6693	6702	6712
47	6721	6730	6739	6749	6758	6767	6776	6785	6794	6803
48	6812	6821	6830	6839	6848	6857	6866	6875	6884	6893

Do Not Interpolate.

PROPORTIONAL PARTS

	22	21	19	18	17	16	15	14	13	12	11	9	8	7	6	
1	2	2	2	2	2	2	2	1	1	1	1	1	1	1	1	1
2	4	4	4	4	3	3	3	3	3	2	2	2	2	1	1	2
3	7	6	6	5	5	5	5	4	4	4	3	3	2	2	2	3
4	9	8	8	7	7	6	6	6	5	5	4	4	3	3	2	4
5	11	11	10	9	9	8	8	7	7	6	6	5	4	4	3	5
6	13	13	11	11	10	10	9	8	8	7	7	5	5	4	4	6
7	15	15	13	13	12	11	11	10	9	8	8	6	6	5	4	7
8	18	17	15	14	14	13	12	11	10	10	9	7	6	6	5	8
9	20	19	17	16	15	14	14	13	12	11	10	8	7	6	5	9

TABLE VII. LOGARITHMS OF NUMBERS

N	0	1	2	3	4	5	6	7	8	9
49	6902	6911	6920	6928	6937	6946	6955	6964	6972	6981
50	6990	6998	7007	7016	7024	7033	7042	7050	7059	7067
51	7076	7084	7093	7101	7110	7118	7126	7135	7143	7152
52	7160	7168	7177	7185	7193	7202	7210	7218	7226	7235
53	7243	7251	7259	7267	7275	7284	7292	7300	7308	7316
54	7324	7332	7340	7348	7356	7364	7372	7380	7388	7396
55	7404	7412	7419	7427	7435	7443	7451	7459	7466	7474
56	7482	7490	7497	7505	7513	7520	7528	7536	7543	7551
57	7559	7566	7574	7582	7589	7597	7604	7612	7619	7627
58	7634	7642	7649	7657	7664	7672	7679	7686	7694	7701
59	7709	7716	7723	7731	7738	7745	7752	7760	7767	7774
60	7782	7789	7796	7803	7810	7818	7825	7832	7839	7846
61	7853	7860	7868	7875	7882	7889	7896	7903	7910	7917
62	7924	7931	7938	7945	7952	7959	7966	7973	7980	7987
63	7993	8000	8007	8014	8021	8028	8035	8041	8048	8055
64	8062	8069	8075	8082	8089	8096	8102	8109	8116	8122
65	8129	8136	8142	8149	8156	8162	8169	8176	8182	8189
66	8195	8202	8209	8215	8222	8228	8235	8241	8248	8254
67	8261	8267	8274	8280	8287	8293	8299	8306	8312	8319
68	8325	8331	8338	8344	8351	8357	8363	8370	8376	8382
69	8388	8395	8401	8407	8414	8420	8426	8432	8439	8445
70	8451	8457	8463	8470	8476	8482	8488	8494	8500	8506
71	8513	8519	8525	8531	8537	8543	8549	8555	8561	8567
72	8573	8579	8585	8591	8597	8603	8609	8615	8621	8627
73	8633	8639	8645	8651	8657	8663	8669	8675	8681	8686
74	8692	8698	8704	8710	8716	8722	8727	8733	8739	8745
75	8751	8756	8762	8768	8774	8779	8785	8791	8797	8802
76	8808	8814	8820	8825	8831	8837	8842	8848	8854	8859
77	8865	8871	8876	8882	8887	8893	8899	8904	8910	8915
78	8921	8927	8932	8938	8943	8949	8954	8960	8965	8971
79	8976	8982	8987	8993	8998	9004	9009	9015	9020	9025
80	9031	9036	9042	9047	9053	9058	9063	9069	9074	9079
81	9085	9090	9096	9101	9106	9112	9117	9122	9128	9133
82	9138	9143	9149	9154	9159	9165	9170	9175	9180	9186
83	9191	9196	9201	9206	9212	9217	9222	9227	9232	9238
84	9243	9248	9253	9258	9263	9269	9274	9279	9284	9289
85	9294	9299	9304	9309	9315	9320	9325	9330	9335	9340
86	9345	9350	9355	9360	9365	9370	9375	9380	9385	9390
87	9395	9400	9405	9410	9415	9420	9425	9430	9435	9440
88	9445	9450	9455	9460	9465	9469	9474	9479	9484	9489
89	9494	9499	9504	9509	9513	9518	9523	9528	9533	9538
90	9542	9547	9552	9557	9562	9566	9571	9576	9581	9586
91	9590	9595	9600	9605	9609	9614	9619	9624	9628	9633
92	9638	9643	9647	9652	9657	9661	9666	9671	9675	9680
93	9685	9689	9694	9699	9703	9708	9713	9717	9722	9727
94	9731	9736	9741	9745	9750	9754	9759	9763	9768	9773
95	9777	9782	9786	9791	9795	9800	9805	9809	9814	9818
96	9823	9827	9832	9836	9841	9845	9850	9854	9859	9863
97	9868	9872	9877	9881	9886	9890	9894	9899	9903	9908
98	9912	9917	9921	9926	9930	9934	9939	9943	9948	9952
99	9956	9961	9965	9969	9974	9978	9983	9987	9991	9996
N	0	1	2	3	4	5	6	7	8	9

TABLE VIII. LOGARITHMS OF TRIGONOMETRIC FUNCTIONS

°	′	0′	1′	2′	3′	log sin 4′	5′	6′	7′	8′	9′	log cos		
0	0		6.4637	7648	9408	7.0658	1627	2419	3088	3668	4180	10.0000		50
	10	7.4637	5051	5429	5777	6099	6398	6678	6942	7190	7425	10.0000		40
	20	7.7648	7859	8061	8255	8439	8617	8787	8951	9109	9261	10.0000		30
	30	7.9408	9551	9689	9822	9952	8.0078	0200	0319	0435	0548	10.0000		20
	40	8.0658	0765	0870	0972	1072	1169	1265	1358	1450	1539	10.0000		10
	50	8.1627	1713	1797	1880	1961	2041	2119	2196	2271	2346	10.0000	**89**	0
1	0	8.2419	2490	2561	2630	2699	2766	2832	2898	2962	3025	9.9999		50
	10	8.3088	3150	3210	3270	3329	3388	3445	3502	3558	3613	9.9999		40
	20	8.3668	3722	3775	3828	3880	3931	3982	4032	4082	4131	9.9999		30
	30	8.4179	4227	4275	4322	4368	4414	4459	4504	4549	4593	9.9999		20
	40	8.4637	4680	4723	4765	4807	4848	4890	4930	4971	5011	9.9998		10
	50	8.5050	5090	5129	5167	5206	5243	5281	5318	5355	5392	9.9998	**88**	0
2	0	8.5428	5464	5500	5535	5571	5605	5640	5674	5708	5742	9.9997		50
	10	8.5776	5809	5842	5875	5907	5939	5972	6003	6035	6066	9.9997		40
	20	8.6097	6128	6159	6189	6220	6250	6279	6309	6339	6368	9.9996		30
	30	8.6397	6426	6454	6483	6511	6539	6567	6595	6622	6650	9.9996		20
	40	8.6677	6704	6731	6758	6784	6810	6837	6863	6889	6914	9.9995		10
	50	8.6940	6965	6991	7016	7041	7066	7090	7115	7140	7164	9.9995	**87**	0
3	0	8.7188	7212	7236	7260	7283	7307	7330	7354	7377	7400	9.9994		50
	10	8.7423	7445	7468	7491	7513	7535	7557	7580	7602	7623	9.9993		40
	20	8.7645	7667	7688	7710	7731	7752	7773	7794	7815	7836	9.9993		30
	30	8.7857	7877	7898	7918	7939	7959	7979	7999	8019	8039	9.9992		20
	40	8.8059	8078	8098	8117	8137	8156	8175	8194	8213	8232	9.9991		10
	50	8.8251	8270	8289	8307	8326	8345	8363	8381	8400	8418	9.9990	**86**	0
		10′	9′	8′	7′	6′ log cos	5′	4′	3′	2′	1′	log sin	°	′

°	′	0′	1′	2′	3′	log tan 4′	5′	6′	7′	8′	9′		
0	0		6.4637	7648	9408	7.0658	1627	2419	3088	3668	4180		50
	10	7.4637	5051	5429	5777	6099	6398	6678	6942	7190	7425		40
	20	7.7648	7860	8062	8255	8439	8617	8787	8951	9109	9261		30
	30	7.9409	9551	9689	9823	9952	8.0078	0200	0319	0435	0548		20
	40	8.0658	0765	0870	0972	1072	1170	1265	1359	1450	1540		10
	50	8.1627	1713	1798	1880	1962	2041	2120	2196	2272	2346	**89**	0
1	0	8.2419	2491	2562	2631	2700	2767	2833	2899	2963	3026		50
	10	8.3089	3150	3211	3271	3330	3389	3446	3503	3559	3614		40
	20	8.3669	3723	3776	3829	3881	3932	3983	4033	4083	4132		30
	30	8.4181	4229	4276	4323	4370	4416	4461	4506	4551	4595		20
	40	8.4638	4682	4725	4767	4809	4851	4892	4933	4973	5013		10
	50	8.5053	5092	5131	5170	5208	5246	5283	5321	5358	5394	**88**	0
2	0	8.5431	5467	5503	5538	5573	5608	5643	5677	5711	5745		50
	10	8.5779	5812	5845	5878	5911	5943	5975	6007	6038	6070		40
	20	8.6101	6132	6163	6193	6223	6254	6283	6313	6343	6372		30
	30	8.6401	6430	6459	6487	6515	6544	6571	6599	6627	6654		20
	40	8.6682	6709	6736	6762	6789	6815	6842	6868	6894	6920		10
	50	8.6945	6971	6996	7021	7046	7071	7096	7121	7145	7170	**87**	0
3	0	8.7194	7218	7242	7266	7290	7313	7337	7360	7383	7406		50
	10	8.7429	7452	7475	7497	7520	7542	7565	7587	7609	7631		40
	20	8.7652	7674	7696	7717	7739	7760	7781	7802	7823	7844		30
	30	8.7865	7886	7906	7927	7947	7967	7988	8008	8028	8048		20
	40	8.8067	8087	8107	8126	8146	8165	8185	8204	8223	8242		10
	50	8.8261	8280	8299	8317	8336	8355	8373	8392	8410	8428	**86**	0
		10′	9′	8′	7′	6′ log cot	5′	4′	3′	2′	1′	°	′

TABLE VIII. LOGARITHMS OF TRIGONOMETRIC FUNCTIONS

°	′	log sin	log tan	log cot	log cos			°	′	log sin	log tan	log cot	log cos		
4	0	8.8436	8.8446	11.1554	9.9989	86	0	7	0	0859	0891	9109	9968	83	0
	5	525	536	464	89		55		5	0910	0943	9057	67		55
	10	613	624	376	89		50		10	0961	0995	9005	66		50
	15	699	711	289	88		45		15	1011	1045	8955	65		45
	20	783	795	205	88		40		20	1060	1096	8904	64		40
	25	865	878	122	87		35		25	1109	1145	8855	64		35
	30	8.8946	8.8960	11.1040	87		30		30	1157	1194	8806	63		30
	35	8.9026	8.9040	11.0960	86		25		35	1205	1243	8757	62		25
	40	104	118	882	86		20		40	1252	1291	8709	61		20
	45	181	196	804	85		15		45	1299	1338	8662	60		15
	50	256	272	728	85		10		50	1345	1385	8615	59		10
	55	330	346	654	84		5		55	1390	1432	8568	58		5
5	0	403	420	580	83	85	0	8	0	1436	1478	8522	58	82	0
	5	475	492	508	83		55		5	1480	1524	8476	57		55
	10	545	563	437	82		50		10	1525	1569	8431	56		50
	15	614	633	367	82		45		15	1568	1613	8387	55		45
	20	682	701	299	81		40		20	1612	1658	8342	54		40
	25	750	769	231	81		35		25	1655	1702	8298	53		35
	30	816	836	164	80		30		30	1697	1745	8255	52		30
	35	881	901	099	79		25		35	1739	1788	8212	51		25
	40	8.9945	8.9966	11.0034	79		20		40	1781	1831	8169	50		20
	45	9.0008	9.0030	10.9970	78		15		45	1822	1873	8127	49		15
	50	070	093	907	77		10		50	1863	1915	8085	48		10
	55	132	155	845	77		5		55	1903	1956	8044	47		5
6	0	192	216	784	76	84	0	9	0	1943	1997	8003	46	81	0
	5	252	277	723	75		55		5	1983	2038	7962	45		55
	10	311	336	664	75		50		10	2022	2078	7922	44		50
	15	369	395	605	74		45		15	2061	2118	7882	43		45
	20	426	453	547	73		40		20	2100	2158	7842	42		40
	25	483	510	490	73		35		25	2138	2197	7803	41		35
	30	539	567	433	72		30		30	2176	2236	7764	40		30
	35	594	622	378	71		25		35	2214	2275	7725	39		25
	40	648	678	322	71		20		40	2251	2313	7687	38		20
	45	702	732	268	70		15		45	2288	2351	7649	37		15
	50	755	786	214	69		10		50	2324	2389	7611	36		10
	55	807	839	161	68		5		55	2361	2426	7574	35		5
7	0	9.0859	9.0891	10.9109	9.9968	83	0	10	0	2397	2463	7537	9934	80	0
						°	′			9.	9.	10.	9.	°	′
		log cos	log cot	log tan	log sin					log cos	log cot	log tan	log sin		

P. P. FOR DIFFERENCE OF 5′

	90	89	88	87	86	85	84	83	82	81	80	78	77	76	
1	18	18	18	17	17	17	17	16	16	16	16	15	15	15	1
2	36	36	35	35	34	34	33	33	32	32	31	31	30	30	2
3	54	53	53	52	52	50	50	49	49	48	47	46	46	46	3
4	72	71	70	70	69	67	66	66	65	64	62	62	61		4

	75	74	73	72	71	70	69	68	67	66	65	64	63	
1	15	15	14	14	14	14	14	13	13	13	13	13	13	1
2	30	30	29	29	28	28	28	27	27	26	26	26	25	2
3	45	44	44	43	43	42	41	41	40	40	39	38	38	3
4	60	59	58	58	57	56	55	54	54	53	52	51	50	4

	62	61	60	59	58	57	56	55	54	53	52	51	49	
1	12	12	12	12	12	11	11	11	11	11	10	10	10	1
2	25	24	24	24	23	23	22	22	22	21	21	20	20	2
3	37	37	36	35	35	34	34	33	32	32	31	31	29	3
4	50	49	48	47	46	46	45	44	43	42	42	41	39	4

	48	47	46	45	44	43	42	41	40	39	38	37	36	
1	10	9	9	9	9	9	8	8	8	8	7	7	7	1
2	19	19	18	18	18	17	17	16	16	16	15	15	14	2
3	29	28	28	27	26	26	25	25	24	23	23	22	22	3
4	38	38	37	36	35	34	34	33	32	31	30	30	29	4

TABLE VIII. LOGARITHMS OF TRIGONOMETRIC FUNCTIONS

°	′	log sin 9.	log tan 9.	log cot 10.	log cos 9.		°	′	log sin 9.	log tan 9.	log cot 10.	log cos 9.		°	′
10	0	2397	2463	7537	9934	**80**	0								
	10	2468	2536	7464	9931		50	**15**	0	4130	4281	5719	9849	**75**	0
	20	2538	2609	7391	9929		40		10	4177	4331	5669	9846		50
	30	2606	2680	7320	9927		30		20	4223	4381	5619	9843		40
	40	2674	2750	7250	9924		20		30	4269	4430	5570	9839		30
	50	2740	2819	7181	9922		10		40	4314	4479	5521	9836		20
11	0	2806	2887	7113	9919	**79**	0		50	4359	4527	5473	9832		10
	10	2870	2953	7047	9917		50	**16**	0	4403	4575	5425	9828	**74**	0
	20	2934	3020	6980	9914		40		10	4447	4622	5378	9825		50
	30	2997	3085	6915	9912		30		20	4491	4669	5331	9821		40
	40	3058	3149	6851	9909		20		30	4533	4716	5284	9817		30
	50	3119	3212	6788	9907		10		40	4576	4762	5238	9814		20
12	0	3179	3275	6725	9904	**78**	0		50	4618	4808	5192	9810		10
	10	3238	3336	6664	9901		50	**17**	0	4659	4853	5147	9806	**73**	0
	20	3296	3397	6603	9899		40		10	4700	4898	5102	9802		50
	30	3353	3458	6542	9896		30		20	4741	4943	5057	9798		40
	40	3410	3517	6483	9893		20		30	4781	4987	5013	9794		30
	50	3466	3576	6424	9890		10		40	4821	5031	4969	9790		20
13	0	3521	3634	6366	9887	**77**	0		50	4861	5075	4925	9786		10
	10	3575	3691	6309	9884		50	**18**	0	4900	5118	4882	9782	**72**	0
	20	3629	3748	6252	9881		40		10	4939	5161	4839	9778		50
	30	3682	3804	6196	9878		30		20	4977	5203	4797	9774		40
	40	3734	3859	6141	9875		20		30	5015	5245	4755	9770		30
	50	3786	3914	6086	9872		10		40	5052	5287	4713	9765		20
14	0	3837	3968	6032	9869	**76**	0		50	5090	5329	4671	9761		10
	10	3887	4021	5979	9866		50	**19**	0	5126	5370	4630	9757	**71**	0
	20	3937	4074	5926	9863		40		10	5163	5411	4589	9752		50
	30	3986	4127	5873	9859		30		20	5199	5451	4549	9748		40
	40	4035	4178	5822	9856		20		30	5235	5491	4509	9743		30
	50	4083	4230	5770	9853		10		40	5270	5531	4469	9739		20
15	0	4130	4281	5719	9849	**75**	0		50	5306	5571	4429	9734		10
		9.	9.	10.	9.			**20**	0	5341	5611	4389	9730	**70**	0
		log cos	log cot	log tan	log sin				10	5375	5650	4350	9725		50
									20	5409	5689	4311	9721		40
									30	5443	5727	4273	9716		30
									40	5477	5766	4234	9711		20
									50	5510	5804	4196	9706		10
								21	0	5543	5842	4158	9702	**69**	0
										9.	9.	10.	9.		′
										log cos	log cot	log tan	log sin		

P. P.

	73	71	69	68	67	66	65	64	63	61	59	
1	7	7	7	7	7	7	7	6	6	6	6	1
2	15	14	14	14	13	13	13	13	13	12	12	2
3	22	21	21	20	20	20	20	19	19	18	18	3
4	29	28	28	27	27	26	26	26	25	24	24	4
5	37	36	35	34	34	33	33	32	32	31	30	5
6	44	43	41	41	40	40	39	38	38	37	35	6
7	51	50	48	48	47	46	46	45	44	43	41	7
8	58	57	55	54	54	53	52	51	50	49	47	8
9	66	64	62	61	60	59	59	58	57	55	53	9

	58	57	56	55	54	53	52	51	49	48	47	46	
1	6	6	6	6	5	5	5	5	5	5	5	5	1
2	12	11	11	11	11	11	10	10	10	10	9	9	2
3	17	17	17	17	16	16	16	15	15	14	14	14	3
4	23	23	22	22	22	21	21	20	20	19	19	18	4
5	29	29	28	28	27	27	26	26	25	24	24	23	5
6	35	34	34	33	32	32	31	31	29	29	28	23	6
7	41	40	39	39	38	37	36	36	34	34	33	32	7
8	46	46	45	44	43	42	42	41	39	38	38	37	8
9	52	51	50	50	49	48	47	46	44	43	42	41	9

	45	44	43	42	41	39	38	37	36	35	34	33	
1	5	4	4	4	4	4	4	4	4	4	3	3	1
2	9	9	9	8	8	8	8	7	7	7	7	7	2
3	14	13	13	13	12	12	11	11	11	11	10	10	3
4	18	18	17	17	16	16	15	15	14	14	14	13	4
5	23	22	22	21	21	20	19	19	18	18	17	17	5
6	27	26	26	25	25	23	23	22	22	21	20	20	6
7	32	31	30	29	29	27	27	26	25	25	24	23	7
8	36	35	34	34	33	31	30	30	29	28	27	26	8
9	41	40	39	38	37	35	34	33	32	32	31	30	9

TABLE VIII. LOGARITHMS OF TRIGONOMETRIC FUNCTIONS

°	′	log sin 9.	log tan 9.	log cot 10.	log cos 9.		
21	0	5543	5842	4158	9702	**69**	0
	10	5576	5879	4121	9697		50
	20	5609	5917	4083	92		40
	30	5641	5954	4046	87		30
	40	5673	5991	4009	82		20
	50	5704	6028	3972	77		10
22	0	5736	6064	3936	72	**68**	0
	10	5767	6100	3900	67		50
	20	5798	6136	3864	61		40
	30	5828	6172	3828	56		30
	40	5859	6208	3792	51		20
	50	5889	6243	3757	46		10
23	0	5919	6279	3721	40	**67**	0
	10	5948	6314	3686	35		50
	20	5978	6348	3652	29		40
	30	6007	6383	3617	24		30
	40	6036	6417	3583	18		20
	50	6065	6452	3548	13		10
24	0	6093	6486	3514	07	**66**	0
	10	6121	6520	3480	9602		50
	20	6149	6553	3447	9596		40
	30	6177	6587	3413	90		30
	40	6205	6620	3380	84		20
	50	6232	6654	3346	79		10
25	0	6259	6687	3313	73	**65**	0
	10	6286	6720	3280	67		50
	20	6313	6752	3248	61		40
	30	6340	6785	3215	55		30
	40	6366	6817	3183	49		20
	50	6392	6850	3150	43		10
26	0	6418	6882	3118	37	**64**	0
	10	6444	6914	3086	30		50
	20	6470	6946	3054	24		40
	30	6495	6977	3023	18		30
	40	6521	7009	2991	12		20
	50	6546	7040	2960	9505		10
27	0	6570	7072	2928	9499	**63**	0
		9. log cos	9. log cot	10. log tan	9. log sin	°	′

°	′	log sin 9.	log tan 9.	log cot 10.	log cos 9.		
27	0	6570	7072	2928	9499	**63**	0
	10	6595	7103	2897	92		50
	20	6620	34	66	86		40
	30	44	65	35	79		30
	40	68	7196	2804	73		20
	50	6692	7226	2774	66		10
28	0	6716	7257	2743	59	**62**	0
	10	40	7287	2713	53		50
	20	63	7317	2683	46		40
	30	6787	7348	2652	39		30
	40	6810	7378	2622	32		20
	50	33	7408	2592	25		10
29	0	56	38	62	18	**61**	0
	10	6878	67	33	11		50
	20	6901	7497	2503	9404		40
	30	23	7526	2474	9397		30
	40	46	7556	2444	90		20
	50	68	7585	2415	83		10
30	0	6990	7614	2386	75	**60**	0
	10	7012	7644	2356	68		50
	20	33	7673	2327	61		40
	30	55	7701	2299	53		30
	40	76	30	70	46		20
	50	7097	59	41	38		10
31	0	7118	7788	2212	31	**59**	0
	10	39	7816	2184	23		50
	20	60	7845	2155	15		40
	30	7181	7873	2127	08		30
	40	7201	7902	2098	9300		20
	50	22	30	70	9292		10
32	0	42	58	42	84	**58**	0
	10	62	7986	2014	76		50
	20	7282	8014	1986	68		40
	30	7302	42	58	60		30
	40	22	70	30	52		20
	50	42	8097	1903	44		10
33	0	7361	8125	1875	9236	**57**	0
		9. log cos	9. log cot	10. log tan	9. log sin	°	′

P. P.

	38	37	36	35	34	33	32	31	29		28	27	26	25	24	23	22	21	19	
1	4	4	4	4	3	3	3	3	3	1	3	3	3	3	2	2	2	2	2	1
2	8	7	7	7	7	7	6	6	6	2	6	5	5	5	5	5	4	4	4	2
3	11	11	11	11	10	10	10	9	9	3	8	8	8	8	7	7	7	6	6	3
4	15	15	14	14	14	13	13	12	12	4	11	11	10	10	10	9	9	8	8	4
5	19	19	18	18	17	17	16	16	15	5	14	14	13	13	12	12	11	11	11	5
6	23	22	22	21	20	20	19	19	17	6	17	16	16	15	14	14	13	13	13	6
7	27	26	25	25	24	23	22	22	20	7	20	19	18	18	17	16	15	15	15	7
8	30	30	29	28	27	26	26	25	23	8	22	22	21	20	19	18	18	17	17	8
9	34	33	32	32	31	30	29	28	26	9	25	24	23	23	22	21	20	19	19	9

TABLE VIII. LOGARITHMS OF TRIGONOMETRIC FUNCTIONS

°	′	log sin 9.	log tan 9.	log cot 10.	log cos 9.		°	′	log sin 9.	log tan 9.	log cot 10.	log cos 9.		
33	0	7361	8125	1875	9236	**57** 0	**39**	0	7989	9084	0916	8905	**51** 0
	10	7380	8153	1847	28	50		10	8004	9110	0890	8895	50
	20	7400	8180	1820	19	40		20	20	35	65	84	40
	30	19	8208	1792	11	30		30	35	61	39	74	30
	40	38	35	65	9203	20		40	50	9187	0813	64	20
	50	57	63	37	9194	10		50	66	9212	0788	53	10
34	0	76	8290	1710	86	**56** 0	**40**	0	81	38	62	43	**50** 0
	10	7494	8317	1683	77	50		10	8096	64	36	32	50
	20	7513	44	56	69	40		20	8111	9289	0711	21	40
	30	31	71	29	60	30		30	25	9315	0685	10	30
	40	50	8398	1602	51	20		40	40	41	59	8800	20
	50	68	8425	1575	42	10		50	55	66	34	8789	10
35	0	7586	8452	1548	34	**55** 0	**41**	0	69	9392	0608	78	**49** 0
	10	7604	8479	1521	25	50		10	84	9417	0583	67	50
	20	22	8506	1494	16	40		20	8198	43	57	56	40
	30	40	33	67	9107	30		30	8213	68	32	45	30
	40	57	59	41	9098	20		40	27	9494	0506	33	20
	50	75	8586	1414	89	10		50	41	9519	0481	22	10
36	0	7692	8613	1387	80	**54** 0	**42**	0	55	44	56	8711	**48** 0
	10	7710	39	61	70	50		10	69	70	30	8699	50
	20	27	66	34	61	40		20	83	9595	0405	88	40
	30	44	8692	1308	52	30		30	8297	9621	0379	76	30
	40	61	8718	1282	42	20		40	8311	46	54	65	20
	50	78	45	55	33	10		50	24	71	29	53	10
37	0	7795	71	29	23	**53** 0	**43**	0	38	9697	0303	41	**47** 0
	10	7811	8797	1203	13	50		10	51	9722	0278	29	50
	20	28	8824	1176	9004	40		20	65	47	53	18	40
	30	44	8850	1150	8995	30		30	78	72	28	8606	30
	40	61	8876	1124	85	20		40	8391	9798	0202	8594	20
	50	77	8902	1098	75	10		50	8405	9823	0177	82	10
38	0	7893	28	72	65	**52** 0	**44**	0	18	48	52	69	**46** 0
	10	7910	54	46	55	50		10	31	74	26	57	50
	20	26	8980	1020	45	40		20	44	9899	0101	45	40
	30	41	9006	0994	35	30		30	57	9924	0076	32	30
	40	57	32	68	25	20		40	69	9949	51	20	20
	50	73	58	42	15	10		50	82	9.9975	25	8507	10
39	0	7989	9084	0916	8905	**51** 0	**45**	0	8495	10.0000	0000	8495	**45** 0
		9.	9.	10.	9.	° ′			9.	9.	10.	9.	° ′
		log cos	log cot	log tan	log sin				log cos	log cot	log tan	log sin	

P. P.

	28	27	26	25	24	23	22	21	19		18	17	16	15	14	13	12	11	
1	3	3	3	3	2	2	2	2	2	1	2	2	2	2	1	1	1	1	1
2	6	5	5	5	5	4	4	4	4	2	4	3	3	3	3	3	2	2	2
3	8	8	8	8	7	7	7	6	6	3	5	5	5	5	4	4	4	3	3
4	11	11	10	10	10	9	9	8	8	4	7	7	6	6	6	5	5	4	4
5	14	14	13	13	12	12	11	11	11	5	9	9	8	8	7	7	6	6	5
6	17	16	16	15	14	14	13	13	13	6	11	10	10	9	8	8	7	7	6
7	20	19	18	18	17	16	15	15	15	7	13	12	11	11	10	9	8	8	7
8	22	22	21	20	19	18	18	17	17	8	14	14	13	12	11	10	10	9	8
9	25	24	23	23	22	21	20	19	19	9	16	15	14	14	13	12	11	10	9

TABLE IX. MERIDIONAL PARTS

1°	59.6	6°	358.2	11°	659.6	16°	966.3	21°	1280.8	26°	1606.2
2°	119.2	7°	418.2	12°	720.5	17°	1028.5	22°	1344.9	27°	1672.9
3°	178.9	8°	478.3	13°	781.5	18°	1091.0	23°	1409.5	28°	1740.2
4°	238.6	9°	538.6	14°	842.8	19°	1153.9	24°	1474.5	29°	1808.1
5°	298.3	10°	599.0	15°	904.4	20°	1217.1	25°	1540.1	30°	1876.7

°	0′	10′	20′	30′	40′	50′	60′
30	1876.7	1888.2	1899.7	1911.2	1922.8	1934.4	1946.0
31	1946.0	1957.6	1969.2	1980.9	1992.6	2004.3	2016.0
32	2016.0	2027.7	2039.5	2051.3	2063.1	2074.9	2086.8
33	2086.8	2098.7	2110.6	2122.5	2134.4	2146.4	2158.4
34	2158.4	2170.4	2182.5	2194.5	2206.6	2218.7	2230.9
35	2230.9	2243.0	2255.2	2267.4	2279.7	2291.9	2304.2
36	2304.2	2316.5	2328.9	2341.3	2353.7	2366.1	2378.5
37	2378.5	2391.0	2403.5	2416.1	2428.6	2441.2	2453.8
38	2453.8	2466.5	2479.2	2491.9	2504.6	2517.4	2530.2
39	2530.2	2543.0	2555.9	2568.8	2581.7	2594.7	2607.6
40	2607.6	2620.7	2633.7	2646.8	2659.9	2673.1	2686.2
41	2686.2	2699.5	2712.7	2726.0	2739.3	2752.7	2766.0
42	2766.0	2779.5	2792.9	2806.4	2820.0	2833.5	2847.1
43	2847.1	2860.8	2874.4	2888.2	2901.9	2915.7	2929.5
44	2929.5	2943.4	2957.3	2971.3	2985.3	2999.3	3013.4
45	3013.4	3027.5	3041.7	3055.9	3070.1	3084.4	3098.7
46	3098.7	3113.1	3127.5	3141.9	3156.4	3171.0	3185.6
47	3185.6	3200.2	3214.9	3229.6	3244.4	3259.3	3274.1
48	3274.1	3289.0	3304.0	3319.0	3334.1	3349.2	3364.4
49	3364.4	3379.6	3394.9	3410.2	3425.6	3441.0	3456.5
50	3456.5	3472.1	3487.7	3503.3	3519.0	3534.8	3550.6
51	3550.6	3566.5	3582.4	3598.4	3614.5	3630.6	3646.7
52	3646.7	3663.0	3679.3	3695.6	3712.0	3728.5	3745.1
53	3745.1	3761.7	3778.3	3795.1	3811.9	3828.7	3845.7
54	3845.7	3862.7	3879.8	3896.9	3914.1	3931.4	3948.8
55	3948.8	3966.2	3983.7	4001.3	4018.9	4036.7	4054.5
56	4054.5	4072.4	4090.3	4108.4	4126.5	4144.7	4163.0
57	4163.0	4181.3	4199.8	4218.3	4236.9	4255.6	4274.4
58	4274.4	4293.3	4312.3	4331.3	4350.5	4369.7	4389.1
59	4389.1	4408.5	4428.0	4447.6	4467.3	4487.2	4507.1
60	4507.1	4527.1	4547.2	4567.4	4587.8	4608.2	4628.7
61	4628.7	4649.4	4670.1	4691.0	4712.0	4733.1	4754.3
62	4754.3	4775.6	4797.1	4818.6	4840.3	4862.1	4884.1
63	4884.1	4906.1	4928.3	4950.6	4973.1	4995.6	5018.4
64	5018.4	5041.2	5064.2	5087.3	5110.6	5134.0	5157.6
65	5157.6	5181.3	5205.1	5229.1	5253.3	5277.6	5302.1
66	5302.1	5326.7	5351.5	5376.5	5401.6	5427.0	5452.4
67	5452.4	5477.1	5503.9	5529.9	5556.1	5582.5	5609.1
68	5609.1	5635.9	5662.8	5690.0	5717.3	5744.9	5772.7
69	5772.7	5800.7	5828.9	5857.3	5885.9	5914.8	5943.9
70	5943.9	5973.2	6002.8	6032.6	6062.7	6093.0	6123.5
71	6123.5	6154.4	6185.5	6216.8	6248.4	6280.4	6312.5
72	6312.5	6345.0	6377.8	6410.9	6444.3	6478.0	6512.0
73	6512.0	6546.4	6581.0	6616.1	6651.4	6687.1	6723.2
74	6723.2	6759.7	6796.5	6833.7	6871.3	6909.3	6947.7

SUPPLEMENTARY READING IN MATHEMATICS FOR HIGH SCHOOLS AND JUNIOR COLLEGES

PRINCIPLES OF MATHEMATICAL LOGIC, by D. Hilbert and W. Ackermann
Intended for students with no previous knowledge of formal logic, this has become, by virtue of its clarity and readability, a classic text on the subject. "The best textbook in a Western European language." —*Bulletin of the A.M.S.*
—1950-59. xii + 172 pp. 6 x 9. [69] $3.95

HISTORY OF THE THEORY OF NUMBERS, by L. E. Dickson
"A monumental work... The ability to reduce complicated mathematical arguments to simple and elementary terms is highly developed in Dickson." —*Bulletin of the A.M.S.*
—Vol. 1 (Divisibility and Primality) xii + 486 pp.; Vol. II (Diophantine Analysis) xxv + 803 pp.; Vol. III (Quadratic and Higher Forms) v + 313 pp. [86] Three vol. set $19.95

SET THEORY, by F. Hausdorff
"We wish to state without qualification that this is an indispensable book for all those interested in the theory of sets and the allied branches of real variable theory." —*Bulletin of the A. M. S.*
—2nd edition. 1962. 352 pp. 6 x 9. [119] $6.95

ELEMENTARY NUMBER THEORY, by E. Landau
The present work is a translation of Prof. Landau's famous *Elementare Zahlentheorie*, with added exercises by Prof. Paul T. Bateman.
—1958. 256 pp. 6 x 9. [125] $4.95

INTRODUCTION TO MODERN ALGEBRA AND MATRIX THEORY, by O. Schreier and E. Sperner
"Outstanding... good introduction... well suited for use as a text... Self-contained and each topic is painstakingly developed." —*Mathematics Teacher*
—2nd edition. 1959. viii + 378 pp. [80] $6.95

THE CALCULUS OF FINITE DIFFERENCES, by G. Boole
A standard work on the subject of finite differences and difference equations by one of the most original minds in the field of finite mathematics.
—4th edition. 1958. xii + 336 pp. 5 x 8. [121] cloth $3.95
[148] paper $1.39

A HISTORY OF THE MATHEMATICAL THEORY OF PROBABILITY, by I. Todhunter
Introduces the reader to almost every process and every species of problem which the literature of the subject can furnish.
—640 pp. 5¼ x 8. [57] $6.95

DIFFERENTIAL AND INTEGRAL CALCULUS, by E. Landau
A masterpiece of rigor and clarity.
—2nd edition. 1960. 372 pp. 6 x 9. [78] $6.00

THEORY OF NUMBERS, by G. B. Mathews
—2nd edition. 1892-1962. xii + 323 pp. 5⅜ x 8. [156] $4.95

PROJECTIVE METHODS IN PLANE ANALYTICAL GEOMETRY, by C. A. Scott
—3rd edition. xiv + 288 pp. 5⅜ x 8. [146] $3.95